How Papa Won the War

Gordon Wagner

Published by the
Flying -W- Publishing Co.
P.O. Box 3118 Courtenay, B.C. V9N 5N3

Canadian Cataloguing in Publication Data

Wagner, Gordon, 1914-
   How papa won the war

   ISBN 0-9693329-2-0

   1. Wagner, Gordon, 1914-   2. Canada.
Royal Canadian Air Force - Biography.   3.
Canada.   Royal Canadian Air Force - Anecdotes.
4. World War, 1939-1945 - Personal narratives,
Canadian.   I.   Title.
D811.W33 1989   940.54'81'71   C89-091576-8

First Edition published September 1989

Soft Cover ISBN 0-9693329-2-0

Printed by Kask Graphics Ltd., Campbell River, B.C.

Acknowledgements

Uncollected Stories of William Faulkner, ed. Joseph Blotner. N.Y., Random House, 1979; N.Y., Vintage, 1980.

I thank Cecil Law author and publisher of *Chinthe* the story of RCAF Squadron No 435 in India. *A true labour of love.*

I thank George Jenkins of Victoria, B.C. for permission to photograph his painting "Mainstreet, Markinch, Saskatchewan".

*For Lorne Taylor, Paul Soder, Whitey Holton,
Noel McPhee and all the other non-returnees
wherever you are*

Table of Contents

Prologue

I write this story without malice. No offence is intended or misdeed impugned to the military establishments of today, yesterday or tomorrow. I have long believed that the instinct to hunt and kill, so vital for most species to survive, is innate also in human beings.

Why else would a prairie boy and his dog both await the spring thaw with restless anticipation? Was it to find the first furry crocus that pushed its purple-coated bloom through the last year's grass so he could give it to his teacher? Was it to watch the first crow refurbish last year's nest so he could rob the green brown-speckled eggs and add them to his collection? Oh no! It was to hear the clear, shrill whistle of the gopher announcing the end of his winter's sleep, and to see his periscopic eyes peering above his burrow. The harbinger of spring aroused the killer's instinct and sent hot blood racing through human veins.

Why else would a prairie boy and his dog, both suffering the lethargy of spring-fever and adversity to any kind of work, carry countless buckets of ice-cold water from a spring-time slough and dump it down a gopher hole? Was it for the one cent the Rural Municipality of Markinch paid him for the gopher's tail? Or was it the thrill of the kill that made the boy and dog tremble as they waited for the half-frozen rodent to crawl from his flooded home?

It is not the intention of my book to discuss the "killer instinct." I snared gophers as a boy, joined the Air Force to fight a war, hunted deer for meat that went to waste, caught salmon beyond my limit and shot grouse out of season. Nowadays I neither hunt nor fish, but I still enjoy a tender roast of venison and a fresh salmon steak.

When my grandsons, Andrew and Geoffrey Clements, were preschoolers and they learned their grandfather had been in the war, they pestered me to tell and retell my stories. One day four-year-old Geoffrey looked up to me, squinted his eyes and with shades of doubt in his voice, said, "Papa, are all dem tories for true?"

Bear with me, as Geoffrey and Andrew did, as I relate the story of my five years of Air Force life. Whether or not the "killer instinct" helped a would-be pacifist survive the harsh climate of the Canadian prairies, the hungry thirties of the Great Depression and five years of disciplined living in the Royal Canadian Air Force, is for you, the reader to decide.

I thank my wife, Ivy, for believing, Roger for inspiring, and Jane for perfecting.

Gordon Wagner

"Think of all that has happened here, on this earth, "
the father tells the boy. "All the blood hot and fierce and
strong for living, pleasuring . . . But you can't be alive
forever, and you always wear out life before you have
completely exhausted the possibilities of living. And all
that must be somewhere."

William Faulkner

Markinch

War has always seemed an exciting adventure. Men, dogs and roosters love to fight. As Canadians, our children and our grandchildren are the first two generations of Wagners in five hundred years who have neither fought nor been involved in a war. My own genealogy reveals military ancestors since 1066. Jacob Wagner, a German mercenary and a captain in Napoleon's bodyguard helped in the retreat from Moscow; Robert De Blais, a Huguenot mercenary and a colonel in King William's army helped in the conquest of Northern Ireland; John Warren, born in Nayland, England in 1585 claimed that a Warren had fought in the Battle of Hastings and married Jundred, daughter of William the Conqueror.

My grandchildren play war with sophisticated electronic toy weapons. But when my chum Roy McInnes and I were five we used sticks. The Germans had killed his father in World War I, and Roy's mother hated living in Markinch, Saskatchewan with its predominantly German population. She taught us to hate Germans and we learned the lesson well. Roy and I built forts, dug trenches and took pot shots at Germans all day long.

One day I put an extra charge in my stick-gun. I covered the end with a wad of excreta I just passed. Roy came sneaking around the corner of their wood shed ready to shoot me dead. He ran into the messy end of my stick. His mother made me clean his brand-new jacket and forbade Roy to play with me. Our war games ended. That war had cost me my best friend.

Over the years, I learned to hate the savage brutality of war. I would never volunteer to fight Hitler. But when France fell and London was in flames my hate turned to fear. In the Air Force I learned to tame my hate, to mix fear and fun, to find new friends and to enjoy my unexpected world tour. For five years I went where the "Gods of War" sent me. I made it back. But again war cost me friends who were not so lucky. My war wasn't all that bad.

Born and raised in a tiny Saskatchewan village called Markinch, I was four and half when World War I ended.

I was just a toddler but I knew that:

> Kaiser Bill went up the hill
> To take a look at France.
> Kaiser Bill came down the hill
> With bullets in his pants.

And I knew that my Uncle Carl Wagner was in France fighting the Germans. I recall how great he looked in his soldier's uniform and how my parents said he could be killed any day, just like my Uncle Jim was.

Even now, decades later, I can still see them reading a list of names in the newspaper and recall how angry they got when they read that the Germans had shot the British nurse, Edith Cavell. I have a vivid memory of the first Armistice day parade and a dray full of boys and men with an effigy of the Kaiser dangling from a scaffold.

I got my first pair of glasses before I knew the alphabet because I remember telling Dr. McClung the letter "E" was a three legged table standing on its end. I didn't mind wearing glasses until I started school. I used to enjoy the attention I got from grown-ups when they saw a little four-year- old wearing glasses. But at school I was the only kid with glasses, and the other kids teased me calling me "four-eyes" or "storm windows."

John Albus, one of the school's big-guys, teased me incessantly. So I called him the worst thing I knew, "You're a dirty German and so are all your family."

"You should talk!" He sneered. "You Wagners are Germans too. Why don't you wipe your snotty nose before I punch it!"

But I couldn't be a German! I'd been killing Germans all my life!

My child's world started to crumble! There must be some mistake. I'd ask my Mom and Dad — they'd know. After all, Uncle Carl came back shell-shocked. He couldn't be a German. He fought on our side.

After school I couldn't get home fast enough. "Hey, Mom, are we Germans?"

"You'll have to ask your father."

My Dad had Markinch's only garage and sold "John Deere" farm implements. He always whistled as he walked from the back gate to the kitchen door, rattling the coins in his pocket to keep time with his tune. I met him at the screen door.

"Dad, are we Germans?"

"Why do you ask?"

"John Albus said I was a dirty German. We're not German, are we, Dad?"

"You are the fifth generation to be born in Canada, but your great-great-grandfather came from Germany. You're a Canadian. Be proud of it."

"But is Wagner a German name?"

"Yes, it is. It's a good name and you needn't be ashamed of it."

"But the Germans killed Uncle Jim and Roy's father. Mrs. Mc-Innes says we shouldn't play with German kids. She really hates Germans."

"Mrs. McInnes is still suffering from the loss of her husband."

"Didn't take her long to get another man," my Mother said. "Roy's name isn't McInnes. His father's name was Walker."

"Are there many Germans in Markinch, Dad?"

"Not many, son. Brandt the blacksmith, Ehmans and Kriekles in the hotel and Ollinger the shoemaker. Most of the farmers came from Germany and were here before the war. They're fine people and good farmers. And now that we have a consolidated school district I guess half the children in school are from German families, but you shouldn't call them 'dirty Germans'."

The British had just won the war. English was the language of the country. I thought we were all one big family until my fight with John Albus. Later, I perceived that the British with their ingrained class distinctions, considered themselves superior. Markinch was divided into cliques ... with the village Anglo-Saxons at the top of our social structure. The different nationalities kept to themselves in their own churches. The Germans schooled their young and formed small cooperatives to compete with the village merchants. The British considered Canada a colony.

The village's Anglo-Saxons never accepted the so-called foreigners, and we were caught in the middle. The Wagners had been in Canada for almost a hundred years, fought in the British wars, and yet we were made to feel that we didn't belong. My father could speak German but he was as bad as the snobby British. He spoke "high" German while most of the Germans in the area spoke "low" German. But to survive on the cold, rugged plains of Saskatchewan, we had to learn to live together and to appreciate each other's talents and abilities.

Markinch had one of the first consolidated school districts in Saskatchewan. Horse-drawn vans brought children to school each day. The village of Markinch, with a population of less than a hundred and fifty people, had a school with a hundred and thirty pupils. We had Germans, Austrians, Hungarians, Rumanians, Russians, and a Jewish family to mix with the Anglo- Saxon people who had settled the town.

By the time I graduated from our one-room, four-grade, one-teacher high school, I believed that World War I was the war to end all wars and I'd never have to die for King and country. My classmates and I believed the League of Nations would save us from future wars. Then Japan invaded China and the League of Nations stood idly by. Pete, the Chinaman, owner of the Maple Leaf Cafe, got upset and smashed all his "Made in Japan" dishes but no one else seemed to care. We read about Hitler but he was far away. Until Harmon Schmidt, a farm hand and a recent immigrant from Germany addressed a public meeting in Markinch's town hall. He praised Hitler and blamed the Jews for all of Germany's problems. It was less than twenty years since "Kaiser Bill came down the hill." Although *Liberty* magazine's cartoons showed Hitler pushing the black clouds of war across the map of Europe, I began to wonder.

I went to the University of Saskatchewan in Saskatoon in the fall of 1935 with sixty dollars I had made in the harvest, enough to pay my first month's room and board and to buy my books. Markinch still suffered from the depression and the dust of the "dirty thirties." Bob Buchanan, who ran the North Star grain elevator, was my mother's star boarder. Mother sent the twenty-five bucks he paid in room and board to me each month. The university took my personal note for my tuition. I had a new leather jacket which I wore for the next three years.

I found a boarding house on Temperance Street with eight other fellows. I had barely unpacked my trunks when Tom Watt, doing his master's degree in agriculture, gave my roommate and me my first lecture on communism. He tried to get us to stand on a downtown corner and hand out pamphlets extolling the virtues of the Soviet Republic. When he and his roommate tried to get me to donate to the war in Spain I decided to move.

I found an empty bed at 2110 Aird Street to share with Markinch's Howard Edwards. Our landlady, Mrs. Herman, fed us three good meals a day, gave us cocoa and cookies before bed and did our washing for twenty dollars a month. There were four of us — Howard and I and two girls, Eleanor McDougall and Kay Johnston. We played a lot of bridge. We would start to play as soon as we finished supper and set the alarm to ring at eight to begin our studies, but many a night we turned off the alarm and played until midnight.

Pacifism ruled the campus — damned if we'd lay down our lives for king and country. But the threat of war streamed across the headlines. Nazi propagandists invaded the University's Convocation Hall. German societies in Saskatoon openly supported Hitler's Germany. The university paper *The Sheaf* called them the "Saskatoon Bund". We still hated war. We'd never fight. The League of Nations would save us — man had learned to settle his quarrels.

By graduation in 1938 Hitler had marched into Austria, Franco had trampled Spain, and our politicians guaranteed there would be an upturn in the economy because of the war scare. Yet jobs were hard to find, and I was still wearing the same leather jacket.

My years at the University of Saskatchewan were tough, but I could add BA to my name and try to find a job where I could make use of all the biology and chemistry classes I had taken. I found it in Markinch on Eddy Blaser's farm. I had a cozy corner in a granary, five weary, over-worked and underfed horses to look after, two hundred acres of summerfallow to plough, and a couple of ornery cows to milk. I worked six days a week. Every other Sunday I had to baby-sit the horses and cows. For this Eddy was to pay me $20 a month, but I'd have to wait till the crop was threshed before I'd see the cash. With the dawn-to-dusk farm routine, I figured I was making about five cents an hour. But I had one privilege. I was a good baseball pitcher so they allowed me to go to one tournament a week. I was given a meal and, if we won, a share of the prize money.

In 1937 we had poor crops, and we had no feed for the horses. Each horse got a gallon of oats at noon. That was all Eddy could afford. We worked in the fields from seven in the morning until noon and from one until six at night. The horses were turned out to feed in the sloughs of the summerfallow. Eddy farmed his section in three fields — 200 acres in wheat planted on the previous year's summerfallow, 200 acres planted to barley and oats on last year's stubble and 200 acres in summerfallow. A section is a mile square, and we ploughed through the mile with a two-furrowed gang plough, making about four two-mile rounds a day. The horses and the driver got more and more weary, and the weeds higher and higher. The weeds finally won, until Eddy's father loaned Eddy his tractor to finish ploughing the summerfallow.

Nellie Boychuk was the Blaser's hired girl. She worked longer hours than I did without a day off and got five dollars a month. She had been in Regina's reform school. The mention of the institution sent chills of fear through any teenager. We heard horrible rumours of how these "young criminals" were treated as their guards tried to beat them into better citizens. Once you were "reformed" you could be placed in a foster home as "hired help." This arrangement relieved the congestion in the school and provided cheap and almost slave-like domestics.

I never paid much attention to Nellie. She was short, a little chunky, with straight fine blondish hair that hung at right angles around a pleasant face that had never learned to smile. Long blond lashes surrounded her protruding sapphire-blue eyes that shifted like those of a frightened rabbit.

One Saturday night, after Eddy had started threshing, there was a little cash around, so my brother Carl and I, Eddy's brothers Lorenz and Norman, Nellie and her girl friend all piled into Blaser's 1927 Dodge and went to the dance at Cupar, our neighbouring town. On the way home we picked up four hitchhikers and Nellie ended up sitting in my lap.

I didn't need the excitement of the dance, and the waning effect of a couple of beers to react to a woman's fanny parked on my groin. It was my Sunday off. Charlie, Eddy's other hired-man, would be sleeping in the granary. On Sunday mornings all the Blaser family attended church and quite often went to friends for dinner. Nellie and I would have to wait.

All day Sunday I fantasized as I contemplated my first experience with real sex. I'd fooled around like most fellows but we weren't as promiscuous as we liked to pretend. We didn't have cars and the girls' dorms, boarding houses and the YWCA were strictly out of bounds. I had never had the chance to combine the maximum of temptation with the maximum of opportunity. I didn't know how the hell I'd wait for Sunday.

Monday morning and all the rest of the week she ignored me. I tried to catch those shifty eyes. I thought she'd at least smile when she said good morning. I had never noticed the soft silkiness of her hair as it swayed seductively each time she moved her head, nor how her fine features and her baby-like complexion blended with the colour of her hair, nor the smooth reverse curves of her bare legs, nor her nicely rounded bum nor the deep and almost hidden plunge-line leading to her firm, upright breasts.

Sunday morning, sitting on the granary steps soaking up the late September sunshine I watched the Blaser's car drive down driveway and turn onto the highway. I opened the screen door wondering if she'd still ignore me.

She was standing on her tip toes putting dishes onto a high shelf with one side of her skirt pulled halfway up her thigh. I almost turned and ran. She glanced over her shoulder her soft bangs hanging at a saucy angle, her blue eyes peaceful and I watched a smile caress her face.

"Oh, Gordon! I thought that Sunday would never come," she said as she took a step towards me, "and I'm so afraid."

"I was beginning to wonder if it was you I had held on my knee."

"I know, and I'm sorry if you thought I was rude. But I was so afraid that Mrs. Blaser might be suspicious if I even smiled at you. She watches me like a hawk when her husband is around. I'm so afraid I might get sent back to the reform school. I'd couldn't stand another day in that hell hole. I'd kill myself before I'd go back."

I took her hand. I felt her go tense and her sapphire eyes began to flash and she looked over both her shoulders. She was terrified. I put my arms around her she was stiff as a corpse and began to tremble. Suddenly she went limp and almost collapsed to the floor. I grabbed her, and held her close. Slowly she relaxed and nestled her soft hair under my chin and began to sob. She put her arms around my neck, raised her face to mine and gently kissed me. Her lips felt soft and yielding as she snuggled her body close to mine. I tried to lead her to the small bedroom off the kitchen.

With an unexpected push she sent me sprawling. "No! No! Not in there! Not anywhere!" She wailed and she ran out the screen door and slammed it. I found her in the granary sitting on my bed her face buried in her hands and hidden by the soft tresses of her hair. I put my arm around her and felt her body tremble. She fell back across the bed and pulled me with her. We lay in motionless silence, each breathing hard and with hearts pounding.

She raised herself on her elbow and turned my face to hers. She kissed me and I smelt the womanly freshness of her silky hair as it buried our faces. I put my arms around her and held her close.

"Gordon, I've thought of you all week. When I made your bed I smelt your manliness and cuddled your pillow. I want you so much! But I'm so afraid."

I rolled over and we lay firmly against each other in the silky softness of her hair I found her ear and whispered, "There is nothing to be afraid of, just let me love you."

"I feel so wonderful and safe in your arms. I could stay here forever but I can't go all the way."

"Why not?"

"I'll tell you later. We'd better get out of here. The Blasers will soon be home from church."

"I heard Eddy say that they might go to Uncle Lorenz's after church."

"Let me up. I'll make a sandwich and a cup of tea."

The day passed too quickly. Nellie and I watched the setting sun grow larger as the red disk tucked itself behind the flat prairie horizon and splashed a brilliant red across the western sky. In the distance the silhouettes of Markinch's four grain elevators poked into the sky. In the foreground Eddy's barbwired fence looked like toothpicks marching along the horizon across the cherry-coloured sky. Then the outline of the 1927 Dodge flicked by the toothpicks and turned into the lane. With a quick embrace and one last kiss we parted, Nellie to her kitchen and I to my cozy granary corner.

We had two more Sundays and some other stolen minutes of bliss before the harvest finished. I learned that she came from a large family of five brothers and six sisters that had immigrated from Russia in the early thirties. She had been sexually abused by her grandfather and when she told her parents they wouldn't believe her. When the abuse persisted she ran away from home. The police brought her home and she ran away again. When she was home once more her grandfather tried to rape her. She stabbed him in the groin with a pitch fork. She spent two years in the reform school where some of the guards were no better than her grandfather.

After the war, on a visit to Markinch I learned Nellie had joined the Air Force and been posted overseas. She had married a RAF pilot and was living in England.

Sudbury

I had sixty-three dollars coming when I threw the last sheaf into Blaser's threshing machine and vowed I'd never milk a cow, plough a field or work in the harvest fields again. I paid twenty-six bucks for a bus ticket to Sudbury. A week later I joined a line-up of three hundred men in front of the employment office of the International Nickel Company.

Markinch's Lloyd Edwards pulled me from the line-up, and took me to the front of the line. An hour later I was on a bus to Inco's mine at Levack.

The town of Levack sat in a narrow clearing in a narrow valley thirty miles west of Sudbury. Long narrow bunk-houses lined one side of the tracks; across the tracks tattle-tale-grey frame houses squatted along narrow lanes. Up the tracks the narrow headframe of the mines pierced the cloud-cramped skyline.

I found the time office and they gave me a shiny silver badge with the number 8118 and told me to wear it at work and in the camp. At the commissary, Inco financed me to a hard hat, safety shoes, underwear, jeans and a carbide light. Crawley and McCracken rented me a room to share with Ray Negus and told me to find a seat in their dining room.

Ray was a machinist. He and his friends all worked on the surface: Mac McDougal, the good looking warehouse-man who played poker almost every night and usually won; Don Walker, the first-aid man and lady killer who never had enough money to pay his way; Earl Beggs, a blacksmith, who was a quiet man, with a fine-tuned sense of humour and a taste for good whisky; Red Jenkins, a skip tender, who lived in the married quarters, drank only Sudbury's Silver Foam beer and couldn't stay away from Annie's whorehouse on pay day; Doc McCready, a mining engineer, who had a cabin on a lake near the camp and was always beating off the Toronto girls wanting to spend weekends and holidays in the wilds of Levack's tiny lake.

Levack had no theatre, no library, no store (the company ran the commissary), no post office, no recreation hall or playground, but it did have a bootlegger. At five every afternoon, Bruno's pickup truck,

11

piled high with cases of Sudbury's Silver Foam, parked in between the long, narrow, concrete-block buildings. If you could holler loud enough, "Bruno, bring a 24 to room 17," Bruno's boy delivered the beer to your room at the same price you'd pay at the government beer store.

In the bunk-house at night you listened to your short-wave radio. Or you could take a trip up a one-way road to a tarpapered shack. In this kerosene-lighted, smoke-filled shack a narrow-necked bottle of beer cost two-bits, or a short shot of rye cost a quarter, or for two bucks you could join the line-up at the bottom of the stairs waiting for your turn to visit one of Annie's girls.

At the mine, the change house had long rows of slender lockers — double lockers, one up, one down. The "up" one was for street clothes, the "down" one for dry sweat-soaked underwear, socks and jeans. We never washed our work clothes; we replaced them every two weeks, every payday. Fine coal-black dust saturated the fabric; after two weeks the board-stiff underwear stood unassisted, ready to rasp the skin. We broke the clothing to fit as we climbed into it.

The days were lightless. In the winter it was still dark at seven am The plunging skip whipped you down the steep, inclined shaft 2000 feet into the black bowels of the mine. Eight hours later you were coughed back to the surface. It was dark again. We worked six days out of seven without seeing daylight.

Underground, rock-walled tunnels grooved by narrow-gauged rails led to smaller tunnels. The air in them was narrow. Each day huge pumps compressed more tons of air into the mine than tons of ore were hoisted to the surface by whizzing buckets. It was dark in the hole. The fork-tongued flame of the carbide lamps cast a spooky glow. The weak light struggled against the forbidding wall of the dark. The weight of the heavy hard-hat holding the carbide lamp pressed you against the rock floor. My partner's light snaked through the dark like the dancing head of a cobra.

With dynamite we blasted a hunk of ore too big to smash with the ten-pound sledge hammer. The stope boss cleared the area, guarded the entrance, lit the fuse runs and yelled, "Fire!" We waited. **B-A-N-G!** The swooshing air blasted down the tunnel. The carbide light died. The darkness was absolute. Only if you lost both eyes would it be that dark again. The darkness narrowed to an infinity unlit by stars.

On our days off we could take Beauchamp's orange and yellow bus into Sudbury, but if we got a ride in a friend's car we'd stop at Henri and Marie's, a small, badly weathered clap-board cottage about halfway to Sudbury. We would sit at their round oilcloth-covered dining room table, and for fifty cents we got a boiler-maker and his helper (a shot of straight rye with a beer chaser) and a big bowl of pickled pigs-feet. We often had two and sometimes three boiler-makers while we devoured the appetizing and succulent treat.

Sudbury was full of men. Men came from all over Canada looking for work. They were single. Dates and women were hard to find. So we'd go to shows or hockey games. The Sudbury Wolves had tough battles with the Kirkland Lake Blue Devils and we enjoyed them, but we spent a lot of time in the beer parlours, especially those of the Nickel Range and the Coulson hotels. There were no beer parlours for women. If you wanted female company, you went to the speakeasies half-hidden at the end of lonely roads in the surrounding country side.

The speakeasies, with names like Chi Chi's, the Silver Slipper and the Red Barn, opened just before the beer parlours closed and stayed open until four or five in the morning, catering to the men coming off work at midnight. You could buy only Sudbury's Silver Foam, but at the same price you paid in the beer parlours — two bits. For fifty cents you got a heaping plate of Italian chicken and spaghetti. For five cents (a nickel) nickelodeons swung the jazz of Tommy Dorsey, Benny Goodman and Artie Shaw and if you were lucky and reasonably sober you might find a woman whose partner would let her dance with you — but you were allowed only one dance.

I met her on Christmas day. I had spent Christmas in Sudbury with Lloyd and Hazel Edwards. I took the only vacant seat on the last bus to Levack. She sat comfortably huddled against the window, bundled in her silver-grey fur coat. Soft, silky, auburn hair escaped from beneath a small tam and cascaded with a gentle curve over the collar of her coat — it was "hair you'd love to touch." As she watched the activity around the bus station I admired her delicate profile silhouetted against the window as the dim lights of the bus cast a velvet glow across her face. Just to sit near her warmed my heart and I wondered who she was and where she was going. To Levack, I hoped. But she was probably married. Weren't all the women in Levack? I hadn't talked to a beautiful woman for a couple of months. *So forget your shyness, Gordon! After all it's Christmas, so what the heck.*

"Merry Christmas!"

She looked startled as she turned. Then she smiled. "Merry Christmas to you."

"Are you going to Levack?"

As she tilted her head, and in the dim light her blue eyes smiled, adding a misty softness to her complexion, "Yes, we are."

"Was Santa good to you?"

"Very good. He brought me this fur coat."

"I've been admiring it. It looks lovely on you, so warm and cuddly."

"Thank you. Did you have a good Christmas?"

"I spent it with some friends here in Sudbury. I was happy to get away from Levack. I find it lonely living in the bunk house and eating at Crawley and McCrackens. Do you live in Levack?"

"Yes, we do. We spent Christmas eve with my sister in Copper Cliff and had our dinner there."

"So you are married?"

"Oh no!"

"I thought when you said 'we' you meant your husband."

"Oh no!" she chuckled, "I was with my brother and my twin sister. They are in the seat across the aisle."

"What do you do in Levack? I've been there for six weeks and you are the first girl I have talked to. My name is Gordon Wagner and I work underground as a mucker. My home is in Saskatchewan and I'd like to know your name."

"I'm Irene Browne and I attend a convent in North Bay. I'm studying to become a nun. I hope to find the strength and courage to enter the order."

"You're a Catholic then. I used to room with a Catholic at university and I admired his devotion and the strength he found in his religion. He was taking medicine and he had no trouble adjusting his faith to the questions and doubts that science brings to Christianity."

"I am not a Catholic. I enjoy living in the convent and I love the help and understanding I receive from the sisters. It's so peaceful there and everyone is so kind."

"Looks like we are going to stop here in Chelmsford."

"Yes, and when we stop I want to introduce you to my sister and brother."

We chatted as the bus wound around the curves to Levack. An hour later when we arrived in Levack, I had met her twin sister, Eileen and her brother, Neil. I knew that her father was a widower and that her mother had died when Neil was born. I learned that her father was a mine captain; that Neil was attending high school in Sudbury; that she was taking an arts course at the convent in North Bay and that her sister Eileen kept house for her father.

We warmed to each other. She had the ability of giving you her complete attention, making you feel you were the only person in the world that mattered. A sweet sincerity flowed from her smiling eyes. Her gentle voice calmed my lonely heart. I wondered if I would ever see her again.

The bus stopped on the west side of the railway tracks. "This is where we get off," she smiled.

I stood in the aisle and as she rose to follow her brother and sister she turned and I was surprised to see how tiny she was. She had to tilt her face to look up at me. Her auburn hair fell from her face, revealing the gentle curves of her neck and breasts. Her eyes, bluer and more beautiful in the overhead light, sparkled like sapphires in the delicate pink of her face. She looked like a cameo snuggled into the cozy collar of her coat.

"I've enjoyed our time together, Irene. That bus ride was too short. I'd like to see you again before you go back to North Bay."

"Would you like to come to the house tomorrow? Daddy always has a few people in on Boxing Day."

"Thank you, I'd love to come"

"We live in the last house on the street right next to the Engineers' Club. Why don't you come about four-thirty or five, by that time most of the callers will have left and you can stay for dinner. Ileen is a great cook and we'll enjoy having you."

She offered me her hand. It felt firm and delicate in my work-calloused grip, and its warmth cruised through my being. I squeezed it gently and felt her return the caress. "It's been wonderful Irene, and you're a beautiful woman."

"Thank you, Gordon, we'll look forward to seeing you tomorrow. Good night and Merry Christmas."

I watched as she joined her brother and sister under the street light. She turned and waved as they headed up the snow- covered street. She had made my Christmas and I would see her again!

She met me at the door. Her page-boy hair rested on her shoulders and glistened against the white collar topping the plain nun-like dress that failed to hide the soft curves of her slim body. She looked delicate, petite and lovely.

"I'm so happy you could come. Let me take your coat. Most of father's guests have gone. Ileen is over at the Club and Neil is skiing. Come on in and meet Daddy and the Thompsons."

The living room held a chesterfield, with matching chairs semi-circled around a glass-topped coffee table and the fireplace. Large windows on both side by the fireplace looked like landscape paintings. To the west, the snow-covered-hills reflected the baby-pink of the sun's fading light. In the east, the sky above the horizon darkened into shades of cobalt-blue, waiting for the night's first stars. In a corner, almost hidden in the gathering dusk, fireflies flicked through a Christmas tree. From a radio, hidden nearby, carols echoed quietly. The forest smell of spruce, the tinge of wood smoke mixed with the smell of a good cigar, and the aroma of fine perfume flooded me with such homesickness that I was almost unaware of the people in the room.

"Daddy, I'd like you to meet Gordon Wagner. He is the young man we met on the bus."

He rose from his chair with studied deliberation. His stocky frame was topped by black, well-groomed hair, with a widow's peak that threatened to join the bushy-black eyebrows shading his soft blue eyes. His well-jowled face seemed to frown and smile at the same time. He looked like Edward G. Robinson. On his left hand he wore a leather glove. "Welcome, Gordon and a belated Merry Christmas."

"Thank you, Mr. Browne, compliments of the season to you, Sir."

16

He introduced me to his guests, Jim and Nancy Thompson, a couple in their mid thirties. Nancy, a buxom brunette, well dressed, but slightly over-decorated, did nothing to conceal her lavishness. Jim, tall and athletic, with a trace of grey in his thin brown hair, looked uncomfortable in his suit and tie."Irene, perhaps Gordon would enjoy a drink?"

"Yes, Daddy," she said. "Gordon, follow me. Daddy keeps his bar in the kitchen, and besides I promised Eileen I'd get the vegetables ready. You can keep me company."

"We must be going," said Jim. "My hockey team has a game tonight. It's been a pleasure to meet you, Gordon."

"We were hoping you'd stay for dinner," said Irene. "Why don't you stay Nancy? Jim can pick you up after the game."

"He never comes home after the game," said Nancy. "There's always beer after the game."

"You might as well stay. Daddy will see that you get home. Won't you Daddy?"

"I'll see she gets home, Jim." said Mr. Browne. I watched the blue eyes begin to grin.

Jim left. Irene led me to the kitchen leaving Mr. Browne and Nancy side by side on the chesterfield.

"Daddy has a crush on Nancy but it doesn't really mean anything. Daddy's too old for any hanky-panky. Would you like a beer?"

Turkey seems to taste better the second day and after supper we gathered round the fireplace and traded yarns. Mr. Browne, or "Jack" as he liked to be called, told us about the big silver rush in Cobalt at the turn of the century, about finding nuggets of silver on the lake shore, and tripping over veins of pure silver.

They say it's not what you know but who you know. Jim Thompson was the foreman of the "toplanders" (the men who work on surface). He needed a goalkeeper for his hockey team and he got me transferred from underground.

I worked with Scotty, the cage tender. We helped load the cages that took men and supplies underground. Scotty, with a Scottish accent almost as broad as his thick shoulders, was short, dark and wide, wore a heavy black sweater and a black hard-hat and chewed tar-black tobacco. And I never ever saw him spit.

At lunch time, after he'd finished his sandwiches and pie, he would fill his thermos cup with steaming ink-black tea. He'd cut off a big piece off his coal-black plug of "Big Ben" chewing tobacco and tuck it into his chipmunk-cheek. Then with obvious relish, that nearly turned my stomach he'd drink his thermos of tea.

Scotty had a girl friend, Sue, who worked nights in Sally's narrow tarpapered-shack at the end of the one-way road. On her days off she and Scotty shacked up in the Nickel Range Hotel. He got all he needed for the cost of the room and two dozen bottles of Sudbury's Silver Foam. "Sometimes we take time to see a show," he told me with a twinkle in his eyes.

He liked to talk about his Sue, and I heard later they were married and living in a company house. The hard-rock miners claimed you couldn't get a better woman than one of Sally's girls.

Irene's sister, Barbie lived in Copper Cliff, and her husband Lawrence worked in Inco's assay lab. I made an application for a transfer to the lab. The white-collar job paid better but we still had shift work. The lab assayed for nickel, copper, silver, gold, platinum, iron and sand, doing twenty-five thousand samples a month. Inco made enough money out of their precious metal sales to pay all their operating costs. The nickel and copper produced in 1938 gave the company a profit of fifty-two million dollars. A million bucks a week. Not bad for the dirty thirties. Inco's shares rose to seventy-two dollars but there was no increase in wages and there was no union to fight for the miners.

Inco's salaried employees could join the supposedly elite Copper Cliff Club with its lounge, dining room, bar, billiard room and swimming pool. I had finished a couple of lengths when I heard "That's a good stroke you use." I looked up to see a well-dressed red-headed man. "What do you call it?"

"I don't, it's a cross between the crawl and the trudgen."

"You use the stroke well and you're a strong swimmer."

"Thank you," I said and continued swimming. He was sitting at the bar when I had showered and changed.

"May I buy you a beer?"

"Thank you," I said.

We spent a pleasant evening together. Clarence James, single, in his mid-thirties was an accountant in Inco's Copper Cliff office. At his suggestion, we took the streetcar into Sudbury for an evening snack and he insisted on paying for it. I appreciated his friendliness and when we said good night he asked me what I was doing on the weekend. I told him I planned to visit my brother in Kitchener.

"I'm going to Toronto Friday after work. When are you going?"

"On Thursday evening or Friday morning and back Sunday night."

"I may see you on the way back."

Irene was staying with her sister Barbie so I dropped by to see her. I mentioned meeting Clarence.

"You must mean Clarence James."

"Yes, that's his name. Why?"

"Clarence likes the boys. He'd really go for you Gordon with your head of curly black hair."

"I thought he was a little too attentive. I've had trouble before with my curly hair."

I had attended Dr. Manning's lectures in biochemistry at the U of S. A tall well-built handsome man, with a head of fine white hair, he handled a piece of chalk like a woman smoked a cigarette. He led the choir in Saskatoon's Knox United Church and was the faculty's only Doctor of Science. In the lab he took a special interest in me. He started with asking me for afternoon tea — he asked all the men, but nobody ever went. Then he used to muss up my hair and called me "schafkopk" (sheep's head in German). That was embarrassing enough. But if I happened to be sitting sideways on my lab stool he would wedge my leg between his and squeeze it.

I felt like hitting him. I jammed the heel of my shoe down on his toes and that kept him away for awhile. I didn't know what to do. I had to pass his exams because I needed the class to graduate.

One day I had to see him in his office. There was no one else around. He walked towards me and before I knew it he had his arms around me. I gave a mighty push and sent him sprawling across his desk. "Leave me alone, you son of bitch or I'll smash your bloody face." I left his office. He never bothered me again and I got a B in biochemistry.

On the way back from Kitchener when I went to get on the day coach at Toronto, Clarence James was waiting.

"I have a compartment, Gordon, I'd be glad to share it with you."

Well you little bastard! You must be queer! But what the hell Gordon, you can handle him. No reason why you should sit up all night in the day coach. You take the upper berth and if he tries anything let him have it.

"Thank you, Clarence, but only if you'll let me have the upper bunk."

Things went fine, except that half way there the train ran off the tracks and we were twelve hours late getting into Sudbury. When we got off the train, we ran into Herbie Fitzgerald, who worked with me in the assay lab. For a while I took a lot of good-natured teasing but I never saw Clarence again.

I rented a room in Sudbury and ate at restaurants travelling the six miles to Copper Cliff on the street car. Neville Chamberlain had made his "peace in our time" speech. In mid-August we were assaying samples marked "Rush — Matte for Germany." I was eating breakfast in a small Chinese restaurant the Sunday morning September 10, 1939, when a barely audible radio squawking from across the counter, paused and then BBC's "London Calling" program announced that Great Britain had declared war on Germany.

I had a spoonful of cornflakes halfway to my mouth. The spoon clattered on the counter. Momentarily stunned, a cold fear goose-pimpled my skin. The hair on my arm bristled. A mouthful of coffee seemed to curdle in my throat. *Well I'll be damned if I'll go to war. I'll go back underground before I'll join the bloody army.*

But ironically, the war found me a new home. Jim and Gladys Davidson's star boarder, Ernie, joined the Air Force. I got his room.

Gladys, a caring mother, a good cook and a fine woman, together with Jim and their young daughters Rita and Irene, gave me a new

My home with Gladys and Jim Davidson, 207 Paterson St. Sudbury.

home with a love and respect that I never received from my own parents. I came to love them and I didn't want to leave my new home. I'd be damned if I'd go to war to stop a German bullet made from nickel I helped to mine.

Jim had been in a cavalry regiment in World War I. His sword and spurs hung on the fireplace. He told me how he faked his birth certificate and joined the army when he was sixteen. In the first six months we would often talk about the phoney war and Jim knew my feelings. I used to hear a lot what a fine fellow Ernie was, doing his thing for "King and Country", especially after we'd had a beer or two. Jim would say, "Gordon, if I could find a horse and a cavalry

Rita, Gladys, Jim and Irene

regiment I'd strap those spurs on tomorrow." I'm sure he would have.

I admired Jim. He worked as a hoist man at Inco's Frood mine. He was good mechanic and his greatest love, next to his wife and family, was a big, long, maroon-coloured 1930 Cadillac loaded with chrome. He was the first man I had ever known who shaved everyday and I asked him why.

"I learnt that in army, Big John." Jim had a nickname for everybody. "When you get called up, Big John, you'll have to shave every day. Makes you feel clean. Real clean."

"I shave most days but I'll be damned if I want to join the army to learn to shave. If they ever get conscription I hope they don't take anybody under fifty. I don't know why they have to use all us young guys for cannon-fodder. I'll be damned if I'll go."

"You must have been listening to those slope-headed Bulgarians and those pink Finns you work with. For two cents I'd put on the spurs and take the sword to you, Big John."

He'd have hit me, or may have grabbed his sword and chased me down the street, if Gladys hadn't intervened. Jim was quick tempered but he never held a grudge and I started to shave every day. He spread his big grin across his face and with a chuckle in his voice, said, "I see you're shaving everyday, Big John. We'll make a soldier out of you some day."

In the spring of 1940 I decided to go underground again. If I got in a good bonus stope I could earn twice as much as I made in the lab. I got into the Frood mine — Inco's biggest, over half-a-mile deep and employing five-thousand men and with over a hundred miles of underground-roads.

The Frood mine was located in the geological formation known as the "Sudbury Basin." Imagine a huge saucer a hundred miles wide half-filled with a gooey mess of red-hot nickel ore. Into the bubbling saucer pour a lighter mixture of equally hot igneous rock and let it cool in a moderate oven under tremendous pressure. The result is that molten mass hardens to form a pair of crescent-shaped discs, one of solid ore covered by one of igneous rock.

In the Frood mine a perpendicular shaft penetrated through the rock and the ore body to a depth of twenty-eight- hundred feet with a mining level every hundred feet. The shaft had two hoists (elevators), one to move men and materials and another for carrying ore to the surface. On each level, adjacent to the shaft, a brightly-lit station with white-washed walls of solid rock had a double set of narrow gauge railway tracks and switches.

On one side of the tracks a spooky catacomb housed the "grizzly." A grid of heavy railroad rails spaced a foot apart, and set below the level of the tracks, covered the gaping hole that swallowed the carloads of ore. A pair of "grizzly-dancers", anchored with safety-belts to the rock walls, wearing big mesh-wire safety-goggles, their broad Stanfield-covered shoulders wet with sweat, dodged the bouncing hunks of ore unloaded from the electric ore trains. Then, armed with ten-pound sledgehammers, they broke the large hunks of ore into pieces small enough to go through the grid. A tough and dangerous job. You never argued with a grizzly-dancer. They were the strongest, toughest and often the meanest men in the mine.

Across the tracks, guarded by an automatic air-tight safety-door, was the lunch and mine-rescue safety room. Narrow-gauged railways ran down the main drifts (tunnels) to gather the coal-black ore from the stopes.

The Frood, like all mines, was designed to let gravity do most of the work. You started at the bottom of the level and worked up a hundred feet to the next level.

Stopes were mining units sixty feet wide, sixty feet apart, parallel to each other and if possible at right angles to the main drift. As you removed the ore you built a square-set to six-foot posts, put a roof over your head and a floor under your feet. When you had drilled, blasted, and shovelled all the ore from the first six-foot level and timbered the mined-out area, you mined the six-foot level above. The empty space below was filled with crushed rock sent down chutes from the surface. The process was repeated until you reached the next level a hundred feet above.

The sixty feet of ore left between the stopes was called the pillars. When all the stopes were mined and back-filled with rock, the pillars were taken out and also filled with rock.

Compressed air ran the drills and supplied fresh air to the work place. When the stope got half way up, heat generated by timbers rotting in the fill raised the temperature into the eighties with a humidity of a hundred percent. By the time you climbed sixty feet of ladder your clothes were saturated. We cut holes in our shoes so the sweat could drain.

It was hard work, dirty work and I wasn't making the big money I had expected. The Germans had conquered France and it looked like England would be next. A friend was going to North Bay to inquire about enlisting in the Air Force. I went along. I passed the medical examination for aircrew but I would have to wait two or three months to be called up and sworn in.

I had left my options open. If conscription came, there was no way I could escape the draft. When I graduated in '38 an Air Force recruiting officer had visited our campus. Prior to '38 recruits needed a degree in Engineering, now they accepted other graduates. In my desperate search for work I had an interview. The life of commissioned officers sounded attractive. If I had a choice I would take the Air Force.

"How did you make out in North Bay, Big John?" Jim asked.

"I passed the medical but it will be two or three months before I'll get a call-up."

"Well if you can't get a horse to ride, Big John, you might as well fly a plane. We used to call you guys, pigeons. While you're away you needn't worry about Inco nor your pinko friends. I'll see that the smoke keeps rolling from Copper Cliff's big stacks.

It was a warm August morning and I was having a late breakfast in Gladys Davidson's kitchen. "Mummy, can we go to Lake Ramsay this morning?" asked five-year-old Irene.

"What about Rita and your cousin Joan?"

"They told me to ask you."

"What about Gordon? He's on afternoons."

"He can come. Can't he?"

"Would you like to come? I'll pack a lunch and we'll get you home in time to go to work."

"I'd love to go. I'd enjoy a swim and a picnic with you and the girls. Sounds great."

We had a wonderful time! A great lunch, a cool swim and a snooze in the warm sun. "Gladys, I've thoroughly enjoyed myself. You are always so good and kind to me. I hate the thought of going from this sunshine into that black hell-hole at the Frood."

"You could play hooky and miss a shift."

"They'd send me home to take another three days off. I can't afford that. I'm saving for a car. Remember?"

On afternoon shift we had to punch time by 3.30 pm If you were late you only got paid for seven hours instead of eight. We had to leave the lake during the best part of the afternoon.

Payday was only a couple of days away. My work clothes, stiff and dirty, almost stood by themselves and scraped my new sunburn. I was wringing wet by the time I climbed the ladders for sixty feet, and the stope boss asked me to run fill. To do this you used a bucket that ran on a narrow track. You filled the bucket with the crushed rock from a chute, pushed it along the track and dumped it into the level below. I had to lay a new track to make a right-angle turn just before the dump. The turn had to be made within the six foot squares. I super-elevated the curve, and wrapped a logging chain around the end of the track to stop the bucket from tumbling in to the hole below. It was a tedious, dusty, lonely and frustrating job. Nobody liked to run fill.

My elevated curve worked better than I expected. When I gave the cart an extra push to make the turn, it jumped the chains and buried itself in the fill below. *To hell with you, you little bastard. You can stay there. It's time I got out of this bloody hole.*

I picked up my shirt and had one foot on the ladder. From behind a light the stope boss asked, "Where do think you're going?"

"I'm going to the surface. The damn fill-bucket is hooked behind a post below and as far as I'm concerned the bloody thing can stay there."

"You better finish the shift. You can help the timbermen. I'll get somebody else to run the fill."

"No. I have had this f——- place!"

At the bottom of the ladder I met the shift boss. I don't know how the underground telegraph works but he said, "I hear you're quitting.

You'd better go back and finish the shift. I'll put you timbering and get you into a good bonus stope as soon as I can."

Damn it all. Maybe I shouldn't quit. I had a hell of a time getting this job. I don't want to be out of work again. Lord knows when the Air Force will call me up. Besides I really don't want to fight this war. "No, I have had it. I'll be on the next cage to surface."

"Go home and think about it. Come back tomorrow, I won't show you as leaving early."

Now I'm too damn proud to turn back but I got a knot in my belly. I shouldn't quit.

In the lunch room I met the mine captain. "Wagner, I hear you're quitting." More underground telegraphy.

"That's right, sir."

"You should go back and finish the shift. We've been watching you, Wagner. Your reports are good. We need men like you. In a couple of months you could be a stope-boss."

Damn it! They aren't making it any easier. I'd better get out of here. "I'm sorry sir, I want to catch the next cage."

By the time I got to the surface I was feeling almost as bad as I felt when I heard that war had been declared. I darn near walked past the time office. *What's the matter with me. What have I done to myself. I need this job. I don't want to join-up. I want to save some money, find a woman like Gladys and have a home and family.* But I was too damn stubborn. "I'd like to draw my time," I told the clerk in the time office.

"I'll have to get your time card. It will only take a minute. Superintendent O'Brien would like to see you. He is in his office across the hall."

He had also been on the telegraph line. "What's the trouble Wagner?"

"Just a bad day, Sir. I'm joining the Air Force and I want to get back home before I'm called up."

"I can't fault you for that. We're sorry to see you go but there'll always be a job for you here. Good luck."

The Medical Corps

In early September the CPR had an excursion rate. Day coach to Regina and return was sixty bucks. The Air Force call-up was still at least two months away. I would go home for a couple of weeks.

There were four soldiers in our coach and we got a case of Molson's at White River. A group gathered in the coach's smoker singing and yarning while the "Canadian" clickity-clacked across the Canadian Shield. That's where I met Bunny.

Sort of cuddled in the corner of the smoker, she hadn't joined the party. Dressed in a plain grey suit with mannish- looking blouse she looked professional and older than the rest of us. Her chin-length, straight-combed, coal-black hair, so soft and silky that it swayed with the rolling rhythm of the train, glistened halo-like around the delicate complexion of her finely featured face and soft blue eyes. She looked distant and unapproachable . . .

From across the aisle I discovered she was a nurse from Sudbury and she invited me to sit beside her. We had dinner in the dining car enjoying the CPR's Lake Winnipeg goldeyes. Twilight blurred the landscape flashing by the window until the black of night turned the windows into mirrors. I listened as she told me her recent heartbreak. As a nurse-receptionist she had also been the doctor's mistress for several years. Now his wife was threatening to divorce him, so Bunny had to go.

We told our life stories to each other as lonely strangers do. The train lights dimmed and the man across the aisle snored. We held each other's hands, kissed and hugged and fell asleep in each others arms.

We awoke to find the scrubby oaks of eastern Manitoba flashing by our window. We got tidied up for breakfast. We sat at breakfast. Just looking at her sent thrills racing through my mind.

"Gordon, do you have to be in Regina today?"

"No. Not really."

"Our train gets into Winnipeg this morning at nine. Why don't we got off and spend a day in Winnipeg?"

"What would we do in Winnipeg?"

"There must be lots of hotels close to the station. I need you Gordon, I want to go to bed with you."

My heart trip-hammered. The saliva drained from my mouth. I was twenty-five but I had never been in a bed with a woman! My first impulse was to get up and run. She reached across the table and took my hand. Electric shock glued my feet to the floor. I wasn't a virgin but I sure as hell felt like one.

We found a hotel and I felt queer signing the register as Mr and Mrs Gordon Burke. At least I didn't use John Smith. Young and strong after a year of heavy work in the mine, I was as hard as nails. She was an experienced lover but not quite prepared for the young bull she had met on the train. She mothered me. She bathed me and scrubbed my back. We collapsed with exhaustion when we boarded the train the next morning, and cuddling together we slept half the way to Regina.

We said goodbye in a long embrace while the train waited to leave Regina. I never saw Bunny again. Two weeks later I received a bamboo back-scratcher with a note saying, "I found this in Vancouver's China-town. Sorry I can't be there to scratch and wash your back. Maybe this will help. Think of you often. Love, Bunny." I still have the back-scratcher.

I had not been home for a week when there was a big write-up in the Leader Post about the Royal Army Medical Corps. The British Commonwealth had decided to make Canada the training ground for the aircrew to drive the German Luftwaffe from the skies. The RAMC would look after the sick, the lame and the lazy. They needed bodies. You could sign on in Regina.

"Gordon, why don't you join the Medical Corps. I don't like the thought of you flying."

"I'd rather fly, Mother. But if it will make you any happier I'll go to Regina tomorrow and check it out."

I had no trouble getting in to see Captain O'Berne. I had trouble getting out. It took me five years.

He told me about all the training schools that were being built on the prairies. "Wagner, we really need men with your qualifications. You should be a corporal in a couple of weeks and a sergeant in a month. Of course you'll never receive a commission —that's reserved for doctors and nursing sisters. But you can become a warrant officer. That's the best rank in the service. The Air Force is stepping up its own medical branch. So you'll soon be wearing the Air Force blues."

It sounds pretty good to me. I won't have to wait around for my aircrew call-up. Even if I qualify for aircrew there's no assurance that I'll ever get to fly. Besides I'm running out of money. I hate being broke. I'll only be getting a buck fifty-five a day. So what's the difference, I never saved a dime in Sudbury. Mum will be happy.

I took the oath of allegiance, signed on the dotted-line and was told to report for duty the next morning at the Regina Normal School.

I knew my hair was too long to suit the army. "Cut it short," I told the barber. "I'm going into the army tomorrow." He ran the clippers high and sheared off most of my curls. I felt like a freshly plucked chicken. The next morning on our first parade I was told to get a haircut. A week later I got nicked again.

Sergeant Gaffney, small, short and snappy, with a bull horn for a voice blared, "You're a motley-looking bunch of farmers. We'll soon change that. Go to 'stores' to draw your uniforms and equipment. You have the rest of the day off. You fall in tomorrow at 08:00 hours properly dressed for inspection."

The World War I uniforms they issued us had been mothballed for twenty years. The 1916 khaki tunic, with a high collar wrapped round your neck, felt like coarse sandpaper. The brass buttons, hat badge and belt buckle gleamed green with more than envy. I wondered how they'd ever shine again. The leather belt, crusted with dried-out mold, crackled when you touched it. The heavy clods we got for boots were coated with a layer of lard.

We shined, pressed and polished. The brass sparkled. The leather belt relaxed and looked like leather. The pants and tunic were crease-less. But I couldn't get those damn boots to shine.

A sergeant and a couple of corporals spent hours marching us around the parade square. We had some stretcher drill, and learned how to make our beds and store our kits so they would pass the CO's

R.C.A.M.C., No. 2 ITS, Regina

inspection. Then Madeleine Carrol came to town.

She and Preston Foster were in Regina for the world premiere of Metro-Goldwyn-Meyers' *Royal North West Mounted Police,* and there had to be a parade. The military was prominent, with the Navy leading, followed by the Army with the Air Force bringing up the rear of the mile-long procession. Our platoon of twenty new recruits dressed in that damned sandpapered-khaki was tacked on behind the Air Force.

We marched for seven miles at attention. The skin under my arms, between my legs and around my neck was rubbed raw. My feet were blistered. And I thought the mines in Sudbury had been tough!

Next week they put us in the hospital. I was stunned. I never realized I'd joined the Air Force as a nursing orderly. I had completed my premedical classes, studied parasitology, bacteriology and biochemistry at university. I expected the medical corps would have some use for my qualifications.

We learned how to take and record a patients temperature, pulse and respiration, how to give a bed bath, an enema, and empty sputum cups, how to make a bed and envelope the corners, how to give medication and keep the charts, how to give prophylactic irrigation to an airman who been exposed to gonorrhea. *My God! What have I got myself into? I'll find someway of getting out of this schamoozle! No damn way am I going to spend my military career juggling piss pots and bedpans in a bloody hospital!*

Things got worse. After a week at nursing school we went on duty in the hospital for twelve hour shifts. Regina College, next door to the Normal School, housed the Air Force's No 2 Initial Training School (No 2 ITS). The ground floor of the women's residence had been converted into a hospital. Captain Latchford, a doctor from World War I, steeped in military tradition, was the hospital's Medical Officer (MO). Nursing Sister Hastings, who never smiled when on duty, was the hospital's only nurse.

Private Gordon Wagner

Our day started at seven when we carried breakfast trays to the patients, then retrieved the tray and helped the patients make their beds. Next was broom and wash patrol. We had to keep the hospital spotless. If Captain Latchford or the Sister passed us we snapped to attention. Nurse Hastings had a pair of white gloves she used to search for dust we might have missed.

Each patient had a four-inch brass box with a cup-like handle and a hinged-spring-loaded lid. The inside was a waxed cardboard box. It was a sputum cup — the damnedest designed contraption ever. I bloody near puked every time I emptied one. With its spring-loaded lid it was hard to spit into and damn near impossible to get the cardboard box out.

One morning, with my stomach still woozy after emptying sputum cups, Sgt Little said, "Private Wagner, get Captain Latchford's tea from the kitchen and take it to his office."

"Yes sir, Sergeant."

I stopped at Captain Latchford's open door, walked in and put the tray on his desk. "Here's your tea, Sir."

"Private Wagner," he shouted, "you take that tray off my desk and go and stand at attention at my door until I tell you to come in."

31

He made me stand there for at least ten minutes. I hoped his bloody tea was cold.

It was not all bad. Regina people were friendly. The girls loved to date the fledging pilots in their Air Force uniforms. Three pay phones in the barrack's vestibule rang constantly.

"Hello. Is that Air Force barracks?" a sweet young voice would ask.

"Yes, it is."

"Could I speak to Jimmy Stewart, please."

You could pretend you hollered for Jimmy, or better yet, tell her Jimmy had been posted and ask if you would do. Young girls with the family car cruised the streets and often took us to their homes and fed us, especially on Sunday afternoons. Western hospitality, a pretty girl, and a home-cooked meal with her family was a delightful combination.

Following two weeks on night shift, and after making a horrible mess giving an enema to a constipated patient and having a patient sneak out a hospital window in his pyjamas, I asked to be paraded before Captain Latchford. I asked permission to remuster to aircrew. I filed the application but I remained a nursing orderly.

The staff at No 2 WTS, Calgary, left to right, Sgt. Blair, AC1 Peebles, Cpl Hardy, AC1 Parry, AC1 Matthews, Sgt Gaffney.

In mid-November Roy (Punchy) Matthews, Doug Parry and I were transferred to No 2 Wireless School in Calgary. The Air Force had taken over Calgary's Normal School and the adjoining Technical School. The buildings sat high on the north bank of the Bow River, now the growing campus of SAIT (Southern Alberta Institute of Technology).

I enjoyed Calgary. The people were more friendly. The girls seemed prettier. The weather was warmer. The MO was a doctor, not a bombastic soldier. We had no parades and we had a permanent reveille pass. We had a two-hundred-bed boudoir, our own mess and a great cook. And there was Sergeant Blair.

The school's gymnasium had been turned into a barrack. Sleeping in the double bunk-beds jammed side by side, lining up to use the washroom and the showers, watching the early morning parade of nudity by the braggarts and the bashful, trying to sleep with an anvil chorus of snores, keeping a snore-stick to poke into the ribs of the sleepers in the adjacent bed, listening to the nightly pre-sleep banter, the vulgar boasting of sexual conquests and after-lights-out bellowing the familiar battle cry, "F—- the East" echoed by "F—- the West" shocked and surprised many a new recruit.

The hospital, located on the third floor of the Normal School, used two classrooms as twelve-bed wards and another classroom for sick parades, treatment room and dispensary. The kitchen and our mess was in the basement.

The first time I heard the strains of *Clementine* echoing through the hospital I wondered what the hell was going on. From the class-room below a chorus of thirty untrained and off-key male voices shook the walls and windows with this song, but instead of singing:

O my darling, O my darling, O my darling Clementine,

You are lost and gone forever, O my darling Clementine.

They belted out, loud and clear:

De dah "A", de dah "A", de dah "A", de dah "A",

De dah "A", de dah "A", de dah "A", de dah.

There were three classes every morning and they continued until the alphabet and the numbers of the Morse Code became a "direct" language. In aircrew a year later I had to be able to receive and send the code at a minimum of ten words a minute. I wished I had sung *Clementine* instead of the "dots and dashes" I had learned as a boy scout. I never was able to think in Morse Code. I had to translate.

Sergeant Blair was our NCO (Non Commissioned Officer) in charge. He had been an orderly in the Weyburn, Saskatchewan, Mental Hospital. We thought he might have been a patient. Small for a sergeant, his uniform hung on his rounded shoulders like a muumuu on a ruptured coat hanger. His shirt, a size too big, with his tie knotted like a lazy lasso, sagged under his receding chin. A strand of his well-greased, washed-out, blonde hair dangled over his right eye. His pasty complexion with a nicotine stain on his upper lip made him look like death warmed over.

We all liked Sergeant Blair, mostly because he didn't throw his rank around. He was drunk nearly every night and we covered for him.

Charlie, the hospital chef, had worked on a CPR diner, and he could change the worst of Air Force rations into tasty meals. Most Air Force cooks had been recruited from factories or farms, given a six week course and then turned loose to spoil good food. Charlie introduced me to clam chowder. I still think of him every time I enjoy a bowl of good chowder.

The first class of wireless operators was still in training when we arrived. Everybody in aircrew wanted to train as a pilot. When they needed a hundred bodies to train as WAGs (Wireless Air Gunners) they lined them up, counted down the line and sent a hundred off to No. 2 Wireless. Two airmen in the first class had their private pilot's license. They would do anything to get out of wireless school. Half our patients were these "lead-swingers."

We had to carry trays of food up four flights of stairs to feed those lazy s.o.b.s. With our limited staff we had to make two or three trips and often Sgt. Blair helped. But we found ways of getting even.

One of the lead swingers favourite complaints was a bad back ache. It was difficult to diagnose. The MO would give them the benefit of the doubt and put them in the hospital. But they kept coming back. We watched them carefully. When the MO was sure they were faking, they got the doctor's "No 10 Special." Our druggist, mixing potassium permanganate, coloured concentrated epsom salts purple and added a dash of quinine to make it bitter. The MO ordered three ounces daily.

They got one ounce immediately, some came back for the second, but nobody ever came back for the third.

Short-arm inspections were more talked about than done. But Dr Finlayson, Punchy and I made a midnight visit to our two-hundred-bed boudoir. Without any warning, and one at time, we got everybody out of bed and took a smear from the end of his penis, got his name and number and tucked him back into bed.

As a biologist, I stained the slides and looked for the coffee- bean shaped bacteria that caused gonorrhea. A few tested positive. Many had an infection caused by not washing under their foreskins. All the suspects had to be interviewed by the MO who ordered treatment.

Dr. Finlayson, a meticulous red-headed man with a fading crop of freckles and with an abrupt bedside manner, listened to the excuses and ordered sulfa, the new wonder drug. One young airman, barely eighteen, with tears rolling down his cheeks as he stood at attention in front of Finlayson, said, "Please, Sir, I have never been with a woman in my life."

Dr. Finlayson, with an uncalled-for cockiness said, "Well if you can't get a clean old woman get a clean old man." I felt sorry for the kid and wondered if we had got some of the slides mixed up.

We always had a few patients with VD. It was routine to find the woman who infected the patient and make sure she reported to Calgary's treatment centre. One young lady, over a period of two months, had put three airman in our VD ward. We now had her fourth victim, a New Zealander.

He developed venereal warts. When he pulled back his foreskin the warts looked like the frilly toadstools you see growing out of rotten logs. We cauterized the warts with silver nitrate. It burned like hell and took damn near a month before they all fell off.

We got to know her for she used to visit her casualties. One day she was in the ward visiting the New Zealander. When we told Dr. Finlayson he grabbed her by the collar, pushed her into the hall and for a moment I thought he might throw her down the stairs. We never saw her again.

We were still short of staff and working twelve-hour shifts and seven-day weeks. We hadn't had a day off since coming to Calgary and we were still wearing our khaki uniforms. I still didn't have a good shine on my lard-covered boots. A week before Christmas we were transferred from the RCAMC to the Medical Branch of the Royal Canadian Air Force. At the Calgary recruiting centre I took the oath of allegiance and enlisted for the second time. Two months later we received our official discharges from the RCAMC, saying we had been honourably discharged on the 14th of November. I had missed my chance. Damn the Air Force. Damn the Army. I could have escaped from the hospital, the bedpans and the VD warts. I had been a civilian for nearly a month, just plain Gordon Wagner. Now I was AC2 Wagner with a new blue uniform and a pair of boots that would take a shine. The girl count improved but the pay was the same — a buck fifty-five a day. I put in a new application to remuster.

Daily Routine Orders (DRO) announced that grades would be assigned to all the different trades in the service with an increase in pay. An assessment officer would visit the station and all personnel would be interviewed, including nursing orderlies.

"Sergeant Blair wants to see you, Gordon," said Punchy, "It's our turn to take the trades test."

"I'm not taking the test."

"Tell that to Blair. He's really hung over this morning."

His door was open. I knocked and waited. He sat slouched behind his desk with a cigarette dangling from his lips. His head nodded. I knocked again. He looked up and blinked. I thought his eyes would bleed. "Come in," he sighed.

I stood at attention in front of his desk and waited. He shuffled himself to attention, found a list of names and in a whisky whisper said, "AC2 Wagner, this morning at 10:10 hours you will report to Flying Officer Downs in Orderly Room and take your trade test."

"Sergeant Blair, you know what you can do with that trade test."

"AC2 Wagner that's an order. If you choose to disobey, you'll be put on charge."

In the service you soon learned that an order is to be obeyed even when it comes from a hungover sergeant. At 10:10 hours I stood in front of F/O Downs desk. "AC2 Wagner, reporting as ordered, Sir."

"At ease, Wagner, have a seat. I see you're a graduate of the University of Saskatchewan."

"Yes, Sir."

"That should help advance your career as a nursing orderly. You'll find this test relatively easy."

"Flying Officer Downs, I'm not interested in taking the test."

"Wagner, you can't be serious. If you don't take the test I'll have to show that you failed. You'll remain an AC2 and you won't get the ten-cents-a-day pay increase."

"Sir, I'm not interested in advancing my military or my financial career."

He dismissed me and I remained an AC2 at a buck fifty- five.

In Calgary we never lacked for entertainment. Beer was ten cents a glass. Service personnel were still a novelty in Calgary. If you were in uniform, and everybody at your table bought a round the next round was on the house. We were often treated by strangers. Hospitable Calgarians were like that.

Men and women drank in separate rooms but were served from the same bar. It is difficult to understand those puritanical regulations our legislatures made to save us from the sin of drink. In Saskatchewan women were not allowed in beer parlours at all.

If you got a table near the swinging doors you could see the girls next door. We would wave back and forth and, if we could afford it, buy the girls a drink. Often a friendly bartender would carry notes back and forth. The place closed at ten, and a mass of confusion clogged the sidewalks, as husbands located wives, and boyfriends found their girlfriends. We didn't always find our note-writers but we could always find a girl. The communication system worked well, in spite of the segregation. It gave both parties a chance to pick and choose.

We would go to a cafe if we could afford the nickel coffee or where the girls could splurge for a sandwich. Occasionally when you took them home you might spend the night. That was when the reveille pass saved you from trying to climb the fence and dodge the sentries guarding No 2 WTS.

I learned to dance in Calgary. In Markinch I used to go to dances but I didn't dance unless I got a little drunk. Besides you couldn't go for less than fifty cents — two-bits for admission and two-bits for a midnight lunch at Chinaman Pete's Maple Leaf Cafe. Sam Eros, the bootlegger, hovered in the shadows around the dance hall door, and for fifty cents you could buy a beer bottle of his potent homebrew. He used Watkin's Red Liniment to flavour his fire-water, and when it was poured into a saucer and lit, it burnt completely.

Five of us would each chip in ten cents and share a bottle. Sam, a bearded gorilla, would hulk off into the prairie darkness, never going the same way twice nor returning the way he went. We huddled behind the dance hall and killed the bottle. We drank it straight each getting two or three swigs. Each gulp curled your teeth, and grabbed your throat. It burnt travelling down your esophagus and boiled in your stomach. Those few slugs slushed away my shyness and I shuffled around the dance floor until daylight.

Calgary had two hostess clubs, one downtown operated by the Red Cross, the other in the suburbs of Scarborough operated by the United Church. They both provided a homey atmosphere where you could read, play cards, write letters, have tea and cakes served by charming women. The Red Cross had a dance every Friday night, and Scarborough had one on Saturday. There was no shortage of girls. Gracious matrons introduced strangers, making sure you enjoyed yourself.

The hostesses were mediocre dancers, especially when they had to follow a clumsy stubble-jumper. But every Wednesday night there was a dance in the Elk's hall. It cost two-bits to get in but could those girls dance! By attending three dances a week my dancing improved considerably.

Flight Lieutenant Ashburn was the Protestant "Sky Pilot" at No 2 WTS and a regular hospital visitor. I was surprised to see him at the Scarborough. The club was for other ranks.

"Hi, Padre, you're a long way from home."

"Hello, Gordon, nice to see you." He turned to the attractive woman beside him. "Penny, I'd like you to meet Gordon Wagner."

"Hello, Gordon. Reverend Ashburn used have this charge. It was he who got this club organized. He drops by quite often."

"Excuse me. I must see the ladies in the kitchen. Why don't you two dance?"

"May I?"

She wore her hair turban-like with a small braid resting on her neck. It glistened with the rich-brown colour of a freshly peeled chestnut. Her deep-set grey-blue eyes, with a brown ring around the iris, smiled as she talked. High cheekbones, her finely chiselled nose with its tiny bump, and her dew-fresh skin framed a classic oval face.

She gave me her hand. Benny Goodman was playing *I Met a Million Dollar Baby in the Five and Ten Cent Store*. There was never an awkward second. We danced in perfect harmony, the way you do in dreams, defying gravity and flowing through the air.

Penny

"You're a wonderful dancer, Penny!"

"I enjoyed it. You're easy to follow."

"May I have the next dance?"

"I'd like to, but I'm duty hostess tonight."

"The second one then?"

"Hmmm! With pleasure, thank you."

Dressed in the look-a-like, long-sleeved, white blouse and the flared black skirt worn by all the girls, she moved with poise amongst the dancers. I watched as she introduced a young sailor to one of the girls, and felt a tinge of jealousy when she coaxed a shy soldier to dance. I had good vibes for this woman and I sat and wondered why.

"I always enjoy dancing to Mark Kenney's music," she said. "He still plays at the Banff Springs Hotel during the summer."

"Did anyone ever tell you that you're a lovely woman?"

"Not lately, but flattery will get you nowhere."

"You smile with your eyes. Not many people add that to a lovely smile."

We danced every second dance. "May I have the home waltz?"

"I came with my girl friend, Doris. We live at the same boarding house. We'll catch the last streetcar at eleven fifteen, you're welcome to join us."

On the ride home I learned that she worked behind the perfume counter at the Bay (Hudson Bay Department Store), and that she had grown up in Drumheller. Then I noticed the ring. She must be married, but I hadn't noticed it at the dance.

"Are you married?"

"Well, yes. Sort of."

"I didn't notice the ring at the dance."

"I suppose I should wear it, but I feel more like a hostess without it. But let's talk about you."

I told her about my beginnings, where I had been and where I hoped to end, when suddenly she announced, "We get off at the next stop. You might as well stay on this car, it goes past the Normal School. It's a long walk across the bridge and up the hill."

"I want to see you again, real soon. How about tomorrow? I'm off this Sunday."

"I go to church in the morning. Why don't you phone shortly after twelve?"

"I haven't been in church for ages. Why don't we go together?"

"I'd enjoy that. The morning service starts at eleven."

"I'll call for you about half-past-ten. Good night, Penny, I've had a lovely evening."

"Good night, Gordon."

Sunday morning I walked down the hill and across the bridge. Calgary was enjoying a chinook. The winter's snow was blackened by the early thaw. The temperature had climbed from thirty degrees since the early morning frost. In the west the Rocky Mountains seemed close enough to touch. I expected to hear a crow caw, a robin to sing or a meadowlark, perched on top of a telephone pole to puff his yellow breast skyward and sing, "I love Canada, Canada!"

She waited in the sunshine drawing imaginary figures on the snow-covered sidewalk with her toe. A small white hat sat saucily on the waves of her brown hair, the soft oval of her delicate complexion snuggled into the silver-grey fur-collar of her black coat.

"Good morning, Gordon, what a lovely morning."

"Hello, Penny, I can't believe it's late November. I like your outfit, it goes well with your smiling eyes." I offered her my arm. " You're like a breath of spring."

"That's the name of my perfume."

"It smells like lilacs. I almost expected to see a tree in bloom."

We walked in the silence kindred souls find precious, both immersed in our thoughts and so aware of our arm-linked communication. In church we held hands, enjoying our nearness and the quiet holiness of the service.

"Memorial Park is just a few blocks from here. Would you like to sit in the warm sun for a while?"

We sat on a bench near the cenotaph. The warm winter-sun bounced little stars off the grey granite. The list of names, weathered black, threatened our enjoyable morning. I looked at Penny, she smiled and the sunshine brightened.

"I didn't sleep well last night. I felt terrible when you noticed my wedding ring. I think we have a warm feeling for each other, Gordon. I know I do."

"I want to know you better. It's a long time since I've had such good feelings for anyone."

"I married when I was seventeen and I have a daughter who will be seven in April. I haven't lived with the man I married for seven years. Angela lives with my parents in Drumheller. She adores her grandparents. I try to see her as often as I can, but it is difficult for me to get to Drumheller so my parents bring her to Calgary at least once a month. She is coming in next weekend so I won't be at the dance next Saturday."

"I'd like to meet Angela. I'm fond of children. My younger sister is just a couple of years older than your daughter. We've always been very close."

"We'll see how things go. Her father does his best to make life difficult for Angela and me."

Things didn't go well. It was ten days before I would see Penny again. I was on ward duty Monday morning, and Dr Finlayson and Nursing Sister Germain had just completed their daily rounds. I was on my way to the bathroom when I met Sgt Blair at the door.

"AC 2 Wagner, this ward has been put under quarantine. One of the patients has meningitis. You'll be confined to this ward for the next ten days."

"What do mean confined? You mean we're going to be locked up in this ward for ten days?"

"You'll eat and sleep here, and be responsible for all the ward duties. The adjacent washroom will be for the use of this ward only. I'll have Punchy bring your gear from the barracks."

"What if I refuse?"

"You'll likely end up in the guard house and for a hell of a lot longer than ten days. Wagner, why do you have to be so damn negative?"

"I just want to get out of this bloody outfit. But I won't go to jail to do it."

They took the meningitis patient to the Colonel Belcher Military Hospital in downtown Calgary. I got his empty bed. I had eleven patients, one with a bad back, some with the flu, a twisted knee and another with cracked ribs. Jim was the only patient with a temperature. His chart showed he had influenza and he was to get 500 mg of sulfa twice a day with an antacid if he needed it. Each time I gave him sulfa he became violently ill and no amount of antacid seemed to help.

During the second night he got the shakes and his temperature was 104 degrees. Dr. Finlayson was on call; I located him in the officer's mess and he brought the Nursing Sister with him. He was well into his cups.

"Wagner, get a thermometer, I'd like to check Jim's temperature!" he said with a slur in his voice. He checked his pulse and listened to his chest with a stethoscope. "Your temperature is still up. Can you roll over Jim, I want to listen to your back." I watched as he moved his stethoscope over Jim's back. "Hmmm, there is something here. Do you have a pen, Wagner?"

He took my pen and put a big X on Jim's skin. "I'll have another look at that in the morning. In the meantime Wagner, give him two aspirin every four hours until you get his temperature down."

Next morning I was almost afraid to touch Jim, he looked and smelled like death warmed up. His skin had the cold sweat of death. His heavy eyelids opened when I put the thermometer in his mouth. His temperature was down and his pulse regular and strong.

"Take these pills, Jim."

"Do I have to take those damn pills?"

"These are aspirin, Jim. I won't give you any more sulfa until the doctor make his rounds."

I had the ward pretty well organized. Everybody made their own beds, the up-patients helped serve the meals, swept the floors and had the place shipshape for the MO's rounds.

"How are you feeling today, Jim? I see your temperature is down."

"I feel a little better today, Sir."

"We'll continue with his treatment, Wagner."

"Aren't you going to look at the mark put on his back last night?"

"Was I in here last night?"

He rolled Jim over and listened to the spot he marked. "Yes, there is some congestion there," he mumbled and marked the chart with a "CT" for "continue treatment."

Well I'll be God damned. The little freckled-faced bastard was so drunk he didn't remember being in the ward. I'm not going to give Jim anymore sulfa. He has a tight chest cold. Mother always put mustard plasters on us when we had the croup. Maybe I should try a mustard plaster. I'll see if Punchy can smuggle in what I need. I'll have to make sure the plaster is off his chest when "the weasel" makes his rounds.

Punchy got the mustard and I strapped the plaster to his chest, continued with aspirin and flushed the sulfa down the john. The next morning the sticky sweat was gone from his face, his temperature was almost normal and he ate three good meals that day. The next day he was sitting up, and the third day he was walking to the bathroom.

I talked to Penny every evening. I waited until after "lights out" and I took the phone with its long extension cord into the bathroom to have a quiet visit.

The ten days were finally over. I thought I might get at least a forty-eight hour pass. "How about a weekend pass Sergeant Blair? I've been cooped up in isolation for ten days and I haven't had a 'forty-eight' since I left Regina."

"You did a good job, Wagner, but we just don't have the staff to give you time off. But I'll put you on steady days."

"I'd appreciate that, Sergeant."

I did a daily check on Jim. Finlayson was still writing the CT on his chart. I watched his temperature climb and he puked each time they gave him sulfa. It wasn't long before he was bed-ridden again. He was sent to the Colonel Belcher Military Hospital in downtown Calgary.

Admittance to the Belcher called for a Wassermann test. Jim had syphilis. No wonder he was so sick. I never did find out if mustard plasters could cure syphilis or how Jim helped to win the war. Finlayson continued to get plastered every evening. Perhaps he should have tried mustard.

The Bay was busy. I watched Penny from a distance while she waited on customers. *I wonder why I find her so attractive. There is a graciousness glowing around her. She carries herself well and she adds elegance to her clothes. She's making that little old lady feel she is the only person in the store. She smiles beautifully. She's free now. She sees me. There are those smiling eyes. Take it easy, Gordon, don't get so excited it's hard on your racing heart.*

"Oh, Gordon it's so wonderful to see you!"

"I've been watching you. You look lovelier than I remembered. I've missed you, Penny. I thought those ten days would never end."

"I missed you too. I'll meet you at the side door right after six. One of the girls got fired last week for spending too much time talking to her boyfriend. I'll see you in an hour."

A fresh winter's chill hovered over Calgary. I stood at the Bay's side door, watching snowflakes swarm around the street light like summer moths, then float earth-wards freshening the white on Calgary's roads and sidewalks. I listened to the crunch of people's feet echoing in the cold air, wondering where they were going, what their hurry was, and what they were expecting to find when they reached their destination. Most wore the frown of worry. There couldn't be that many unhappy people in the world. Most avoided eye contact, and if they did look my way, the glance was quickly diverted without returning my smile.

I didn't see her come out the door. Suddenly she had both my hands, pulled me towards her and kissed my lips. "It's wonderful to see you again, Gordon. I missed you."

"It seems like ages to me. Time passed slowly in the isolation ward. Oh! you look so yummy! I got paid today, so why don't we splurge for dinner downtown?"

"I'd love to. I'll have to phone to say I won't be home."

She took my arm and we exchanged connecting squeezes. "Let's go to Jimmy's, the food isn't too bad and they have booths. I insist on paying for my own meal. Don't argue."

We held hands across the table and played a little footsy. It filled my heart with joy just being near her. We lingered over coffee. "Would you like to come back to the boarding house? We're allowed to have visitors, but only in the parlour. Sometimes it gets a little crowded."

"That will be fine. What are your plans for Christmas?

"Christmas is on Wednesday, so we have to work Friday and Saturday. I'll spend Christmas Day and Boxing Day in Drumheller with Angela and my parents. What are your plans?"

"I'm on duty both days. But we will be off at seven pm."

"Angela and my folks will be in the weekend before Christmas. I want you to meet Angela. I've told her about you, she likes the Air Force uniforms. Let's go back to my place, I have some new photos of Angela."

I helped her on with her coat and was stirred by the warm firmness of her body and the cleavage she hid beneath her coat. She kissed me with a quick peck and the soft lusciousness of her lips flip-flopped my heart. We walked, arm in arm through the falling snow, to her boarding house.

In the dimly-lit parlour a gas fireplace flickered shadows on the over-stuffed chesterfield and the pair of matching chairs. In a rocking chair a middle-aged woman knitted under the room's only lamp.

"Good evening, Mrs. Fraser, I'd like you to meet my friend, Gordon Wagner."

"Hello, Mr. Wagner, so you're the young man we've been hearing about. Well, I am sure you young people have things to talk about that would likely interfere with my knitting. Besides I've got a million things to do in the kitchen. Susie arrived home today, so that's another one to cook for. Good night, you two."

"Mrs. Fraser is a real doll. Susie, her daughter is supposed to be at school in Edmonton. She thinks she God's gift to men. As soon as she knows you're here she'll be down to work her charms on you."

We sat watching the flickering fireplace.

She turned to face me, took my hand and let the smile fade from her face and eyes. "Thanks for taking me to dinner, Gordon, I did enjoy it."

"It was my pleasure. You know, when I dance with you I want to dance forever."

"Oh, Gordon. It's been a long time since I've allowed myself to have a good feeling for anyone. My husband is an absurdly jealous man. Though I haven't lived with him for five years, he still thinks of me as his wife. I live in constant fear that he will do something to Angela. He has threatened to take her from my mother. He is almost insane at times."

"Does he know about us? I've only seen you half-a-dozen times."

"If he doesn't he'll soon find out. His mother and sister live in Calgary and they watch me like a hawk. A year ago I went with an army captain for awhile. My husband picked up Angela on her way home from school and kept her for the week end. I had to promise not to see the captain again. We went to the police but there was nothing they could do."

"Why don't you divorce him?"

"He won't give me grounds for divorce. He just wants to make life as miserable as he can for me. I'm his prisoner. There is nothing I can do until Angela is twenty one. Even then I'll never feel really safe."

"Do you mean I won't be able to see you anymore."

She put her head on my shoulder and cried like a broken-hearted child.

"I don't know! I don't know what to do! I want to love you, Gordon. I need your love. But this situation with my husband is so hopeless I wonder if it will ever end."

I gathered her in my arms as I would a sobbing child. I kissed the tears from her eyes, caressed the softness of her hair and held her close. She quieted to a whimper. For a moment I thought she had fallen asleep. Then she put her arm around my neck and pulled my head to hers and kissed me.

The parlour door exploded open with a bang. "Well, I hope I'm interrupting at the right time. Penny, I wouldn't want you taking advantage of one of our airmen. I heard you had a good-looking man in the parlour so I just had to see him. My name is Susie, soldier. I love you service men. Where you find this handsome devil, Penny? At the Scarborough hostess club? Or was it at your perfume counter?"

We untangled ourselves and I stood up ready for the attack of this amazon. She was a brazen little bitch. She wore a lacy black dress that showed off her white skin and raven-black hair. She walked right up to me, smoothed the lapels of my uniform. Her well-endowed and bra-less breasts threatened to pop out of her blouse.

"This guy is all man, Penny. When you're finished with him let me know. You're my kind of man. What's his name Penny?"

"Don't pay any attention to her Gordon. She talks to men like that only when there are other women around. Her bark is worse than her bite."

Mrs. Fraser rescued us. "I have a cup of tea ready. Give the other girls a call, Susie."

We sat around the kitchen table and I listened as the women chatted. Then Penny said, "Gordon, a matron at the club tells me you read tea cups. Have a look at mine and tell me what you see."

I have pretended to read teacups ever since I listened to Uncle Carl tell fortunes from tea. Because he'd been shell-shocked in the war my mother believed he was left with a psychic power. I had a good imagination and I always forecast the good things people wanted to happen to themselves. It's good fun and occasionally your generalizations are right on. I told Mrs. Fraser that she was going to receive an unexpected sum of money. "It should be in the mail any day," I told her. Two days later she received a money order from a former boarder who owed her three months rent. After that, every time I called on Penny, Mrs. Fraser made a cup of tea. I'd tell her fortune and we'd get am extra hour of parlour time.

Now that I was on steady days, I saw Penny often. On Fridays I'd meet her at the Bay's side door and we'd go to the Red Cross dance and on Saturdays we'd dance at the Scarborough Club. We always left early so we'd be home before Mrs. Fraser went to bed. We'd have a cup of tea and I'd tell her fortune. "Thank you, Gordon. It's past parlour time, but seeing it's Sunday tomorrow you can sit her till twelve. Mind you turn off the gas when you leave Penny. Good night you two. I envy the love I see in your souls. God bless you, my dears."

The parlour was cozy-warm. We cuddled into the corner of the chesterfield and sat in studied silence watching the flames dance behind the screen. "Angela will be in town next Saturday, Gordon. I'm trying to get the afternoon off. My boss has always tried to date me — I guess it's because he knows I'm not living with my husband. I hate to ask him for the afternoon off. He'll have some scheme. It makes it difficult. I can't afford to lose my job. He's awful. I just hate the thought of Christmas because I won't see you and I can't see my daughter without compromising my job. Now that I am seeing you so often, I expect my mad husband to do his best to spoil my holiday."

"I'm supposed to be on duty Saturday, but I can probably trade a shift with someone. I'm sure something will work out. Maybe we could get your boss fired. Cheer up, Penny. Things are never so bad that they can't be worse. Remember to live in the 'here and now'. We can't live in the distant past nor in the imagined future. Cuddle a little closer and let me tell you how wonderful you are and let me bite your ear."

"I wish you didn't have to go. Why do we have to be such slaves to convention? I really need you, Gordon. I need to bare my soul to someone I can trust and love. I've tried to talk to our minister but he doesn't understand. He prays for me. People have been praying for me as long as I can remember. But nobody seems to help. You're the first person in years who seems to care and understand and you're only here until the Air Force moves you."

The mantle clock struck twelve. "You must go. We must honour Mrs. Fraser's curfew. Let me help you with your overcoat."

She stood in front of me, a little shorter in her stocking feet. She snuggled close. I wrapped her inside my great coat. We kissed long and hard.

"Now I've got you. I'll keep you inside my great coat and you'll never have to worry again."

"Good night, dear Gordon. I do love you."

"Good night, sweet love, I live for you."

"Will I see you tomorrow?"

"Why don't you come down tomorrow night? Everybody gathers in the parlour Sunday evening to listen to Jack Benny, and to Edgar Bergen with Charlie McCarthy. Mrs. Fraser serves cookies and cocoa. She'll likely have tea."

"Thanks, Penny I might do that."

I took my time walking across the bridge and up the hill wondering where my life was headed. I stopped in the middle of the bridge. The Bow River, silenced for its winter's rest, would live again. I leaned on the rail watching the northern lights unfurl the curtains of the north. Could those mysterious phantoms reveal my future? I watched and wondered. Mrs. Fraser had no trouble a tea cup couldn't solve. The war, my fear, and my peacock-pride had changed my life. How long would I have to wait for my spring thaw?

Live in the "here and now" Gordon. Enjoy Penny's love while you can. You'll never pass this way again. You both need each other. I suppose someday I'll get married but not on fifty-five dollars a month. Be kind and love her. Be gentle and don't add to her troubles. Enjoy the happiness of your togetherness. It's a jewel. Treasure it. You'd better get moving, you romantic dreamer, you still have that damned hill to climb.

Sunday evening Susie met me at the door. "Come in handsome, I know Penny is expecting you." She turned and shouted up the stairs, "Your beau is here, Penny, but don't hurry I'll entertain him."

She took me into the parlour. I sat in one of the over-stuffed chairs, I was afraid to use the chesterfield. She wore her black, sexy dress and perched herself on the arm of my chair. I could almost bite her boobs. She crossed her legs bringing her short skirt above her silk-covered knee and tucked her foot against my leg. She shook her head and threw her lovely mane over her shoulders.

"Gordon, I can't understand what a good-looking man like you sees in Penny. You know she is married and has a little girl? She's moving, did you know that? Yep. I'm going back to school, so I need the bedroom and she and Doris have to move. I don't know if they found a new place or not."

"No, I didn't know that."

"Why don't you take me out sometime?"

"I might just do that."

"I wouldn't have to entertain you in the parlour. I'd sneak you in the back door. Mum would never know. I'm good in bed. You ever been to bed with Penny?"

"Well if I had, you'd be the last one to know!"

Penny walked through the door, "Oh! Excuse me. Looks like I maybe interrupting something."

"Not really, Penny, I was just trying out my charm on your boy friend. I leave you to him, dearie, he's too good to waste."

"I'll be glad to see the last of that little vixen. Did she tell you we have to move? Doris has a friend who is giving up her apartment, and we're hoping we might get that."

They moved before Christmas into a cozy three-room apartment. It was there that I met Angela.

Her large, brown eyes seemed to use most of her face and with her pugged-nose was almost hidden in a cloud of freckles. Her straight, shiny-black hair was pulled back into a foot-long braid. She loved to play cards — snap, crazy-eights —and never seemed to grow weary. I baby-sat her on a Saturday afternoon a couple of weeks before Christmas while Penny worked and her grandparents did their shopping.

"Can we play another game, Mr. Wagner?"

"Well, one more. Your Mom and her folks will soon be home. You've just about worn me out."

"I like you Mr. Wagner. My Mom said I would. She said I should call you Mr.Wagner but I'd like to call you Gordon. May I?"

"All my friends call me Gordon. You're my newest friend. I'd be happy to have you call me Gordon."

"I'd like to call you Daddy, I never had a Daddy. Then maybe we could live together."

"Your Mom would have something to say about that."

"She really likes you Gordon. I wish you were coming to our place for Christmas."

We played three more games of crazy-eights before I was rescued by Grandpa and Gramma.

I opened the red envelope addressed with the scrawl of a six-year-old, and postmarked Drumheller, happy to get a card from my new freckled-face friend and maybe a note from Penny. I pulled out a blank piece of paper folded like a Christmas card. Inside, scrawled in large, child-like letters and printed with red crayon was—
BEWARE DONT SKATE ON THE BAY THE ICE IS THIN.

When I showed it to Penny she turned white and her eyes quit smiling. "I knew it," she said, "I knew as soon as you met Angela he'd start some trouble. I was so happy when I got our apartment, and I could have Angela with me once in awhile. Oh! Gordon, what will I do? I'm afraid he might pull some dumb stunt at Christmas."

"Try not to worry. I'll stay away when Angela is in town."

"Oh, that won't help. You don't know how irrational he can get."

Penny had to work extra hours the last Saturday before Christmas so we missed the Scarborough dance. She had to work Christmas eve and then catch a bus to Drumheller. She had her afternoon coffee break about three o'clock. We exchanged gifts, held hands and let our love flow across the table and warm our troubled hearts.

Calgary, famous for its western hospitality, outdid itself that second Christmas of the war. I was waiting for a street car at the corner of 8th Avenue and 2nd Street. Big, soft fluffy snowflakes floated into the street light from the black blanket of night-sky, dropping a clean white carpet over Calgary's busy streets. I heard a quiet voice, just barely audible above the street-noise.

"Excuse me, soldier."

I turned to see a tiny woman bundled in a muff and muffler, with a black tam sitting saucily on one side of her head, looking like a tiny snowman.

"Do you have any place to spend Christmas? We'd like you to come and have Christmas with us."

"How kind of you to ask me. I have to work Christmas day but I'm sure there are many who would appreciate Christmas in your home."

On the day before Christmas a draft of a hundred Australians arrived at No 2 WTS. On Christmas morning the only phones on the station were in our hospital and in the guard house. We were inundated by calls asking airman for Christmas dinner. By ten o'clock every airman on the station had been invited to a Christmas dinner, including the hundred Aussies. And the phone rang on and on and on. It was western hospitality at its best.

The hospital was quiet, the M/O had discharged the lame, the lazy and the lead-swinger. We spent most of our time answering the phone. I missed Penny and wondered where our love would lead. I was in love with her. But I realized there was no way I could ever marry Penny. I wrote and told my parents about her, and alarmed that I was seeing a married woman, Mother replied and tried to warn me.

I had only been in the service for four months and it seemed like four years. I disliked most things about the service. Especially the apple-shining, the suck-holing and the brown-nosing. I had no military ambition and the way things were going I'd probably be juggling piss pots for the rest of the war.

What the hell was I doing in this bloody outfit? Anybody could do what I was doing, and might even enjoy it. Then there was Sergeant Blair. I felt he was scared of me and I didn't try to discourage him. Rumour said we were going to get our white pants and jackets to wear when we were on hospital duty. I decided I'd make a stand. I'd refuse to wear the bloody things. If I couldn't work in my blues, they could put me the guard house and stick the whites up their bloody bums.

I could handle Sergeant Blair, and I got along with the MO, but Nursing Sister MacBeth used to like to keep me busy. She had me sharpening hypodermic needles, and wrapping bundles to be sterilized in the autoclave. I found a way to beat her. She couldn't, or didn't, or was too shy to go into the men's washroom and there was no women's bathroom. Nursing Sister MacBeth was the only woman in amongst four hundred men. I don't remember where her quarters were, but she probably had a bathroom all to herself. The window sills in the men's washroom had a casement two-feet wide, and faced the south with plenty of room to sit and read during Calgary's sunny winter days. When I had finished my morning duties and with an hour until lunch, I'd get a book or magazine, and sit and read until it was time to carry those damn lunch trays up four flights of stairs to feed a bunch of lead-swingers. So I was one up on the Nursing Sister. I loved it and got lots of reading time.

Penny was back. I didn't like the arrangements in their new place. I liked it better in Mrs Fraser's boarding house. At least Penny and I could use the parlour after hours. Now we had to share the parlour-come-dining-room with Doris and her boyfriends — the girls shared the bedroom with its twin beds.

As soon as she got back to work I stopped by the Bay. "How did your Christmas go, Penny?"

"Better than I expected. It was a quiet time and I needed the rest. You made a big impression on my daughter. Now Angela thinks we should get married so she can have a Daddy."

"Maybe we should listen to her. I did miss you, Penny. I'll meet you after work. I'll be at the side door at nine."

But Penny didn't show. June Gerow, whose brother I had known at the U of S, worked at the Bay's jewellery counter, and she brought me Penny's message.

"Gordon, Penny had to rush to Drumheller. She's in an awful state. Her nutty husband picked up Angela on her way home from school and they don't know where they are. Penny was almost hysterical when she left."

"My God! What are they doing about it?"

"Lord knows! Penny asked me to give you her Drumheller phone number. She'll be waiting for your call."

I got a pocket full of dimes and found the closest pay phone.

"Hello, is Penny there?"

"Just a moment, please."

"Hello," she said and her voice sounded strained and tired and I couldn't see the smile in her eyes and you could almost hear the tears.

"Penny! How are you? I just got your message!"

"Gordon! How good of you to call. Things have settled down now. Angela is fine. Her father picked her up on her way home from school. A friend saw her get in the car and phoned my mother, but he brought her home just before dinner time. The police saw them in an ice cream parlour but they didn't interfere. They have seen this happen before. Thank God, she is all right. I just tucked her into bed and she's asleep. We've had a hectic day here. I'm going to catch an early bus tomorrow. I can't afford to miss another day's work."

"I'll meet you after work. Try and get a good night's sleep and don't forget I love you."

"I love you, Gordon. Thanks for calling. I'll tell you all the details tomorrow."

Calgary's temperature had dropped to twenty-below-zero. The underfoot crackle of frigid snow echoed with every footstep and I listened as people, with heads pulled into their collars, hurried home.

"Burrrr, it's cold," Penny said, as she grabbed my arm. "It's too cold to stand here and talk. How would you like bacon and eggs? I brought some fresh farm-eggs from Drumheller."

There were three of us for supper, Doris, Penny and I. After dinner, Doris went to a movie with a friend, and Penny and I washed the dishes. Dishwashing is a quiet time, seldom hurried and a great time to visit.

"I suppose I shouldn't worry. But I spent two horrible years with my husband. I was seven months pregnant when we were married. It shocked my parents and I was scared to death. I was only sixteen when he first picked me up. I had been a scrawny kid, not popular with the boys at school. He was in his twenties and drove a Model A Ford. It boosted my ego when he started to meet me after school. Then one afternoon it happened. It is a horrible memory and even now it makes me sick to think about it. I got out of his car and somehow stumbled home and I never went with him again although he pestered me to death.

"Finally I got so big I had to tell my mother. Mom understood but my dad got out the shot gun. Gordon, you grew up in a small town and know the scandal pregnant girls face. I tried my best to make a go of our marriage. I won't ever forget the pain and shame of those years.

"After Angela was born it got worse. If I wouldn't do his bidding he'd threaten to hurt her. Then one day, when she was almost two, I caught him trying to fondle her. We had an awful quarrel and I thought he was going to kill me and Angela as well. He has an violent temper. I was afraid to call the police. I grabbed Angela, packed a small bag and fled to Mom and Dad's. I never went back, not even to get my clothes.

"He is not without his good points. He has always been a good provider and I suppose, in his own way, is fond of Angela. We have a legal separation and he is supposed to stay away from her. He refuses to give me grounds for a divorce and I can't afford to have him followed.

"I suppose his sister has told him about us. I'm sure she has and it is a wonder he didn't react sooner. Thanks for drying the dishes, Gordon. Let's make use of the chesterfield while we're alone."

I sat in the corner, holding her in my arms as she lay across the length of the sofa. She felt firm, warm and so cozy. I snuggled my nose in the soft womanly scent of her hair. I kissed the smile in her eyes and found the warm caress of her lips. We kissed long and hard as if it might be our last. "Oh, Gordon what are we going to do? I missed you so much. I do love you. How am I going to keep you?"

"I think of you all the time, Penny. I love you and need your love. Oh! It is all so damned mixed up. It's the bloody war. We are both trapped in this mess. I can't divorce the Air Force and you can't get one from your husband. But if it hadn't been for the war I would never have met you. I will always treasure our friendship whatever happens. I just don't want to cause you any heartaches, and most of all I don't want to cause trouble for Angela and you."

She sobbed softy and I kissed the tears from her eyes, "Just hold me Gordon, let this minute last forever. I do love you and I need you so much. I feel a strength in you I have longed for all these years. Just hold me close!"

"We all have to live in the here and now. I have no control over my life. I go where the Air Force sends me. I'd marry you tomorrow. You are an attractive, mature woman and so alive. Let me stretch out and lie beside you. I do love you, Penny."

"Your closeness scares me. I want you, Gordon. I need you. But I can't. I just can't! I could never live through another pregnancy alone. Why does life have to be so difficult? I don't want to ever let you go!"

I don't know how long we lay there, but she felt so good against me. We were almost asleep when Doris and her boyfriend returned.

In early February of '41 No 2 Wireless Training School's first class held its graduation in the Palliser Hotel with a banquet and the presentation of newly-won wings, followed by a dance. The station's adjutant, Flight Lieutenant Pilling, an executive with the Calgary Brewery before he wangled a commission in the Air Force, arranged to have the brewery donate the beer. Our hospital staff was given a left-handed invitation by members of the class who had been patients. When Porky Clarke and I got off duty that evening, we decided to visit the Palliser to see how the party was going.

We arrived about nine-thirty but were too late for the free beer. At the entrance to the ballroom in a small room ordinarily used as a checking room, a bar had been set up. Half-a-dozen empty beer kegs lay prostrate on the floor almost afloat in a sloppy sea of beer. The beer had flooded over the door jam into the marble- floored hall and seeped into the carpets.

"Hi, you bloody Medics, sorry the draft's all gone but we have a few bottles of Calgary's best. Have one, and welcome to the party. Glad you could make it. Great bash!"

We stood in the stag line and watched the newly-winged wireless operators dance with the long-gowned beauties, and jawed with the airmen we knew.

"Glad you blokes could make it. There's a bit of a bash going on in my room. Come along and I'll pour you a drink." It was Ron Evans, an Australian, who had been one of our patients.

"I didn't recognize you in civvies," said Porky.

"I like to get out of the blue monkey-suit any chance I get. I'm in room 435. You go on up, I'll be along as soon as I have a word with my Sheila."

Ron's father, a wealthy Australian vintner, gave Ronald a monthly allowance that enabled him to keep a permanent room in Calgary's finest hotel, the CPR's Palliser. He used it for his forty-eights and other leaves. He had offered the key to us but we couldn't afford to live in such luxury.

The door to room 435 was open and the cackle of the drinking voices burst from the room and filled the hallway. We joined the crowd and found ourselves a drink. The room buzzed. Ron arrived and the party slowed a bit as some of the hangers on had worn out their welcome. I found a tall, evening-gowned girl with her coal-black hair pulled tight against her head and wearing a red gardenia behind her right ear. With her dark complexion that complimented her cream-coloured dress, she looked like she had just arrived from Spain.

"The senorita looks unhappy, but very lovely. You should display such beauty in the ballroom. Would you care to dance?"

She took an angry puff on her cigarette and ground it into a ash tray. "Why not," she said with anger straining her voice. "My bloody boy friend has passed out. I'd really like to go home."

"Let's go and dance. You're much too attractive to be angry."

"Okay, but I have to find the guy I came with; he has the keys to my car."

We danced well together. After an intermission my senorita left me to dance with a red-headed airman. I spotted Ron at the door of the ballroom.

"Gordon, I have to be back in barracks at midnight but I left the key for the room with Porky. Just make yourselves at home and I'll see you around the station."

"Thanks, Ron, we'll take good care of your room."

"You pick them well, Gordon. That tall beauty is Sharon Cross. Her daddy owns the Calgary Brewery. Her boy friend is a bit of an ass. He is probably shacked up in another room."

"Senorita, I enjoyed dancing with you and I know your name is Sharon. I suppose we will have to find your boyfriend."

"Oh, he'll show up. He always does. You haven't told me your name."

"I'm Gordon. Would you like to come up to room 435?"

"Not really. I wanted to find my girl friends. I think I see them down the hall."

We found them, two girls and three men, sitting on the steps near a landing in a hall. The men were in civvies and I soon discovered they had no use for the Air Force.

"I'll run along Sharon and leave you with your friends. I enjoyed dancing with you."

"Thanks, Gordon, It was fun. I hope to see you again."

"I'll call you soon. Are you in the phone book?"

"I'll give you my number, it's unlisted."

"Don't you give your number to that damn airman, Sharon. And you, mister, better bugger off before we clean your clock."

I watched as she got pen and paper from her purse and started to write. Then the three fellows got up and surrounded me. I jumped to my feet and tried to get next to the wall. If I was going to take on three of them I had to have my back protected.

Two of them grabbed me from behind, pinned my arms to my side and the third landed a heavy blow on my nose. I heard the bones in my nose crunch and saw the room fill with stars. I pulled myself and the two guys holding me to the wall, and with a quick twist of my body I broke free from the pair holding me, kicked the third guy in the shins and ducked as he tried to hit me again. There was a small jog in the hall wall and when I wrenched myself clear I slammed my elbow against it. It hurt like hell.

When I have a few drinks I don't get quarrelsome and never get into a fight, but with three against one, a broken nose, and smashed elbow, I saw red. I had been shovelling ore for International Nickel and I really didn't know my own strength.

The three attacked me. I charged like a mad bull. I hit one with my shoulder and bounced him off the wall. Another grabbed me from behind. I twisted hard and he cracked his head where I had cracked my elbow. Now I had the guy who punched my nose. I waded in. The basic rule of barroom brawling is to hit first and hit hard. I caught him on the temple and he fell like a pole-axed steer. Two of the women screamed and went to help their fallen heroes. Sharon handed me her phone number. "Nice going, Gordon, the bastards deserved it. Call me soon. Good night and thanks."

Back in room 435 Porky was just pulling on his pants and a fuzzy head of red hair rested on the pillow. "Damn it, Gordon, I thought I had the door locked. I had a hell of a time getting rid of all the people. Now I'll have to get this girl home somehow. The room key is on the dresser and I'll likely be back. Ron said to make ourselves at home."

"Yes I saw him at the dance."

I helped Porky get the redhead to the elevator, and on the way back I met a woman with a drink in her hand. "Do you know big Red Hardbottle?"

"Yes I do. He got his wings tonight."

"I haven't seen him since the dance finished."

"He was in here earlier and he knows Porky and I have the Australian's room for the night, so he'll likely come back. Why don't you come in and wait for him here."

"Thanks, I'll do that. Where did you get that black eye?"

"You should see the other guy. Would you like a drink?'

"No thank you. I'm going to stretch out on the bed. I'm almost asleep on my feet."

"I'll join you."

"I'm not going to bed with you. I love Big Red. You're welcome to lie beside me."

"Well thanks, after all it is my bed."

"Okay. Okay. Just let me sleep."

Red found us sound asleep and she had trouble convincing him of our innocence. He crawled in between us and the three of us fell asleep.

At four-thirty we were awakened by a pounding on the door. "Open up. It's the Military Police."

"Come in, the door is open," I said. Two burly MPs pushed through the door. "What's the trouble, Corporal?"

"The hotel management has complained about the party. You be out of here in half an hour or we'll put you on charge. We'll be back to check."

"Okay Corporal, how's about a ride back to No 2 WTS?"

"Go down and wait in the paddy wagon."

I reported into the hospital and got painkillers to ease my aching elbow and in the morning had an x-ray at the Colonel Belcher Hospital. Around No 2 WTS they said they'd had two graduation parties in the swanky Palliser Hotel — the first and the last — and both in the same evening. It was a warm and sunny chinook day and as I walked the streets of downtown Calgary, with my black eye and my arm in a sling, I heard people say. "Look at that poor airman, he must have been in the plane that crashed at Okotoks the other day."

I stopped by the Bay's perfume counter to see Penny. At first she didn't recognize me. "Can I help you, sir? Oh my gosh! Gordon, whatever happened to you?"

"I didn't realized I looked that bad. I know what you're thinking. No, I haven't been to Drumheller. No, I didn't run into your husband, and I don't know what the other fellow looks like. But if you're not ashamed to be seen with Calgary's first war casualty, I'll meet you at the side door after work and give you all the gruesome details."

"Looks like you need some tender loving care and a good home cooked meal. I'll see you at six and I do love you. Remember?"

Calgary's days were beginning to lengthen. The sunken-sun, hidden behind the Rockies' jagged peaks, tinted a rosy glow on the curdley sky and reflected a delicate pink from office windows and the skiff of new-fallen snow. The deep blue of the eastern skies crept westward, and the last light of day surrendered to the canopy of night. Venus, low on the western horizon, blinked her message of eternal love. I turned. Penny smiled and stepped into my arms. We spoke no words. She took my arm and we walked in silence.

"Come in and let me have a look at your elbow. I don't suppose there is anything we can do for your black eye. They say a beef steak poultice helps but I'd rather have you eat it."

"There is nothing you can do. You might try kissing my elbow. I'm sure that would help."

"What happened? Tell me about it or is that a military secret?"

I told her about the graduation party and how I hurt my elbow and got my black eye. "Gordon, I can't imagine you in a fight. I really can't understand why you're in the service when you are so set against the war."

"I often wonder myself. I'm not a belligerent person. When I have a few drinks I get rid of my shyness and I'm everybody's friend. I've never been in a brawl before. I hate violence."

"What made you join up?"

"I really don't know. It wasn't a rational decision. I felt devastated when war was declared. Then when France fell and the mighty Maginot Line crumbled, real fear struck me. The gregarious instinct urged me to follow my friends. It was the thing to do, almost fashionable. It was an escape from the drudgery of the mines, a chance to see the world, and the charisma of uniform."

"How did you feel after your fight?"

"I felt good. All my reactions were instinctive. I had to defend myself. I was surprised at how easy it was. How strong I was. I suppose I revelled, at least momentarily in my newly-won power."

"Do you feel that you want to exploit your newly-found power?"

"No. I have always believed that we are born with the hunter instinct. It helped our ancestors survive. I remember the thrill of the hunt when we kids used to kill gophers. I believe that the instinctive person is happier, is more successful and certainly less worried than the rational man. Once you start to wonder why, question your reactions or your motives you become confused, irresolute and unhappy. Follow your basic instincts. Keep your stomach full, produce your own kind in abundance and don't be afraid to be selfish. You'll not only survive, you'll be successful and happy."

"It sounds confusing to me and it doesn't sound much like you, Gordon."

"Think about it. Think about how it affects our love. We would never have enjoyed our love and our friendship if we had listened to our minds instead of our hearts. Come here Penny and let me kiss you. I love you."

"And I love you and I hope you don't get into any more brawls. Turn that fighter instinct into love and give it all to me."

"I wonder what I'd have felt like if I had been fighting for my life and I had to kill those people? I hope I never have to find out. I'd be happy if that were the only fight of my military career. I always think of the time I watched some soldiers learning to use a bayonet. The sergeant was showing them how to drive the bayonet through a sack of straw and he said, 'When you pull it out make sure you give it a good twist and tear his guts apart.'"

"Well, it's time to satisfy your hunger instinct. Doris should be here any minute but we'll start without her. We won't have the place to ourselves tonight so how about a big hug and kiss before I serve you your supper?"

I was on light duty while my elbow was tender and accompanied Corporal Smith on his ambulance runs. "Come on Gordon, I might need some help on the trip."

"Where are we going this time?"

"To pick up some airman who has been AWOL (absent with out leave) for weeks. The MPs found him in east Calgary and they need an ambulance, probably a stretcher case. Your arms strong enough to handle one end of a stretcher?"

"Sure, let's go."

I couldn't believe the squalor we found almost in the shadow of the luxurious Palliser Hotel. But not far from the Calgary stockyards we found the MPs waiting. They led us to a long, tumbled-down old building that reminded me of Markinch's curling rink. The inside was divided in five small rooms connected by homemade doors hanging on broken hinges. It looked like an old chicken house. There were no windows and a dull, dirty, chain- pull light dangled from the low-hung ceiling. Stagnant air, warmed by heat from sweaty of bodies, and reeking with stink of excrement and the sour stench of vomit, flipped my stomach. I swallowed hard and tried to breathe through my mouth.

On the dirt floor lying on piles of straw and covered with gunny sacks and raggedy old clothes and blankets lay the homeless people of Calgary. We found our airman. His face, hidden behind a week's growth of silver-tipped whiskers, was scarred and beaten. He whimpered like a baby and sucked his thumb. His lips and nose were blue and the whites of his eyes were clotted with bright red blood. We uncurled him from his fetal position and nestled in the warmth of his stomach was an empty wine bottle and a tattered teddy bear. He screamed when we lifted him out onto the stretcher and messed his already dirty pants.

"We'll take him right to emergency at the Colonel Belcher," Smitty told the MPs.

"Here's his name and regimental number. You'll need that for the hospital records," said the burly MP.

"Corporal, I wouldn't have believed such a place could exist."

"We see it all on our job. You think it's bad now. Just wait until the weather warms up."

Smitty loved to use the ambulance's siren and as we blared our way through the streets of downtown Calgary I wondered what our prostrate luggage was doing in the King's uniform. The Air Force would try to cure him before he killed himself, or they'd give him a suit of clothes, put ten dollars in his pocket and turn him loose on civvy street. He'd likely find his way back to the Calgary stockyards. Maybe those were the people we should use for cannon fodder. *Don't be so damn crude, Gordon. There, but for the grace of God or the blessings of your parents, it might be you back there.*

Calgary was in the grip of an Arctic coldfront, the kind the Americans blame for all their bad weather. In the thirty-below temperature the snow crackled with every footstep. Trees exploded with a rifle-like bang as the frost split them. A full moon, high in the sky, cast stubby shadows across the frozen prairies. Penny and I followed ours from the Scarborough church hall to the streetcar stop and tried to step on our shadows to keep our feet warm. We could hear the tracks squeal their protest at the streetcar when it was half a mile away. It growled to a stop. Sparks crackled from the overhead cable. We welcomed the cozy warmth of the wicker seats.

"Gordon, the tip of your ear is frozen. Let me rub it."

"These Air Force forage caps weren't designed for the frozen north. I did enjoy the dance Penny; that is the first time I danced 'every dance with the same wonderful girl'. I do love you."

"And I love you more than you'll ever know. I think you better stay on this streetcar. It's too cold to walk across the bridge and up that hill tonight. Besides Doris and her boyfriend will be cuddled up on the chesterfield. Are you working tomorrow? Maybe we could go to church?"

"I'll see if I can switch a shift. I'll stay on this car. I'd probably freeze both my ears walking over the bridge to tonight."

"You have battle scars enough. You don't need cauliflower ears. I've been meaning to ask you. June Gerow, the girl at the jeweller counter is fascinated by the scar on your left cheek. She says it looks like a duelling scar. How did you get it? It must have been quite a gash."

"I rode a toboggan through a barbed wire fence when I was a young boy. It should have had some stitches but we were too far from a doctor. Hate to disappoint June, especially with a good old German name like Wagner. Besides I find her attractive. She's a big woman, but carries herself well and I love her wild mane of jet-black hair."

For a moment the smile left her eyes. "You're allergic to black hair, aren't you? I remember how you looked at Susie the first time you saw her."

I rubbed my cheek against the soft frosty-freshness of her hair. "Sure I like black hair but yours shines like the rich-brown colour of a newly-peeled chestnut. I love it. If you're not careful I'll bite your ear."

"Was my jealousy showing? You are a wonderful man, Gordon. But here's my corner. I hope you can make it. In the morning I may have a surprise for you. Good night, sweet boy."

"Good night, Penny." I watched as she got off the street car, turned and waved and blew me a frosty kiss.

I helped serve Sunday breakfast and switched a shift with Punchy. A chinook arch, the telltale cloud that announces the warm winds hung over the Rockies. By the time I arrived at Penny's the snow had started to thaw. The song of the meadowlark listened in my mind and my heart beat faster.

Penny opened the door. She was still in her kimono. "I thought we were going to church."

"I told you I might have a surprise for you. Doris left early this morning to ski at Banff. We'll have the place all to ourselves. I just made a fresh pot of coffee. Can I pour you a cup?"

"Yes, thank you. It's a wonderfully warm morning. I was looking forward to our walk to church. There is a breath of spring in the air."

"Come here you wonderful hunk of man. You haven't kissed me."

She looked seductively beautiful in her baby-pink dressing gown with a lacy nightie revealing her cleavage with her nut-brown hair tumbling over her shoulders. She locked her arms around my neck and I gathered silky hair in both my hands and looked at the smile in her grey-blue eyes with their mysterious brown ring. Running my fingers down through her hair I pulled her closer. We kissed long and hard. She felt so firm, so close and yet so soft and so womanly.

"Penny, did I ever tell you that I love you?"

"Not this morning."

I picked her up and cradled her in my arms and headed for the chesterfield.

"No, no. Put me down. Let's have our coffee."

We sat and nursed our coffee eating each other up with our eyes and trying to keep our feelings under control. I walked around the table lifted the rich-brown chestnut mane and kissed her neck. "Your honeydew tastes good. Did you know that the back of your neck is where honeydew grows?"

"It gives me goose pimples. But I like it."

"Let's stretch out on the chesterfield."

"I think it would be much more comfortable in bed."

"Let me carry you in."

"Just a minute Gordon, we've talked about this before. You know how much I love you and I feel you do love me. But I just can't take any chances. You'll have to respect my feelings."

"I know, I know, but my heart aches for you. Let us love in the best way we can."

I carried her into her bedroom and we cuddled and loved in her narrow bed. In our own way we exhausted each other. She fell asleep in my arms with soft hair nestled on my chest. The sun blinked through shadows of a tree and sunbeams danced with the joy of our love.

Her gentle sobs awoke me. I stroked her hair and kissed the tears from her eyes. "I'm so happy, Gordon. You make me feel so good. It is all so right, so beautiful. It's a new and wonderful feeling for me. I feel sad and happy at the same time. So happy to be with you and sad that this moment can't last forever."

"This moment will last forever. It will never be again. I'll treasure it. I'll frame it with gold and store it in a special part of my heart and write 'Penny' on the door. This moment our love has passed into eternity to dwell in our hearts forever. I love you, Penny."

"It must be warm outside. There is water dripping off the eaves. Let's go for a walk. Come on, get up before I push you out of bed."

"You be careful or I'll pick you up, take you outside and plunk your cute little bum in a snow bank."

"You wouldn't dare!"

It was slushy under foot as the warm west wind caressed Calgary's streets. Penny's thermometer read 50F. Last night when we left the dance it was -30F a change of eighty degrees in fourteen hours. We window-shopped picking out furniture for our dream home. We wandered through the park and then rode the street car out past Bowness Park and stayed on after it turned around and had a free ride back.

"Let's have a cup of tea and a sandwich. Is the Blue Moon open on Sundays?"

"Why don't we go home? Doris made some good scones last night. Besides it's cosier there."

"You mean we might go to bed again?"

"No. I couldn't stand that again. I don't think I'm that strong."

We walked back to her suite, had tea and Doris' scones, lay on the chesterfield and enjoyed our togetherness. Little did we know that it would be the last time we'd ever have to be alone together.

Monday morning the hospital routine continued, carrying breakfast up three flights of stairs, making beds, following the doctor while he made his rounds, helping with sick parade and dodging N/S MacBeth. I was in my reading room, the men's washroom, when about fifteen minutes before lunch time, Sergeant Blair struggled through the heavy washroom door. He pushed his Hitler-like long lock of blond hair out of his eyes, stopped about three feet from my window nook, squared his shoulders and stood at attention. "AC 2 Wagner, you will go to stores and draw your white uniform."

His nicotine-stained lip quivered and I let him wait for my answer. "Sergeant Blair, you know what you can do with your white uniforms."

"AC 2 Wagner that is an order. You will draw your whites and report back to me dressed in your whites by 15:00 hours. If you refuse I'll have no alternative but to put you on charge." He did an about-turn, clicked his heels and marched out of the washroom.

Well, Wagner, you've got three hours to make up your mind. Maybe even less. He could charge you for insubordination right now, but I think he is too scared of me to do that. Well, it's time to lug those bloody trays again. I hope Charlie has a good lunch today, I might be on bread and water for a while.

There were three RCAF bases in Calgary and Warrant Officer Corbett was the senior NCO for the hospitals for all three No 2 WTS's third floor corridor was crowded as the classrooms emptied for the midday break. I was headed for the stairs when Sergeant Major Corbett stepped out of the Orderly Room. "Wagner," he shouted and beckoned me with his threatening index finger, "Come here. I want to see you for a minute."

Wagner you've had it! That damn Sergeant Blair didn't even give you time to change your mind. Why the hell did Sergeant Major Corbett have to be here today?

"Yes, Sergeant Major Corbett, you wanted to see me, Sir?"

"Wagner, you've been here for almost four months without any leave. Here is a week's leave and a couple of forty-eight hour passes to stretch it out, and a warrant to draw a pay advance. Enjoy yourself and we'll see you when you get back."

"Thank you, Sir."

I saw Sergeant Blair at lunch. "Sergeant Blair, did you have anything to do with the week's leave I got?"

"Not really. But Punchy, Parry and you have been damn good around here. Don't worry about the whites. We'll see about that when you get back."

I called Penny. "You going to be home tonight? You are? I'll be down as soon as I finish my shift. About seven-thirty."

What the hell am I going to do with twelve days of leave? I can't stay in Calgary unless I want to live in barracks. I have to get out of NO 2 WTS. I can't stay with Penny. I guess I'll have to go home. My folks don't live in Markinch any longer and I don't know anyone in their new town of Lajord. Maybe Penny would like to come home with me? I wonder what Mother would say. I know she'll like her.

Both girls were home when I reached Penny's. Doris was doing her hair and Penny was ironing. I told them about my leave.

"You mean we won't see you for almost two weeks?" Penny said as she held the iron at ease.

"How would you like to come home with me? I'd like you to meet my folks."

"I'd never get the time off. I don't get my holidays until July."

I decided to delay my trip home for a day. We had dinner with Doris and her friend. They got the chesterfield and Penny and I went off to a movie. We walked home in silence. I didn't go in. We had a long good-night in the hallway. I watched her turn the key and caught her smile as she disappeared through the door.

There was a new chill in the air — another cold front sliding south. I stopped on the bridge and watched a full moon playing hide-and-seek with the fluffy clouds. I watched their moon- shadows chase each other down the frozen river. I had a foreboding that Penny and all that she meant to me was riding on a fluffy cloud and I was helpless to stop the clouds or run after the shadows. I could cherish the dream, but my life was as ice- bound as the Bow River. Damn the war, the Air Force and bloody convention! I could see the windows of the Normal School poking into the sky above the snow-crested hill. I still had that damn hill to climb. Life seemed to be all up-hill.

The ten days of my leave passed all too quickly. The train trip from Regina to Calgary was an all night ride. Punchy Matthews and Doug Parry were also on the train and we caught a ride with an Air Force truck up to Calgary's NO 2 WTS. Porky Clarke was helping with sick parade.

"Well here are the 'Three Musty Steers' back. I suppose you turned Regina and Moose Jaw up side down. But we've got news for you," said Porky as he poured two ounces of the MO's "Lead- Swinger's Special" into a medicine glass and with a twinkle in his eye handed it to an unsuspecting patient. "That should help your back. Come back at 13:00 hours for your second dose."

"What's the news for us, Porky?"

"The three of you have been posted to No. 5 SFTS at McLeod effective today."

"You're kidding," said Punchy, "that's where that son-of-a-bitch Sergeant Pritchard is."

"Yeah. His son is there too. So is Stu Mason," said Doug.

"The station has only been open for six months and they have a new hospital equipped with an OR (operating room). I wouldn't mind going there. I could handle Pritchard," said Porky.

I didn't know the Pritchards or Stu Mason but I didn't want to leave Calgary. I remembered the night on the bridge and the fleecy clouds, the frozen river and the wonderful Sunday I had spent with Penny. Surely to gosh we wouldn't have to go today. How the hell would I get to see Penny?

We reported to the Orderly Room and picked up our posting papers. "There's an MT (Motor Transport) run leaving for Mcleod at 13:30 hours," the Corporal snapped, "the truck will pick you up at the guard house."

It was after eleven before I got my gear together, got cleared from "stores" and headed for the Bay. I stopped and watched Penny from a distance. Her chestnut-brown hair, pulled tight to her head and tied back with yellow ribbon reflected flashes of gold and copper as she move in and out of the sunlight slanting through the store's large windows. She dabbed samples of perfume on an elegant woman's hand. I waited until she was finished.

I was at the counter before she saw me. She turned into a shaft of sunlight. Her plain beauty glowed in a halo of browns, coppers and yellows. Soft shadows mellowed her spring-like complexion, and her rose-like lips and the grey-blue violets of her eyes smiled together. "Oh Gordon, how wonderful to see you! But you don't look very happy. Is there anything wrong?"

"No, not really. Can you get away from the counter for a while?"

"It is almost lunch time. I'll speak to my boss."

"Okay let's go." She took my arm and my heart began to pound.

"Penny I've been posted to McLeod. I'll be leaving in a couple of hours." She turned and faced me. For a moment her smile vanished. Then in the aisle between the ladies' wear and the men's with people all around us she put her arms around my neck and we kissed. People stopped to stare as we whispered our love to each other and both started to cry.

"We'd better get out of here or I'll be losing my job."

Over coffee in the Bay's cafeteria we pledged to love forever while deep in our heart we knew we really had no control over our destinies.

She was married to a stupid man and I was married to a stupid war. I never saw Penny again. There is still a part of my heart framed in gold and with a golden "Penny" written on the door.

McLeod, Alberta, a prairie town of two thousand people, a hundred miles south of Calgary and thirty miles east of the Crow's Nest Pass, sits on a river bank where the Saint Mary's River joins the Old Man River just above the Belly. Originally called Fort McLeod, it was established in 1874 by the Royal North West Mounted Police to wipe out the whisky trade.

In early 1940, the sleepy cow-town watched as construction crews mushroomed runways, hangars, barracks, mess halls, canteens and a hospital on the flat prairie. The invasion of fourteen hundred airmen began in the summer months of '40 and by fall every spare room, many garages and even some chicken coops were rented to airmen and their families.

Canada's good flying weather provided ideal conditions for training aircrew. Towns with good rail connections and above all a good water supply were chosen as sites. Mcleod had all of these. But nobody considered the Crow's Nest Pass.

After living in McLeod for a month you realized why the people of the town walked with a westward lean. The stubby trees and even the grass grew with a prayer-like gesture to the mystic east, and there were no small stones on the gravelled roads.

It was the wind. The prevailing westerlies, calm in the morning, blew briskly by noon and reached almost gale force by mid- afternoon. The west winds, blocked and buffeted by the Rockies Mountains were funnelled into the Crow's Nest Pass, compressed and escaped onto the prairies with added gusto. Many afternoons the winds were so strong that flying was washed out and the canvas- covered Anson airplanes had to be tucked into hangars or anchored to the ground.

The Red Ensign and the Air Force flags, whipping straight out in stiff afternoon wind, snapped with authority over No 5's parade square. We found the hospital and were snapped into Sergeant Pritchard's office by Corporal Gould. "AC 1 Parry, AC 1 Matthews and AC 2 Wagner reporting for duty, Sergeant Pritchard."

Sergeant Pritchard, short, well-built and every inch a soldier, bristled like his well-trimmed mustache. A week-end soldier in Moose Jaw's Militia Reserve, with a St John's Ambulance certificate, Dr. O'Berne had recruited him from Swift's Meat Packing plant, and he had enjoyed the rapid promotion that Dr. O'Berne had predicted for me. He was the senior NCO at McLeod No 5 Service Training Flying School's hospital. He sat behind a meticulously tidy desk studying the file on his desk. He ignored us.

Then without raising his head he lifted his bushy eyebrows closer to his close-cropped hair and drilled us with his small, gimlet- like beady eyes and snapped, "I see Calgary unloaded you three want-me-nots into my hospital. You'll cut the mustard here. I run a tight ship. We've got a new hospital, fully equipped and I keep it in A-one condition. We have three doctors, two nursing sisters and a staff of fifteen. Your quarters are in the hospital. Now follow me."

He led us to a door marked "Morgue" and paused with his hand on the door knob. "Couple of guys spun a Tiger Moth in from twenty-five hundred feet. We just picked them up. They're still warm."

He opened the door and switched on the light. The smell of sweat, feces, urine and blood seared my nostrils and for a moment I didn't realize that the two teddy bears lying on the floor were corpses. They were still wearing their woolly flying suits and helmets. The Sergeant moved one their legs with his foot and it twisted like a rubber hose. "No bones left in that leg," he said, "take a look at this guy's face. He must have been in the front seat. Something drilled that hole in his head and almost popped out his eyes."

My stomach flipped and I headed for the door. "How would you like the job of getting those guys out of their flying suits?"

I'll bloody well refuse. What the hell are you trying to prove you sadistic little bastard. You're not working in Swift's meat packing plant now. I'll keep my nose clean as long as you're around here. You must be as mean as you look.

He showed us our quarters, a good sized room with four double bunks, a few cupboards and a bathroom just around the corner. We met our new roommates, Clarence Fraser, six feet two, handsome with a smile reaching from ear to ear, and Cece Hemming, young, baby-faced with a peaches and cream complexion and a mop of thick wavy hair.

"Welcome to the 'Stud Room.' That's what Sergeant Pritchard calls this place. All the other AC-deuces on our staff live off the station. The sergeants and corporals have their own mess and quarters," said big Fraser. "It's a good hospital. Hope you'll like it."

"Nice to be in a real hospital. I see you still wear your blues. In No.2 WTS you're supposed to wear a white uniform."

"We have white jackets or lab coats but dress is optional."

"Glad to hear that. Sergeant Blair was going to put me on charge because I refused to draw my whites from stores. I want to remuster and if they ever get me into those damn whites I'll end up being an AC 2 nursing orderly for the rest of the bloody war."

"I supposed Pritchard showed you the two guys in the morgue," Cece said. "The Sergeant is a bit of a weirdo. His bark is worse than his bite. He doesn't bother us much.

"Brewster is the Chief Medical Officer and there are Dr. Nelson and Dr. Hogg. Nursing Sisters Winters and Smith live at the other end of the hall. The only time you get in there is to do some cleaning. They're the only two women on the base. They never lack for company.

"Jimmy Barr is the cook. He does a fair job of spoiling good food. He worked in a shoe factory in Kitchener until six months ago. But he's learning and we have access to kitchen.

"The night life of down town Mcleod leaves a lot to be desired. There is the coffee shop at the Bus Depot and the Queen's Hotel "For Men Only" beer parlour. There's a dance every Saturday night in the hall we call the "Gonorrhea Race Track." If you want a date you have to go to Lethbridge twenty-five miles east of here. The hitchhiking is pretty good in the afternoon and early evenings but there is damn little traffic coming this way late at night. If you don't get a ride, there is a freight train that pulls out of Lethbridge bound for Mcleod and Calgary anywhere between two to four in the morning. But that's a damn cold ride at this time of the year.

"I've had an application in for a remuster to aircrew for six months. They claim you should renew it regularly," he concluded.

"You're right Cece, I'm going to get a new application in."

We soon fell into the hospital routine and it was rather pleasant working in a well-equipped facility. But I missed Penny. We wrote long letters back and forth. On a fine April Saturday I hitchhiked to Calgary only to find that Penny had gone to Drumheller for the weekend. I went to the dance at the Scarborough hostess club, but it wasn't the same without her. I stayed over night in an empty hospital bed and enjoyed a couple of Charlie's good meals.

Anson and control tower at No 5 SFTS, McLeod.

When there were planes in the sky an ambulance had to be parked beside the control tower. We worked in four hour shifts with nothing to do but stay awake and alert — great for reading and writing letters. I enjoyed being around the airplanes and we flew as often as we could and actually got paid extra for some of our flying time.

With the hospital fully staffed we got a forty-eight hour pass every other week and a week's leave every three months. It was mid-May when I got my first week's leave and was able to tack a forty-eight hour pass on the front end. I planned to hitchhike back to Saskatchewan to see my parents. We got paid every other Friday but we had to go on pay-parade with the rest of the station personnel. With

Piggy-back landing, No 5 SFTS, McLeod

74

the initial "W" it meant a long wait. It was nearly three-thirty and there were only about ten people ahead of me when Pay-Accounts ran out of money. They would finish the pay parade on Monday.

I floated a couple of loans in the Airmen's Canteen and half an hour later I was on No3 Highway heading east for Moose Jaw and Regina. It took me two rides to get to Lethbridge. One long ride and a couple of short ones got me to the eastern outskirts of Medicine Hat. By that time it was dark and I waited in a filling station and a friendly farmer took me ten miles and dropped me off on the darkest bit of highway in all of Alberta. Traffic was light and nobody stopped. Standing on black highway and dressed in my blues I was hard to see and drivers were hesitant to pick people up at night.

I made myself comfortable on an over-turned bucket and waited. The night began to chill and I could have used my great-coat. Somewhere nearby in a prairie slough a frog's choir filled the silence with their croaking symphony. A slightly lop-sided moon climbed out of the eastern horizon revealing the silver-ribboned highway and the glassy surface of the slough. Excited by the moon, the frogs increased their crescendo, and two coyotes, one on either side of the highway howled their coyote-talk to one another. I was beginning to despair.

Ah. There's a set of head lights. I'll get well onto the road to make sure they see me. They seem to be coming pretty fast. Gee, I think they're slowing up. By gosh they're going to stop. It's a station wagon.

"What the hell are you doing a way out here at this time of night, soldier?"

"I'm trying to get to Regina."

"You'll have a helluva time making it tonight. Get in and we'll take you a few miles."

There were four men in the wagon. They were working on highway construction and had a camp just a few miles down the road. They invited me into their trailer, made me a cup of coffee and fed me some cookies.

"You'll have a tough time getting a ride tonight. You're welcome to stay here. We'll find you a bunk somewhere."

"Thanks, but I'll try my luck."

75

I hadn't been on the highway for ten minutes when a car stopped. A man was driving and his wife was curled up asleep on the back seat.

I got in and as we drove he told me that they were from Blackfalds, a small town a hundred miles north of Calgary. Their son was in the RCAF and he was getting his pilot's wings the next day.

"I'll have to drive all night but I'm getting low on gas. Have you any idea where we are?"

"We're about thirty miles east of Medicine Hat. I doubt if you'll find a filling station open before we get to Swift Current."

"I'm less them a quarter full."

"Just had a ride with some construction workers. I'll bet you could get a tank of gas there."

They filled our tank and wouldn't let us pay for it. We took turns driving and by daylight we were still a hundred miles from Moose Jaw and low on gas again. At five in the morning none of the filling stations were open.

We passed a gasoline-tank truck parked on the side of the road. "Stop the car," I said, "I'm going to ask that driver for some gas."

I woke the truck driver and told him our predicament. With the help of a gallon can my friends had in their trunk we transferred a tank full of gas a gallon at time, and the driver wouldn't let us pay.

We were in Moose Jaw by nine. I had breakfast with my Blackfalds friends. They had plenty of time to get to their son's graduation and I was home before noon.

Hitchhiking was a great way to travel. As long as you were in uniform most people would stop and pick you up. Doug Parry and I decided we would visit the Crow's Nest Pass. "Coleman is the best town," we were told, "and be sure to check with the United Church. They run a hostess club of sorts and will find you a place to stay."

Coleman, the largest of a cluster of small mining towns nestled in the green bottom of a valley, was guarded on both sides by giant mountains tumbling skyward in a struggle to be the biggest. They dwarfed the towns and the people into Gulliver-like miniatures. The

The Crow's Nest

top of the highest mountain had been blunted to either stunt its growth or to make a table for the council of the mountain gods. The Indians in their respect for the sagacity of the crow called the dome-like top "The Crow's Nest,"

The hostess at the United Church arranged for us to spend the weekend with a local doctor and his wife. We spent the first night in their Coleman home and they introduced us to a couple of women school teachers slightly older than Parry and me but not too old.

Sunday morning the six of us piled into the doctor's station wagon and climbed a rough and winding trail to a small lake nestled in a basin near the timber line where our doctor friend had a small cabin.

They had packed a scrumptious lunch and we boiled some tea over an open fire. After being well fed and feasted our host suggested that we climb up the mountain, follow the stream that fed the lake and we would come to the Great Divide, the height of land that was the boundary between Alberta and British Columbia. A small creek trickling across a short mesa was split by jagged rock and became two smaller streams. The dentist pulled one of those collapsible Boy Scout's cups from his pocket and handed it to me.

"Fill this cup and you can send it either to the Pacific Ocean or to the Atlantic Ocean."

I sent a cup full of that ice cold mountain water on its way to both oceans. *If only all life's decisions were as simple. Was my life a mere cupful cast into the eternity of time?. Or was it a mere drop sent to wander haphazardly down the river for three- score-and-ten? Or was it just another molecule of H2O floating through the infinity of time? Perhaps it didn't matter what it was or how long I would be caught up in this bloody war? Nor where I went? Nor whom I loved? Nor if I lived? Nor how I lived? Some Corporal, Sergeant or Air Marshal could toss me into either ocean with a stroke of his blunted pen. Why not take the hand of that lonely school teacher and lead her into the "here and now?" We're two lonely souls adrift in the unknown. Thrown together by chance.*

But it didn't work that way. We had a wonderful day on the mountain and it was dark when we dropped the teachers off at their boarding house and returned to the doctor's home. We enjoyed a night-cap in front of the fireplace and retired early. Doug and I had separate rooms. I had no trouble falling asleep and I don't know what time it was but I awoke to find the doctor's wife lifting the covers of my bed . . .

The eastern sky was brightening when she left and I fell into the deep sleep of exhaustion. In the morning I was tempted to leave without breakfast but she cooked us bacon and eggs and acted so naturally that I wondered if I had an erotic dream. A few days later we happened to mention our stay with the doctor and his wife to one of our friends.

"Which one of you got to sleep with the doctor's wife? She has taken more than one airman to bed with her."

"She crawled into bed with me the first night we were there," said Doug. "I had a hell of a time the afternoon we went to the lake. She just ignored me and I wondered if she'd be back the second night but she never showed."

I kept my peace, perhaps rebuffed by my arrogant maleness that she'd taken Parry before she'd taken me. I never got back to Coleman nor wondered if my cup of water reached either the Atlantic or the Pacific.

Corporal Leadbeater had been hospitalized before and treated for pains in his lower left side. Doctor Hogg had diagnosed it as an attack of appendicitis and prescribed ice-packs and sulfa. The pain had subsided and the patient discharged. But he was back again and this time with a temperature.

I was assisting Dr.Hogg with sick parade. He admitted Leadbeater, prescribed an initial dose of sulfa and put him on a liquid diet.

"Wagner, it's time we put that shiny new operating room to work. Will you contact Nursing Sister Winters and have her prepare the OR?"

I had all but forgotten about Leadbeater and his appendix. It was about three thirty and I was just about ready of go off shift when Dr. Hogg appeared at the nursing station.

"Wagner, we have Leadbeater ready for his surgery. Why don't you get a mask and gown and watch the operation? I'll explain what I'm doing. You never know, after this war is over you might go back and finish the medical career you started."

"How long will it take, Doctor?" I asked. Fraser and I had planned to hitchhike to Lethbridge that evening.

"It's a routine procedure. We should be through in an hour."

The operating room had the smell of ether, lysol and a new car. Dr. Nelson capped, masked and gowned, looked a little-boyish with narrow face and finely-toned skin. Nursing Sister Winters capped, masked and gowned, still looked like the station's sexy pin-up girl. Dr. Hogg, totally uncomfortable in his disguise, looked more like a heavy-duty mechanic than a skilled surgeon.

On the operating table Leadbeater's lay draped with a square opening on the left side of his lower abdomen. The patch-like opening, almost a fluorescent red from the mercurochrome paint-job, glowed like porterhouse steak. Dr. Hogg, with one rubber-gloved hand resting on Leadbeater's gently heaving stomach and the other holding a bright shiny scalpel, which he waved around like a blackboard pointer, explained the procedure.

"I'll imagine a line joining the tip of the hip bone to the navel and about a third of the distance from the hip bone I'll make a vertical incision about three inches long. Just beneath the skin will be a layer of fat, which in this patient will be thin. Below the fatty tissue are two layers of muscle, one vertical and the other horizontal. I will cut those separately so we won't have any trouble when we come to sew him up. That will lay bare the peritoneum which I'll cut through to enter the body cavity. Then I should be able to reach into the incision with my forefinger, find the appendix and pop it up through the incision. I'll tie it off next to the intestine, put a second tie close to the first one, cut in between the ties and remove the corporal's useless appendage. We'll preserve it in formaldehyde for him and his ancestors to admire."

I cringed as he pulled the scalpel gently but firmly over the skin and watched the slit open and little beads of blood seeped from the fatty tissue as he laid bare the bright red muscle.

"This is the first layer of muscle and I must be careful not to cut the layer below." Blood flowed from the wound and they sucked it up with an aspirator and cotton swabs. "Ah, this is the peritoneum. We want to cut as little as possible."

We watched in eager anticipation as he pushed his forefinger deep into Leadbeater's belly. He pushed hard probing deeper and his face began to colour and small beads of sweat oozed from his forehead. "I can't find the damn thing. I'll have to enlarge the incision." He added an inch to the bottom of the cut and got his thumb and two fingers inside the corporal's belly.

"Where in hell is the bloody thing?" His face became crimson and his beady little eyes looked ready to pop and the nurse had to wipe his sweaty forehead. "Give me the scalpel. I have to get my whole hand in there." He added an inch to the top of the incision and we watched his whole hand bury itself inside the wound. The incision fit tightly around his wrist like the collar on a suction cup.

We watched with awed attention as his hand searched inside Leadbeater's belly and the sweat dripped from his beet-red forehead. He withdrew his hand and it sounded like a horse pulling its foot out of a mud hole. He took the scalpel and lengthened the hole (it was no longer an incision). "The appendix has formed an adhesion to the body wall and we have to get the intestine out of the way so we can tie off the adhesion."

The nurse placed a wash basin on the corporal's belly, and lined it with a sterile towel. Dr. Hogg slowly and gently, foot after foot pulled Leadbeater's intestines from the gaping gash and dumped them in the bowl. When it was half full he did an inspection, shook his head and piled some more guts into the bowl. Three times he felt inside and now the bowl was full. *My God*, I thought, *the incision is almost a foot long. The poor guy will die. They must have all his guts laying in that bowl. Its like a damn slaughter house. His guts are steaming just like when you open up a pig.*

"Now I've found the trouble. The appendix is enlarged and is firmly attached to the body wall. It feels like it's ready to burst. I'll have to get both hands inside to make a tie where the appendix is adhered."

He made the incision larger and piled more guts in the basin. He made the ties, cursed and sweated, and when he tried to cut the adhesion away from the body wall the appendix burst. The air turned blue. Aspirators and swabs flew into action and finally the stubby little gherkin-like appendage lay beside the basin.

"Come here you ornery little bastard," said an exasperated Dr. Hogg as he cut between the ties, laid the bloated gherkin to one side and began to put the corporal's guts back where they belonged. "We'll have to leave a tube in here to drain the mess we've made." We watched as he sewed the peritoneum, the two layers of muscle and the skin together.

Corporal Leadbeater had been on the operating table for three and a half hours. I wondered how he would ever live.

Dr. Hogg turned to me and said, "Wagner, the patient may go to his ward and since you saw it all we'll give you the job of looking after him tonight. Nursing Sister Winters will be on call and I'll come by a couple of times to see how he is."

Thanks a bundle, Doc. Why pick me? I don't want to watch this guy die. Besides I'm not supposed to be on duty.

We got the Corporal into bed and propped him up so the fluid in his guts would drain. I sat there waiting for him to gasp for his last breath of air. I watched him breathe and felt his pulse expecting it to slow and weaken. But it never faltered. Dr. Hogg stopped by about midnight. "He'll be fine. Give him his dose of sulfa when its time. He's young and strong and he'll be as good as new in a few days. Do you still think you'd like to be a doctor?"

"I don't suppose you remember but you gave me my medical when I applied to join the Air Force in North Bay."

"Is that so? I was in North Bay for about six months. How come you didn't get into aircrew?"

"A smooth talking Captain O'Berne talked me into this job. I'm still trying to remuster. I'm not thrilled with my military career as a nursing orderly."

"I know O'Berne, you're not the only one he persuaded. I'll do what I can to help you remuster, and I'll send somebody to relieve you. Good night, Wagner."

"Good night, Dr. Hogg and thank you."

Life in the "The Stud Room" was never dull. In the hospital you got all the gossip about the station as well as about the life in downtown McLeod. There was one particularly juicy piece about the newly commissioned pilot who went home on leave, got his wife pregnant and gave her the clap. He was in our VD ward when she arrived to give him the news. You could have heard her all over town.

Our Corporal Gould, in charge of the hospital orderly room, looked and acted like a Dicken's Uriah Heep. We learned he had a girlfriend in Lethbridge. There was nothing surprising about that except that the corporal had a wife in Moose Jaw. He wasn't very popular with the members of the "Stud Room" because we figured he screwed us out of some of our forty-eight-hour passes. He just seemed to enjoy being miserable. Somehow we learned that he often sent his girlfriend flowers—damned if I know how we discovered that and what difference it made to us.

Then one evening I met her at the Henderson Lake dance hall. I kidded her about Corporal Gould and about the flowers and she kind of laughed. I took her home. She lived in an upstairs suite with her mother. We sat on the stairs, talked necked and petted until we both were pretty excited.

There was a school yard right across the street from where she lived. The moon was bright and we found a secluded spot at the base of a large poplar tree. We had just begun to get comfortable and I felt the ants. We had sat on an anthill and they swarmed over us and cooled our ardor. I never saw Gould's girl friend again after that. Sometime later Gould found a place to live and his wife moved to McLeod and put an end to Uriah's love affairs. But it helped to keep the S-Room's gossip pot warm and boiling.

One spring night Fraser and I were on Lethbridge's Railway Avenue waiting to hitch a ride to McLeod. There was damn little traffic and it was nearly midnight.

"Fraser there's supposed to be a whorehouse somewhere on this street."

Small bungalows sat side by side facing the railway tracks. They all looked the same and none of them looked like a brothel.

"Why don't we see if we can find it, better than standing out here," said Fraser. "I'll try that house over there. At least there's a light on."

I stood on the sidewalk and watched as Fraser rapped on the front door. In the dim glow of a nearby street light I could see a short, stout woman standing in the doorway.

"Do you have any girls here?" Fraser asked and I could hear that big smile as it grinned across his handsome face.

I recognized the Japanese accent as she said, "No geel heeh. But me do! Me do!"

"We want young girls," big Fraser grinned.

"Me do bettah. Me do weal good fol you Mistah!"

She opened the door and for a minute I thought Fraser was going to go in. "No. No, not tonight."

"You come moah time. I makee velly good for you. Bling youah flend too."

It was a Saturday night and Fraser and I had hitched a ride to Lethbridge. The town was still small enough that people came downtown and sat in their cars to watch the passing parade. Fraser and I had cruised the downtown streets and checked the parked cars without any luck. It was almost nine o'clock and the stores would close and empty their pretty clerks onto the streets. We stood in front of Kresge's Five and Ten Cent store pretending we were admiring the window display but really watching the parade of pulchritude getting ready to leave.

I turned to Fraser, "Do you see that ...", but Fraser was gone. The street was crowded and it took me a few seconds before I saw him. He was almost half a block away walking between two girls. I had to hurry to catch up to them.

Fraser with the chuckle that went so well with his infectious grin said, "Join us Gordon, these girls are going to the dance at Henderson Lake. Maybe we can tag along."

The tall girl on Fraser's left with her upturned nose tilted in a suggestion of refusal and with a saucy lilt replied, "We're not really looking for company, are we Ivy? Daddy's parked somewhere here and he is going to drive us."

"There they are, Gladys," and I saw Ivy smile. She was neat, trim and attractive.

Gladys's parents were parked in his long black Chrysler and we watched as she talked to her father. "We'll meet Daddy at the house and Mom says these two airmen look a little gaunt and if they'd like to come home with us she'll make us coffee and find something to eat. How would you boys like that?"

"Sounds fine to me," said Fraser, "my name is Clarence Fraser and my friend is Gordon Wagner."

"We're the Harvey girls. I'm Gladys and she's Ivy."

"Are you sisters?" I asked.

"No, we're second cousins," said Gladys, "and we don't live far from here. Come on let's go."

"Let's take the sidewalk," said Ivy.

"It's shorter through the park, come Clarence," said Gladys as she led the way.

Ivy and I followed. In the centre of the park there was another one of those slabs of stone inscribed with names of the victims of World War I. I started around the wrong side, "We go this way," she said and took my hand and led me along a path bordered by rose bushes that filled the warm evening the scent of come-hitherness. I squeezed her hand and felt the vibes stir my soul. The path circled the trunk of a large maple and I felt her hand let go.

"Come on this side, Ivy. It's bad luck to let that maple come between us."

I stopped and gave her hand a pull and she walked into my arms. She gave a little squeak but stopped. She felt good and her soft hair tickled my nose and smelt fresh-washed and womanly. She fit cuddly-like against me, raised her head and I kissed the full flavour of her soft lips.

"We'd better hurry or your friend and Gladys will be home ahead of us."

"Do you live with your cousin?"

"No, I'm spending the weekend with her."

"Do you work in Kresge's?"

"No, I teach school — but here we are. Come on in and meet Fred and Elsie, Gladie's parents."

Fred Harvey was a tall, thin, and gaunt man, darkly tanned with a mop of steel-grey hair too large for his face. With a slightly hooked nose and piercing black eyes, he had the majestic look of a bald eagle. I'd recognize Fred the next time I'd see him.

Elsie, heavy set and bulging front, back and sideways, had her unruly hair tamed under a net and stapled with hairpins. She walked erect and blinked through rimless glasses as she talked with the mannish authority of a boss.

Gladys, tall, well-built and husky for a woman, yet fine-featured and good-looking, resembled her father. She was flippant and cheeky and at times could be offensive to a sensitive person. She was a good match for big Fraser. He'd just make his grin a little bigger and turn up the ends a bit more.

Ivy, with her classical oval face, her luxuriant head of thick brown hair, her fine white teeth and her engaging smile looked beautiful in the better light, reminding me of the "Girl with the Pepsodent Smile."

"Do you people still want to go to the dance at Henderson Lake?" Fred asked.

"Why not?" said Gladys, "It's not every night we get a couple of stray airmen to go with us. We usually have to find them at the dance.

Okay Daddy, let's go."

The hall was crowded, too crowded to enjoy dancing and too noisy for easy conversation but I learned that Ivy was a school teacher and taught in a rural school west of Lethbridge. She lived in a teacherage during the week and spent her weekends in Lethbridge. The dance was over at midnight. Fred picked us up and when we got back to Harvey's Elsie had coffee and sandwiches ready.

It was a Friday evening in early June the next time I hitched a ride to Lethbridge and called Ivy. "Hello, Ivy it's Gordon Wagner. How are you?"

"Just fine thank you. It's nice to hear from you again."

"I was wondering if you are busy this evening? There's a good show in town. It's James Cagney and Janet Gainor in the *Strawberry Blonde*. Have you seen it?"

"I'd love to see the show. I have a tentative arrangement to meet Gladie after work. Can I call you back?"

"I'm at a pay phone. I'll call again in ten minutes."

She was ready and waiting when I got to Fred and Elsie's front door. She looked prettier than I remembered and seemed to be in a hurry to get away from the house. We enjoyed the show and I still remember how she looked in the brightly-coloured flowered dress she wore and every time I hear the music of the *Strawberry Blonde* I still recall our second date.

I was still corresponding with Penny but the letters were fewer. I was genuinely impressed with my new friend and the "S Room" couldn't believe that I might be serious. Neither could I. But I enjoyed Ivy's company and was proud to be seen with her. She taught in a one-room country school and lived in the teacherage nearby. She regaled me with stories about her school and her pupils.

It was a Friday afternoon. Ivy had told me how to find her school. "You know where the highway starts to go down into the Lethbridge coolie? Instead of going down the hill you'll see a dirt road going straight ahead. You take that road until you come to the first crossroad then go south on that trail for about a mile and a half and you'll see the West Lethbridge School on your right. It's quite a walk."

I had no trouble getting a ride to the top of the coolie, finding the dirt-road and heading south. It was a warm afternoon, the road was dusty and the persistent west wind rippled the green fields of grain. I spotted the clump of buildings from a mile away. I watched an Anson aircraft as it did a couple of tight turns high above the buildings.

The clump resolved into the rectangular school house with its double door entrance and four rectangular, curtainless sidewindows staring absent-mindedly over the flat prairie. A square, pyramidal-roofed, chimney-topped bungalow with two curtained- windows and a door facing the road looked like a block-headed man who may have strayed from the *Wizard of Oz*. Behind the school stood a lean-to barn bordered on both sides by lean-to outhouses. A swing dangling a piece of broken rope looked like a gallows in the warm summer air. A shiny black car was parked in front of the bungalow.

My heart sank. How was I, a lowly AC 2 going to compete for the favours of this attractive girl against a fellow who would soon be wearing the wings of an Air Force pilot, or some civvy-type who drove a big shiny black car? If I hadn't already walked a couple of miles and would have to walk another two miles back to the highway I might have turned around. I knocked on the door wondering what I would find.

The swanky car belonged to her uncle, her mother's brother. She introduced me to Uncle Russ Patterson, a jolly Santa Claus-like man and his gentlewoman wife, Aunt Hedrig. They were on a visit from Lake Athabasca and had stopped to see their niece. When they left, Uncle Russ offered to drive us to Lethbridge, but Ivy declined saying that Fred Harvey was picking her up.

She showed me the one-room school where she taught 21 pupils from grades one to ten. I had forgotten those old fashioned doubled-seat initial-carved desks with their inkwells and how they varied in size to fit the smallest to the biggest of the students; forgotten the potbellied coal-burning stove parked next to the door and the small cloakroom off the entrance; forgotten the earthenware water-cooler snuggled in a corner and the raised platform for the teacher's desk; and forgotten the expanse of blackboard across the back wall and the smell of chalk and lunch pails mixed with the odour from old running shoes and smelly feet.

In the tiny cottage she had a piano and she played for me. One of the songs was *Marie Elena* and it became our theme song and still holds a very warm spot in both our hearts.

"When did you eat last, Gordon? I'd get you a bite to eat but I'm right out of food. I get just enough to do me for the week as I spend most weekends at Fred and Elsie's. They are good to me and I'm very fond of them. Elsie has a heart of gold."

"I'm okay but what about you?"

"Fred usually picks me up before this. You know I do have a couple of slices of brown bread and an over-ripe banana. How would you like to share a banana sandwich with me and a cup of tea?"

The banana, black-skinned and mushy, spread between the crusty brown bread and washed down with scalding hot tea helped us survive till Fred arrived in his elongated 1939 Chrysler. I began to see Ivy at every opportunity. I always received a warm welcome anytime I appeared at Fred and Elsie's. Elsie was a dynamo of energy and as strong as a man, a born-again-Christian and a personal friend of Alberta's Premier the Right Honourable William Aberhart, "Bible Bill." She was president of the Southern Alberta Social Credit Party and responsible for the election of John Blackmore, the party's only member in the House of Commons. She did all the manual jobs around the house. I watched her climb an extension ladder to put screens on the upstairs windows. She laid a new concrete floor in their basement, mixed the cement and trowelled it like a master mason. Her energy and abilities seemed endless and she felt it was her duty to save the souls of all sinners, including me.

Fred, quiet and easy-going, let her have her way. He worked for the government as a tax assessor. He had once been a car salesman and admired Chrysler products. He served Sunday breakfast and was justifiably proud of his "Sunday Morning Flapjacks."

They loved to argue and at times it got loud and sarcastic. At first I was embarrassed but I got used to it when they didn't come to blows. They enjoyed their battles. It was part of their life. Most of all I enjoyed their warm hospitality and being there with Ivy.

One evening after a movie Ivy and I walked into Elsie's kitchen just as she tightened the rings of the last jar of raspberries she was canning. "Elsie, we could smell those berries half a block away. Gee! They look delicious and what a lovely colour! They look good enough to eat!"

"Would you like some?" she asked.

In our home you never opened your preserves until the snow flew or extra-special company came. "Sure, I'd like some but you wouldn't dare open a jar just after you sealed them."

She opened a jar. They were delicious and I should have realized there was method in her madness.

"Thanks Elsie, the raspberries were delicious. Now I must get going."

"You're not hitchhiking back to McLeod tonight?"

"There's quite a lot of traffic on Saturday nights and it's warm tonight."

"Are you on duty tomorrow?" Elsie asked.

"No. I'm off until Monday morning."

"You might as well spend the night here. I'll make up a bed on the chesterfield."

"You'll be able to enjoy Fred's pancake breakfast," Ivy said.

"But you'll have to go to church," Elsie interjected.

I didn't mind going to church on Sundays, if that is what it took to enjoy being near Ivy and living in a comfortable home for a day or two. But when a Bible-thumping Evangelist had a two week session in Elsie's church Ivy and I went just a couple of times to please Elsie. My beliefs were well established but I had no desire to impose them on anyone. I sat through those meetings and had the fear of eternal damnation yelled at me and was told that as a sinner I would burn in the fiery furnace unless I accepted Jesus Christ as my Saviour and was washed in the blood of the lamb. I was glad to escape before their angry God collapsed the church on top of us and sent me on my merry way to hell. I suspected Elsie had plans for Ivy and me but she was not going to convert me.

Ivy had a part time job during July and August and we saw each other often. We swam in the Old Man River and picnicked in the shade of its scrubby willows. We picked saskatoons and Ivy made me a saskatoon pie. We hunted gophers with an old twenty-two rifle Elsie resurrected. We dug for fossils on the river bank and found they were too big to lug home.

One weekend, Ivy had to attend a wedding in Medicine Hat with Fred, Elsie and Gladys. Punchy and I had "forty-eights" but no money. Saturday after lunch we were lying on our bunks in the S-room bemoaning the sad state of our finances and wondering how we would spend the weekend.

"Punchy, have you ever been to Waterton Lakes?"

"No. Why?"

"I know Sergeant Pritchard and some of his friends are up there, and I heard Rowdy Dowdy talking to Nursing Sister Winters about going there for the weekend. They say the place is packed with American tourists and those American girls love our blue uniforms. Let's hitchhike up there and see what it's like."

"What the hell will we use for money? All I got is a dollar in change."

"I got fifty cents. Let's pack yourselves some food, take our bathing trunks and get started. Better than moping around here all weekend."

We were in Waterton before four. We swam in the lake and tried unsuccessfully to share our picnic dinner with a couple of American girls. We crashed the dance, found Sergeant Pritchard, his wife and friends and were invited to their motel for a beer after the dance. Pritchard let us sleep in his car. I had the back seat and Punchy used the front.

The next morning, after an early morning swim, we spent the eighty cents we had left on a good breakfast. As we left the cafe a couple of girls were getting into their car.

"Are you girls heading for McLeod?" Punchy asked.

"No. We're not. Are you from the Air Force station in McLeod?"

"Yes. Where are you from?"

"From Cardston. We'll give you a ride as far as Cardston. It's forty miles south of McLeod. I have to pick up my father. We'll meet you here in half an hour."

They took us to Cardston. We were there by noon but instead of going north to McLeod we took the round-about-route to Lethbridge.

There was nobody home at Fred and Elsie's. The day was hot and we sat in the shade of their front steps and waited until they returned from Medicine Hat. Elsie fed us but we had to go to church.

After church we hitched a ride back to McLeod and reported to the S-room about the forty-eight we'd enjoyed for a dollar and fifty cents.

In July I strung some forty-eights together and hitchhiked back to Tugaske, Saskatchewan to celebrate my mother's birthday with my two sisters, Bernice and Phyllis, and my brother Carl. It would be the last time the family would be together.

I boasted to the family about my new girl friend. "Sounds like you're getting serious," my sister Bernice said.

"It's about time you got married, Gordon," Mother added, "I was afraid you were serious about that married woman in Calgary."

"I was very fond of Penny but the whole thing was impossible. I can't get married while I'm in the Air Force, especially as an AC 2 nursing orderly. Who knows how long this crazy war will last?"

"You were twenty-seven in June and you're not getting any younger," said Bernice. "Al and I have been married for three years. He doesn't make much more teaching then you get in the Air Force, and you get your board, room and clothes."

"I'm still trying to remuster to aircrew. If I get flying I'll make more money. I might even ask Ivy to marry me."

"If you get flying you'll end up getting killed. You'd be better off to stay in the Medical Branch and marry Ivy, that's if she'll have you," my sister said. "First thing you know you'll be overseas, marry one of those English girls bring her back to Canada, that's if you're still alive when the war's over."

On my return to McLeod I learned that DRO's had announced that applicants for remustering to aircrew would be interviewed by a recruiting officer. I had my interview a week later. "That will be all for now, Wagner, your application will be processed in due course. With your qualifications you should be near the top of the list."

Well maybe I should get married. I've been kicking around long enough and with nothing to show for it. It's almost four years since I got out of university. You only have four-score-and-ten and I've used up more than a third of that and if I sleep as much as the average person I'll used up a third of what's left. So I don't have a helluva lot of time left.

I'll never be remembered for much. Who is? I've managed to feed myself but I've done nothing about the other basic instinct of perpetuating my kind. Society says you must do that in wedlock.

I'll look a long time before I find a finer partner then what Ivy will make. But this damn war. What if I buy a bill of goods in bloody aircrew and leave her with a couple of kids or worse yet if I get buggered up and be a drag on her for the rest of our lives?

Don't be so goddamn rational, Gordon. Follow your instincts and marry the girl. Or do you have the guts to ask her?

I asked Ivy if she would marry me. She threw her arms around me, held me close and started to weep. I still don't know whether I surrendered or I was captured. Elsie had done her part and more. She even arranged the wedding and the whole shebang.

I got a couple of forty-eights and we were married in Elsie's little Lethbridge church and had a wedding luncheon in Fred and Elsie's home. We caught a bus to Calgary and spent the weekend there.

I took an extra day and when I got back to the hospital Sergeant Pritchard put me on charge for being AWOL. The next day he paraded me before F/L Brewster, our senior MO, and read the charges with his bristling mustache rigidly at attention.

Dr. Brewster smiled. "I understand that you were married on the weekend, Wagner. If I'd been you I'd have taken a couple of more days. Sergeant Pritchard, the case is dismissed. Congratulations Wagner, may you have a long and happy marriage."

Air Force regulations said I had to sign over three quarters of my pay to my wife. I was reduced to less than twenty dollars a month and because Ivy lived in Lethbridge and not in McLeod I wasn't eligible for a living-out allowance. It took three months for my deductions to appear on a cheque for Ivy. Fortunately Ivy had a small bank account.

No accommodation was available in McLeod and it was nearly as bad in Lethbridge. Ivy found a room, a sort of bed-sitting room with an old leather-covered Winnipeg couch. It had coil springs that felt about the size of those used to buffer box cars. Sleep was impossible as the damn coils drilled through the thin mattress and tried to separate your ribs. We spent one night there. Ivy went to stay at Elsie's and I slept in the S-room.

We found a one-room suite with a walk-in clothes closet converted to resemble a kitchen. It did have a good bed, a table and two chairs, though I hitched rides for the first week then found a sergeant who commuted each day and rode with him.

One payday Punchy and I got started in the airmen's canteen and had quite a few before we bummed a ride to Lethbridge. Punchy planned to stay at the YMCA but the "Y" was filled. I took him home and Ivy fed us. When bedtime came we gave Punchy a blanket and he slept on the floor at the foot of our bed.

Hospital staff at No 5, SFTS, McLeod, January, 1942.

Aircrew Training

I had orders to report to No 3 Initial Training School (ITS) in Edmonton, Alberta, on the 6th of December, 1941. The school was on the campus of the University of Alberta and we lived in Pembina Hall where I roomed with Cece Hemingway. Three of us had been selected from McLeod—Cece and I, and a Sergeant Red Rice from aero-engines.

On our first morning that 7th day of December, 1941, Cece and I were on our way to breakfast when the news of Pearl Harbour crackled from our radio. We had several Americans in our class, even one who thought that he'd win the war for Canada and make it pay, and wondered why he had to go to school to do it. His cockiness cooled that day as we listened to the news and the devastation the Japanese had wrought upon the American Navy.

Once again the initial "W" of my name played me dirt. We all wanted to be pilots and the crucial test was the training you took in the "link." The link was a machine built to resemble an aircraft simulating all the conditions of flying a plane. Each student was to have two hours training in the link and it was arranged in alphabetical order. When they got to the W's the time had been cut to fifteen minutes. I had done a lot of bobsledding as a boy and with a bobsled to make a turn to the left you pushed the steering bar with your right foot. The rudder in an aircraft worked the other way. I made a mess of my link time and was sent to Air Observers' School (AOS) No 2 at the airport in Edmonton.

Ivy had followed me to Edmonton and we shared a home with a Mrs. Holmes and her five-year-old son. Her husband was in the Air Force and stationed in eastern Canada. I had sleeping-out privileges but couldn't get a living-out allowance so took most of my meals in the airmen's mess.

We flew Anson aircraft out of the Edmonton Airport, which in those days was located on Main Street in west Edmonton. We all enjoyed flying. On the 6th of February, 1942, I took my first flight in Anson No. 6010 and my pilot was none other than the famed Canadian

bush-pilot, Ginger Coote. It was bitterly cold in winter of '42 and colder still in the drafty Anson.

I was impressed with the training we received. Our instructors were top-notch and we studied navigation, mapping, photography, bombing, meteorology and the theory of flight. We had to learn to work in the cramped confines of an aircraft and to work rapidly and accurately as the airplanes travelled through the air and the air moved with the winds.

I was slated to write my final examination in navigation, the course's most important subject, on the 29th of April. Two days before, Ivy had gone into the Edmonton's Alexandria Hospital to have our first child. I visited her the evening before the exam and she was having a wretched time. When I left after visiting hours I wondered if she'd live through the night. The baby was due momentarily and the nurse assured me they would phone when the baby was born.

The barrack's phone was in the washroom and my bunk-bed was right next door. I got to bed at midnight and left the door ajar so I could hear the phone. I waited and I waited. I couldn't sleep. I worried about Ivy and about the exam due next day. But the phone didn't ring and I didn't sleep. Finally at five o'clock I phoned the hospital.

"How is Mrs. Wagner?" I asked the nurse in Maternity.

"She's resting now. You have a healthy baby boy. He was born at 3:30 am. Your wife asked us not to phone you because you'd likely be asleep."

Half-way through the exam I discovered I had made a mistake and would have to start again. I had visions of failing but we had learned to work fast and I got the navigation problem solved and graduated with the rest of the class.

I visited the hospital that evening. Ivy looked a little peaked but, flashing her smile, showed me our new son. He looked more like a monkey than a boy. His tiny hands were clutched close to his face and he had a lot of hair that seemed to grow right over his face. We decided to call him Gordon Keith. Gordon had been one of my father's names and we both liked "Keith."

A week later I was posted to No 8 Bombing and Gunnery School at Lethbridge. Once again Ivy followed me and I found a place for her to live. We shared a home with a Mrs. McAllister. Once again I had to live in barracks but it worked out rather well, and we both enjoyed being back in Lethbridge. We saw Fred and Elsie Harvey, and Gladys and the rest of Ivy's friends. Punchy, Fraser and Doug Parry were still in McLeod when I visited my old quarters in S-room.

At No 8 B&G we trained in "Fairey Battles", an aircraft built like a concrete outhouse. We learned how to strip down and use the Browning and the old WW II Vickers machine guns. We sat in the rear cockpit of the aircraft trying to hit an eighteen-inch by ten-foot drogue a hundred yards away. The old WW 1 Vickers held a hundred rounds and if you got two or three hits you were doing well. I got frustrated after firing three or four hundred rounds with only one hole in the drogue. I asked the pilot to fly closer and at point-blank range I hit the damn thing thirteen times but I didn't fool our armour instructor.

The bombsight was in the nose of the Fairey Battle. You had to crawl up into the nose, lay on your belly and adjust the bombsight to allow for the speed of the aircraft, direction of the wind and your ground speed and release the damn smoke bomb so that by the time it fell to earth it would hit the target. We dropped the bombs at a target in a dried-up alkali lake bed. In the centre was a five-foot circle called the pickle barrel. It was surrounded by concentric circles of fifty, one-hundred, one-hundred-fifty and two-hundred yards. We had a pool to be won by anybody who could drop a bomb into the pickle barrel. I was lucky if I hit the target.

Then one day we got Sergeant Bloxham for a pilot. He was an RAF type, fresh out of England. Before we took off he admitted it was his first flight in a Fairey Battle and he didn't know too much about the airplane. We left the bombing range flying at five thousand feet. He put the nose down, gave it full throttle and at a thousand feet he pulled up the nose and did a loop. I almost messed my breeches. I didn't know much about flying but I knew you weren't suppose to start a loop under five thousand feet and our brick-outhouse airplane wasn't designed for aerobatics.

We drew Sergeant Bloxham the next day. After we dropped our bombs he decided he'd do some low flying. He skimmed over the prairie at naught feet for half an hour, buzzed a couple of farm houses, and stampeded some cattle. Then he climbed to a thousand feet and was headed for Montana.

"Where the hell are you going?" I yelled over the intercom.

"Back to the air base," he replied.

"That town ahead is Sweetgrass, Montana. You better do a hundred- and-eighty and follow that gravel road. It will take you back to Lethbridge."

"Tally ho! Old man!"

He greased a smooth landing but he forgot to put the propeller into fine pitch. We raced down the long runway. Sped over five hundred feet of grass. Broke through the heavy link-chain fence guarding the airport. Bounced across No 1 highway just missing a car. Ripped up a farmer's barb-wire fence and buried the propeller and nose of Fairey Battle 2104 in an irrigation ditch. Miraculously no one was hurt. The aircraft was only slightly damaged but Sergeant Bloxham was grounded.

We were nearing the end of our training at No 8 and Taylor and I had a night bombing exercise to do. Our flight was scheduled for 22:00 hours. I'd been home most of the afternoon and returned to the base half an hour before our flight time. I found Taylor in the wet canteen and well into his cups.

I thought he'd never make it to the aircraft. But he was determined to go. "I've never missed a day's work in my life," he slurred, "and I'm bloody well not missing my last chance to hit that pickle barrel."

I had to give him a boost to get him into the cockpit. We got airborne and he crawled into the bomb bay. I listened as he gave instructions to the pilot to guide him to the target. We each had five bombs to drop. I heard him curse the pilot, the bombsight and the bombs. He shouted "Bombs away" as he let the last one go.

"I hit the pickle barrel," he screamed. "I really hit it! Really, I really did!"

We landed and the instructor confirmed the hit. Taylor won the jackpot. The canteen was closed but we had to celebrate so we found an all-night restaurant and had their best steak smothered in mushrooms.

Ivy, with baby Keith, was enjoying living with Mrs. McAllister. Keith was a cranky baby and Mrs. Mac seemed to know just what to do. She was a buxom woman about Ivy's age. She picked up Keith, wrapped her thick arms around him and snuggled him against her ample bosom — sometimes I thought she'd smother the child. Then she'd rock him vigorously and sing a lullaby loud enough to scare most babies until Keith was sound asleep. But it was moving time again.

We finished our course in Lethbridge on the 21st of June. We had a week's leave and were to report to No 1 Advance Navigation School at Rivers, Manitoba on the 28th. If we had good flying weather the course would last five weeks. If we passed we would receive our Air Observer's Wing, be promoted to a sergeant and if were lucky might be given a commission. But more important we would get a raise in pay.

My folks were anxious to see their first grandson and we spent my week's leave with them in Tugaske Saskatchewan. With the hospitality so typical of the prairie people, they rented to us a small three-roomed cottage and scrounged enough furniture to make it comfortable. The change agreed with Keith when he was fed the rich milk of Grandpa Moore's jersey cow. She and Keith stayed in Tugaske while I went on to Rivers.

Rivers, a small prairie town about twenty-five miles northwest of Brandon, boasted a peace-time population of five-hundred. Now it bulged with people as did the other small towns nearby. No. 1 ANS bulged with fledgling observers. There were no empty barracks so they gave us double bunks in a hangar along with a hundred other souls.

The hangar doors wouldn't close. We didn't need the privacy but we could have used some screens to keep River's mosquitos from eating us alive. The hanger's roof leaked and I, like everyone else, made sure my bed wasn't under a hole. One hot afternoon we had an extra heavy thundershower and warm rain poured through the roof. We stripped and showered in soft rainwater as it cascaded to the hangar's concrete floor.

Author enjoying thunder shower.

The food was truly terrible. One day at noon when the Orderly Officer asked us about our food, we all yelled, "It stinks!" We turned our plates up- side-down and walked out of the mess. We were saved by the airmen's canteen. They served hot dogs. I learned to love hot dogs smeared with mustard and chased with a bottle of coke. This is still one of my favourite snacks and brings memories of Rivers and how much I missed Ivy and Keith.

On my first flight out of Rivers we had five people in Anson 6207 with Sergeant Pilot Whitney at the controls. We had a radio operator, and a first, second and third navigator. I was the third navigator. I had to sit on the floor near the rear door to practice map reading. We had been warned by the weatherman about thunderstorms. Our pilot tried to fly between two angry, mean-looking black clouds. We were tossed around like feathers in a whirlwind. Hail pounded the canvas-covered aircraft. It got dark. Visibility was zero. I couldn't see the wing tips. I couldn't tell up from down. Then, suddenly the sun emerged and the endless prairie stretched beneath us everlastingly flat. I had no idea where we were. We flew towards the afternoon sun and across a double railway track. I could see the pilot and the two navigators pouring over maps. *My gosh! They're lost. Lost on the prairies? They can't be.*

"Are you having trouble?" I asked.

"We can't find a landmark. All these roads and small towns look the same."

"I haven't picked up a landmark since we came out of the thunderstorm. Did you know that we have some fabric flapping on the right wing?"

"Doesn't look too bad. We should find the nearest airfield and land to have a look at the damage. But where the hell are we?" Sergeant Whitney asked.

"We flew over a double railway a few minutes ago. There is only one of those on the prairies. It's the main line of the CPR. If we turn around and fly back we'll find it."

"Yeah, and what good will that do?"

"All the Wheat Pool elevators have the name of the town on them. You can read it from half a mile away."

We found the double railway. The Pool elevator said "Grenfell." "We're in Saskatchewan. About eighty miles east of Regina. That's the nearest airport." If we had to land I'd enjoy a few hours in Regina. I had two aunts there and several cousins.

Sergeant Whitney found Grenfell on the map. "There's an emergency landing strip at Broadview. It's only about ten miles east of here. We'll have a look at the strip. I don't want to go any farther than we have to."

We landed on the Broadview strip. There were five or six rips in the fabric of our canvas-covered Anson. Our pilot got in touch with Rivers. They told us to stay put and they would send an aircraft to pick us up and bring an airframe mechanic to patch up the damaged aircraft.

Half the town turned out to see us. The starry-eyed teen-aged girls asked for autographs. Some people offered to put us up for the night, but we stayed in Broadview's Maple Leaf Hotel and had our meals in Don Wong's chinese restaurant.

The next morning our pilot didn't show for breakfast and his hotel bed hadn't been slept in. Our rescue plane arrived from Rivers just after nine. The air-frame mechanic got busy mending number 6207.

Two of the navigators flew back to Rivers in the relief plane and I stayed as Sergeant Whitney's navigator.

When the plane's fabric was repaired and we were wondering what had happened to our pilot, he emerged from the nearby red-roofed cottage that housed the caretaker of the landing strip. He'd spent the **night with the caretaker's promiscuous wife.**

Course No. 42, No. 1 ANS, at Rivers, 1942.

They kept us busy at Rivers. In addition to flying we took crash courses in astronomy, spherical trigonometry and astro-navigation. We learned to use a sextant and took hundreds of observations both on the ground and in the air. We used seven-place logarithms with a formula we didn't need to understand to use. We had to learn to work fast and accurately. Today those tedious observations and calculations are done by computers. We flew by the stars and by the sun. I felt good the night I navigated our Anson from Rivers to Regina, from there to Saskatoon and back to Rivers without looking at the ground and had my ETA (estimate time of arrival) within minutes. I learned to appreciate the importance of time. I still like to have a chronometer that keeps accurate time to the second.

The great day finally arrived. On the 5th day of August, on River's hot parade square, the station's Commanding Officer pinned the "Flying O" on our tunics and wished us well. More important was the notation on the next day's DROs of our promotions to the rank of sergeant and the subsequent pay increase.

Then came the postings. *I wonder why everybody wants to go overseas? We know damn well if we get posted to Bomber Command the chance of completing two tours of thirty raids are worse than poor. They lose fifteen percent of the squadron on every raid. That means a complete turnover every tour. Who the hell wants to fight those odds to be a bloody hero? I'd be scared shitless and so would most other guys. Maybe I should have stayed in the Medical Branch. If I hadn't been so damn stubborn I could have gotten some "rank" and my chances for survival would have been a helluva lot better. They say if you're married they tend to keep you in Canada. You're supposed to bitch like hell if you're not in the overseas' draft. I'll bitch but I'll be glad to stay in Canada, so will most guys. But I'll have bugger-all to say about it. Whatever the draw, I'll have to go where they send me.*

On Active Service in Canada

Three of our brainy guys went to Air Observer Schools as instructors. Six were posted to Coastal Command on the east coast. Myself and five others were sent to Western Air Command and the rest of the class went overseas.

Three days later we arrived in Vancouver and were the first observers to join "Bomber and Reconnaissance Squadron No 147" at the Vancouver airport on Sea Island. But with the usual cufuffle the squadron didn't know we were coming and they had no place to put us. We didn't get a chance to unpack our kit bags. They gave us a week's leave. I got a return ticket to Tugaske.

It was wonderful to be with Ivy and Keith again. Keith had put on some weight and looked so much better. Ivy had the small cottage real homey like. While I was in Tugaske I received a notice that I had been awarded a commission in His Majesty's Royal Canadian Air Force.

A lot of goodies came with a commission. Whether they were deserved was questionable. The RCAF commissions a large percentage of its aircrews. There seemed to be no rhyme or reason to their choices. We had all been trained to perform similar duties yet the hierarchy was not based on ability.

Well Gordon, congratulations! You made it. I wonder how many of the class did? You made it in spite of the B.A. you've carried around since 1938. It never did do you a hell of a lot of good. There were some clever guys in Class No 42. You'll have to change your tune. You won't be dealing with the likes of Sergeant Blair. They say in aircrew your promotion from a Pilot/Officer to Flying/Officer is automatic and the same with F/O to Flight Lieutenant, so you'll have to keep your nose clean. It will be nice to get the increase in pay and find a decent place for Ivy and Keith. But I suppose it will be like Jack Brown warned me in Levack when he said, "Gordon, it doesn't matter how much you make they'll always find some way of taking it away from you. I didn't see Taylor's name on the commission-list. Fifteen of the twenty-two got commissions. Doesn't seem fair. But life never is. When your number comes up it won't make any difference. A German or a Jap will use the same ammunition, and you'll be just as dead. Might help your wife or your parents. I wonder what we'll be doing on the West Coast?

I soon discovered.

We reported to Squadron 128's orderly room and Adjutant F/O Bird, a thin, hollow-cheeked man with a whisk of greying hair spread carefully across a bony skull. He looked out of place amongst the youth of our aircrews. He was a native of Vancouver and had flown a desk for C.M. Oliver and Company on the Vancouver Stock Exchange. He always had a stock market tip for everyone. I often wonder if he got a commission. He gave us a requisition to buy our officer's uniform. "Any of the downtown stores will fit you for a uniform. Pick up some P/O ribbon and sew it on to your epaulettes and get those sergeant's stripes off your sleeves. The Officer's Mess is in an old farm house on the other side of the runway. The sergeant will assign you your quarters."

The mess sergeant put the six of us in an old garage adjacent to the fine old farm home. "This place is getting crowded. They'll be using tents pretty soon."

I met my first earwig my first night in our garage-cum-boudoir. I had never seen the flat little beetle with hook-jawed mouth and a pair of forceps attached to its rear end. I was almost asleep when I felt something in my ear. I caught the wiggly little bugger before he'd gone too far.

The flight room and the orderly room were in a Quonset hut on the south side of the runway. The squadron's commanding officer S/L Anderson briefed us. "We are in the process of assembling the crews and aircraft for a unit that will be used for reconnaissance. You are all aware of the recent shelling of Estevan Point and the invasion of the Aleutian Islands by the Japanese. We will be flying the Mark IV Bolingbrook which can carry bombs or depth charges. When we are up to full strength we will, in all probability, be sent to Alaska. We have six aircraft, five of which are air-worthy. More are on the way. We have a few bombs but we don't have any armourment personnel. We'll try to get a few hours of flying-time in for all of you. In the meantime you'll have to be patient.

"Married personnel and those whose homes are in the Vancouver area will be given living-out allowances until we have quarters on the station. Are there any questions?

"Good! I want you to baby those airplanes. Your mothers may have told you to fly low, and slow and go easy on the corners, but anyone caught low-flying or disobeying squadron procedures will be grounded. You fly those Bolingbrooks as if both wings were going to fall off. And remember, the day you think you know all there is to learn about flying is the day you quit."

I started to look for a place to live. The Red Cross had a housing service but accommodation was as scarce as it had been in McLeod. A few rooms were available but nobody would rent to people with children. Then one day the Red Cross phoned.

"Mr. Wagner there is a lady who has a room to rent and she won't mind the baby. Her name is Mrs. Hern. The house is at 2260 Collingwood. It's near the intersection of Collingwood and Marine Drive. Take the Dunbar streetcar at 41st and Granville."

"Thank you, I'll get over there right away."

I found the large mansion-like house sitting on an acre lot fronted by a raggedy lawn and overlooking a golf course with patches of the Fraser River peeking over the fairways. A slightly-built man in his sixties, with a wisp of fine blond hair brushed to cover as much of his skull as possible, was raking leaves.

"Excuse me, sir, are you Mr. Hern?"

"That's right, soldier," he replied with an asthmatic sputter in his voice.

"I understand you have a room for rent?"

"That's right sonny. All I know is we got too damn many rooms, too big a lawn, too many trees and I'm too bloody old to look after it. I think the war department has a room to rent. She's in the house. Can you parley voo fransay? This is her day to speak French. She'll be in the front room yakking to one of her French friends. Go on in."

I mounted the steps just as the visitor was leaving and waited until she had said "bon voyage" to her friend.

"Are you Mrs. Hern?"

"Oui Monsieur, parlez-vous francais?"

"No I can't but do you have a room to rent?"

She stopped looking down her nose and unpuckered her lips, "It is unfortunate that you don't speak French. But do come along and I'll show you the room."

She led me upstairs and showed me a good-sized bedroom with a walk-in clothes closet and a couple of chairs. "You'll be sharing the bathroom with the family. You'll have use of our kitchen stove and use our dining room. I've decided we must do something to help you boys. You'll be our only tenants and we hope you become part of our family."

"How much is the rent?"

"How does twenty five dollars a month sound?"

"Sounds fine to me. You won't mind our baby?"

"Oh no, we have a crib you can use. It used to belong to Shirley."

I gave her a month's rent, and she showed me through the house. There were four bedrooms upstairs, a large living room with a fireplace, a den with a fireplace, a dining room and a kitchen downstairs. A double garage adjoined the kitchen and the servants' quarters were over the garage.

Ivy arrived a week later and we moved in. Mr. Hern's first name was Lou. He had been manager of Eaton's big store in Edmonton and had to retire because of his asthma. Her name was Sue and they had two daughters, Jane, who was at UBC in her third year and majoring in French and twelve-year-old Shirley, with a blond braid that hung to her waist, was still in grade school. Mrs. Hern, with her shiny-black, lightly-silvered hair combed straight back, looked much younger than he. She had taught French in an Edmonton High School, had lived in France and was active in the French community in Vancouver.

She was determined to have her family learn to speak French. Tuesdays and Sundays she refused to talk English. Jane spoke the language fluently; Shirley was quite good and Ivy managed fairly well. I didn't try and Lou would say in a loud sarcastic voice, "Mercy beau cup," when she handed him his cup of tea.

We had been there a week when Sue rented the den to a couple,

Margot and Michel. They had a baby boy the same age as Keith. They cooked on a hot plate in their room but it added another family for the washing machine and the kitchen sink. I told Ivy the only reason we didn't get the den was because we couldn't speak French.

I was away for a week and when I came back they had rented two more rooms upstairs. Jane and Shirley were moved to the servants' quarters over the garage. Now there were five women cooking on one stove, washing in one washing machine, feeding their air force husbands at one table and trying not to have a nervous breakdown.

Vancouver had a cold November in '42. Coal was in short supply and they had the army cutting wood to keep the people in Vancouver warm. By now we realized the Herns had to rent the rooms to augment their income. It was no patriotic gesture now and they could not afford to buy fuel. The big lot had lots of firewood and Lou Hern tried to cut enough wood to keep that big house warm. We all gave him a hand. It was pitiful to watch him try to drag that crosscut saw through those logs.

The house was never warm. In the evenings we'd all huddle around the living room fireplace to warm up before we jumped into bed. Keith was old enough to sit on the floor and play. I bought a one-burner hot plate and leaned it against the wide enamelled base and sat Keith in front of it while I played with him. We burnt the pattern of the hot plate onto the base board.

We started training in the Bolingbrooks with flights up and down the coast of Vancouver Island and in and out of the long winding fjords of the mainland. On the fourth night in our garage-cum-boudoir we awoke to the whine of an air raid siren. The city of Vancouver had had full blackout since Pearl Harbour. But it was the airport siren and we scrambled into our clothes and headed across the runway to the Quonset hut.

"There's been a report of enemy ships approaching the west coast of Canada," said a bleary-eyed S/L Anderson with his pyjamas showing under battle-dress tunic. "There's a red alert. You're to sit in the aircraft ready for takeoff. You've got two armour- piercing bombs in the bomb bay. I don't know if the bloody things are properly fused, but it's the best we can do."

We sat there until daylight when the alert was cancelled. Damn good thing we didn't have to go after a Japanese cruiser. We'd have been shot out of the sky before we'd ever have gotten near enough to let an armour-piercing bomb go. The enemy ships never did appear. Somebody probably saw a whale and mistook it for a submarine. It wouldn't be the first time this happened, nor the last.

Two days later on a beautiful September morning one of our Bolingbrooks failed to return from a routine flight over Vancouver Island. I had flown with P/O Thorn just the day before. We searched for that plane for a week without success. After the war, when I became a surveyor and worked in the mountain wilderness of the rain forest, I realized how easily a plane could disappear in the dense growth that covers most of the Island. It wasn't until 1975 that loggers found the wreckage of P/O Thorn's plane.

Gee whiz Wagner, and you thought it would be safer on the West Coast. Why Taylor and the rest of the overseas draft aren't in England yet. Whatever happened to the Bolingbrook and P/O Thorn could have happened the day before and you'd be rotting in some lonely valley, impaled upon a mountain peak or under salt water providing food for hungry crabs. Don't be so damn morbid, Gordon. When you're number's up there's bugger all you can do about it. I really don't believe that bull. Surely I have some control over what I do. I'll never be killed in an aircraft if I refuse to fly. The thing to do is to be careful. Don't fly with those hair-brained pilots who like to skim the tree tops or do tight turns around smoke stacks. The other day I sat in the nose of that Bolly while Tex Steveson flew from Duncan to Qualicum Beach and was never above 200 feet. He started to do the same thing on the way back and I told him I'd had enough and to get the hell up where he should be flying or I'd turn him in when we got back.

In mid-October a submarine had been reported as having been sighted in Sydney Inlet about seventy-five miles north of Tofino. A fisherman claimed he had seen it near an abandoned mine at the head of the inlet. The Vancouver Sun got hold of the story and the paper's imagination ran wild, claiming the Japanese-Canadians had stored supplies there in preparation for the Japanese invasion of Canada. It all helped to justify the action taken by the Canadian government, when in February under the War Measures Act, it had ordered the removal and internment of all Japanese from an area within a 100 miles of the Pacific coast.

P/O Jay Ronalds, with a radio operator and me aboard, landed the first twin-engined aircraft on the newly-completed runway at Tofino.

The new station, about five miles south of the small fishing village, was within easy walking distance of Long Beach. On this three miles of hard-packed sand, England's racing hero Sir Malcolm Campbell had set a world's speed record. Now it was considered Canada's first line of defence with an anti-tank regiment camped near the new air base and with pilings driven deep into low-tide sand to deter the expected invasion.

We spent six days cruising around, over and sometimes under the scud-cloud cover of Sydney Inlet with never a sign of the submarine nor the suspected whale. We were blessed with a week of Indian summer. Although radio reception on Vancouver Island's west coast was notoriously poor we were able to pick up an American station that was carrying the World Series and listened to the St. Louis Cardinals beat the Brooklyn Dodgers in five games.

Since August, rumours (all air force intelligence starts as rumour) had 147 B-R Squadron on its way to the Aleutians. I watched the apple-polishers and the porch-climbers try to advance their military careers. By late November the squadron had a surplus of air crew and with the move to Alaska just a week away the scramble became brutal. When we returned from Tofino the broadaxe had fallen. I was with the rejects. I had been posted to 149 Torpedo and Bomber Squadron at Patricia Bay near the town of Sidney on Vancouver Island, thirty miles north of Victoria.

If you had to fight a war there couldn't be any better place to do the fighting than in the beautiful city of Victoria. Experiencing the odd skirmish in the Bengal Room, taking afternoon tea and crumpets in the lobby listening to the music of Victoria's finest string quartet, or having a payday celebration in the alcohol alley of the stately Empress hotel was a "piece of cake." We occasionally invaded the sacred lounge of the "very British" Union Club and met the "Colonel Blimps" of Victoria comfortably entrenched in their black leather armchairs.

It's a tough war, Gordon. Sure as hell beats living in a tent and being lashed by the horizontal rain of the Aleutians. A great way for some of those porch-climbers to get the brown washed off their noses. But I don't suppose those apple-polishers will ever change. It seems to be a way of military life. Just take it easy Gordon and keep your nose clean.

I had to find a place for Ivy and Keith. She couldn't take much more of crowded Hernsville. Victoria had the Navy, the Army and Air Force scouring the city and its suburbs for accommodation. I looked at horrible places: summer cottages with the inside-studs uncovered and daylight showing through the shiplap; converted garages that reeked with the smell of oil and one room suites with hot plates and communal bathrooms.

Then, through the Air Force grapevine I heard someone was moving out of the Brentwood Autocourt. We got a small suite in the motel's office building. It was right over the furnace room, toasty warm and a pleasure after the wintry chill of Hernsville. Ivy and Keith loved the cozy comfort.

There were twelve units in the Brentwood Autocourt, all occupied by air force officers and their wives. We visited back and forth, respecting each other's privacy. We got caught up in the Christmas parties. Johnny Higham, who had done a tour in Bomber Command and wore the DFC (Distinguished Flying Cross) received a turkey from his mother in Saskatchewan and Ivy cooked it. Johnny, Jimmy Shaw and Jocko Van Nostrand came to Christmas dinner. We sat on the green lawn in our shirt sleeves that Christmas afternoon and I decided that after the war someday, somehow, we'd live in British Columbia.

149 (T-B) Squadron was to be equipped with Beauforts, twin-engine airplanes designed to carry torpedoes. With the typical air force cufuffle they got the personnel together but couldn't get us aircraft to fly. So, somewhere they found a couple of Bolingbrooks that some other squadron had discarded. Our innovative ground crew got them airworthy and our pilots got some hours in. Meanwhile, our Beauforts were at No. 9 Repair Depot having their "British Bristol" motors removed and "American Pratt and Whitneys" installed. My log book shows I flew six hours in December, five in January and three in February — not many hours for a guy who was supposed to win the war. It was a damn good thing the Japanese didn't decide to take the west coast of Canada and the United States. There was bugger all to stop them.

With twenty crews for the two Bolingbrook strays and one Beaufort that had wandered into camp equipped with Bristol engines, it kept the squadron's Commanding Officer, Squadron leader Wilson, and his two Flight Commanders busy trying to find things to keep us occupied. We took hours of military drill on the tarmac in front of the hangars. We took a refresher course in aircraft recognition and the theory of flight. We improved our gunnery skills shooting skeets. We played a lot of cards, mostly poker and blackjack. At times the games got a little rough and they'd be shut down for a week. Crap games in the flight room were tabooed.

There were addicted gamblers like Doug Marshall, Junior Knowlan and Gus Reid. There were the hanger-on-ers like myself, who liked to gamble but really couldn't afford it. And there was Tommy Thompson. Tommy was half way through Osgoode Hall law school when he joined the Air Force. He looked distinguished even in his pyjamas. He didn't drink, smoke or tell dirty stories but he was fascinated by the dice.

There would be a game almost every night. They played in someone's bedroom with a grey-blanketed single bed pushed tight against the wall. They bounced the dice off the wall and piled the money on the bed. On paydays they'd use the billiard table with twenty or more players in the game.

Tommy watched for a long time and he used to talk to me about the odds. When he thought he had it figured, he got in a game. He won. The next night he won again. He was hooked. He got to be a good crap player — when he was up he got out. He didn't figure he had to be a good sport and hang around giving the losers a chance to recoup.

S/L Wilson had been in the Battle of Britain and had flown Hurricanes. Nobody could figure out how he got to command a squadron of Beauforts without any twin-engine time, especially with his senior flight commander S/L Ron Gilmore.

At the age of sixteen Gilmore had joined the permanent Air Force as a boy-apprentice and he enjoyed throwing his rank around. Short and stocky with a walrus mustache that he kept well waxed, he was strong and wiry and when he had a few drinks he became sadistic. At our Christmas stag, for some reason he grabbed my arm and pulled it up behind my back and nearly broke it. I had to cry "Uncle" before he would let me go. I damn near hit him but I held my cool.

On a fine April morning the airfield gleamed with the velvets of spring. The runways crisscrossed the fresh green carpet as if a giant had left a game of tic-tac-toe. A border of dark green firs and hemlocks mixed with the lighter greens of the maples and alders rimmed the base and was punctuated with white periods of flowering dogwoods. The end of the north runway dipped to reveal the seaplane hangers hugging the shoreline of Pat Bay. A pair of Stranrear seaplanes floating at anchor on the sparkling waters of the bay looked like awkward ducks dozing in the morning sun. On the sapphire horizon a fleecy cloud fluttered like a cotton batting flag from the top of Salt Spring's rounded mountain, and the snow-covered peak of Mount Baker glistened in the clean spring air. In the front of our hanger, radiant in a new coat of paint and proud of its new Pratt and Whitney engines, our first Beaufort gleamed like a virgin in the refreshing light of spring.

"Attention! This is your Commanding Officer speaking," blared our hangar's PA. "All 149 squadrons flying personnel report to the flight room at 09:00 hours."

Noisy with voices, the flight room silenced, and then filled again with the noise of scraping chairs as we stood to attention when our Commanding Officer S/L Wilson entered.

"At ease men," he said.

With his field cap squashed against his black Bryl-creamed hair, and his chubby neckless face squeezed through his collar, he stood behind a lectern that nearly hid the row of ribbons under his pilot wings. He looked like Humpty Dumpty with a whisky rash preparing to preach a sermon.

"You've all seen our first modified Beaufort sitting out there on the tarmac. We should be getting two or three a week until we're up to strength. This is a hot airplane. You all know it had no single-engine performance with the old motors, we'll soon know how good it is with the Pratt and Whitneys. I want you to treat these machines with silk gloves. We've got a job to do here on the coast and I'm going to see we do a damn good one. I'm going to test fly 9160 this morning. Are there any questions?"

A murmur of approval rippled through the room. Bill Switzer, sitting next to me, whispered, "Saskie, I just hope he doesn't want a navigator for his test flight."

"So do I, Bill. I hate being baggage when a pilot is doing circuits and bumps. I don't need hours that badly."

"Thank you gentleman. I'll give you a debriefing after the flight," said the C/O as he left the flight room.

"I hope the hell he doesn't want a copilot," said Johnny Higham. "I wonder how many hours he has on twin-engined aircraft? Damn few I'll bet."

The squadron had been without airplanes for almost five months. The war would be over and the Japanese brass entrenched in the Victoria's Union Club, before we learned to launch a torpedo. We had learned and relearned all the drill maneuvers on the parade square. The poker and blackjack games were almost part of routine orders. I was knocking clay pigeons off the skeet range at twenty out of twenty-four. But I had flown less than forty hours. Even I was anxious to get some air time.

It was about 10:00 hours when S/L Wilson, dressed in his brown "issue-tissue" flying suit and looking like a teddy bear, climbed with two of our mechanics into Beaufort 9016 and taxied to the south end of the runway. The aircraft sat there. We could hear the roar as Wilson revved the engines but the aircraft never moved.

"It's just about lunch time," said Jimmy Shaw. "Come on Saskie, he won't take off on an empty stomach."

Bill Switzer joined us. To get to the mess we had to cross the runway near the north end. We were about half way across when we heard a plane thundering towards us. "My gosh it's the C/O in the Beaufort," hollered Jimmy. We ran to the edge of the blacktop. The plane was still on the ground when it passed us. There was a drop-off at the end of the runway, where the ground sloped down to the seaplane hangars. The Beaufort struggled for altitude as it leapt off the hill. The right wing dipped. For an instant a top view of the Beaufort was silhouetted against the sky, then it cart-wheeled nose first into an abandoned farmhouse and exploded into a ball of dust, smoke and flames.

We were the first to arrive. S/L Wilson, his face bloodied and one arm dangling helplessly by his side,staggered in the long grass. "My God! My wife's in there! Get her out. She'll burn to death. That bloody car hit us head on."

"Was there anyone else in the plane?" I asked.

"Yes, my wife! You get her out," he screamed and began to cry.

"He's in shock and has no idea where he is. Look there's someone under that apple tree," said Johnny. "It's getting damn hot. We've got to get him away from there."

It was one of the mechanics. We pulled him clear. He was alive but unconscious. The ambulance and the fire truck arrived. They took Wilson and the mechanic to the hospital. There was little the fireman could do to save the house or douse the fire in the plane. They found the body of the other mechanic when they got the fire out. We never saw S/L Wilson again. S/L Gilmore was made acting C/O and immediately put us back on drill and refresher programs. He shut down the card games.

Gilmore's days of glory were short lived. Wing Commander Ronnie Dennis, who with his crew of F/L Norman Altstedter and F/O Doug Stallard, had survived five days floating in a rubber dinghy in the English Channel, became our new C/O.

W/C Ronnie Dennis was a popular C/O. He had our respect and he treated us like human beings rather than numbers. I hated being a number at the disposal of a lot of people who couldn't add.

Al Watts had done a couple of tours and got himself the DFC. He had been in the desert and helped Montgomery chase Rommel out of Africa. He married a girl from Calgary called Judy, and she was staying at the Dominion Hotel until they could find a place to live. There were no bars or beer parlours in Victoria, so Al and his crew were celebrating in their room.

They had finished a late dinner in the hotel's dining room and were waiting for the elevator to take them back upstairs. The hotel, built at the turn of the century, had a brass-cage elevator and required an operator. In the evenings the elevator man had other duties and often left the elevator unattended. The four of them decided they couldn't wait for an operator. They got the elevator working but they couldn't get it stopped and jammed it three feet above the top floor. Somehow they got the door open and wiggled free and got to Judy's room.

The hotel had called the police and when they rapped on Judy's door the three men decided to escape. But more police spotted them in the lobby and chased them onto Victoria's rain-slicked streets where the three tried to hide behind parked cars. The police called for reinforcements and cornered them in a used car lot. Watts and crew spent the night in jail.

Next morning Ronnie Dennis was in court to plead their case. He apologized to the judge and assured his Worship that the squadron would discipline F/O Watts and his crew. The judge dismissed the charges.

We got some more Beauforts and we finally began to get some hours in. Things were just getting back to normal when J.K. Macdonald and Al Watts' Beaufort lost an engine coming in to land. The aircraft bounced off the roof of a hanger and pancaked itself on the air-field grass. They both walked away from the wreck without a scratch. But that was the end of the Beauforts.

In early May a rumour, that reliable source of information often in the ears of the civilian population before we heard it, said I49 was going to be equipped with new aircraft, probably the "Lockheed Ventura PV 1."

"Good morning, Gentleman," said W/C Dennis as he entered the flight room. We didn't have to stand at attention when he came in. "I have just received word that we are to take delivery of our new aircraft. The machines are at the U.S. Naval Base in Alameda, California. They have seven planes ready. My crew and I will be going and the other six will appear on DRO tomorrow. Those chosen will attend to pay accounts and pick up their temporary duty pay-allowance. We will fly to Vancouver and go from there to San Francisco by train."

With a hundred and forty dollars each for fourteen days of temporary duty tucked into our wallets, twenty-one of us boarded the Great Northern Railway train for San Francisco. We were all in the same sleeper and it didn't take us long to discover the parlour car at the rear of the train.

British Columbia had begun to ration booze. You had to have a permit for your monthly ration of one twenty-six ounce bottle of liquor or two dozen beers. The train stopped just across the border at Blaine, Washington to clear United States customs. There was a liquor store across the street and before the train pulled out we had eight cases of beer piled in the parlour car — a real bonanza for us booze-rationed Canadians.

When we went for dinner there was a long line-up waiting to get into the diner. There were a dozen people in front of me when the headwaiter beckoned. A woman with two small children stood next to the door.

"Come in soldiers, I have a table for four," he said.

"Take this lady first," I said. "We don't mind waiting."

"Nobody eats in my dining car until all the service men are fed."

"Thank you. We're not used to that in Canada. We're usually last and we can have only certain items on the menu."

"Order what ever you want. Your voucher will cover anything on my menu. Enjoy your dinner, Canada."

"Some different than the CPR. Eh Saskie?" Switzer said.

We had a great party in the parlour car. We were friends with everybody. We treated the porter, brake man and the conductor. The trainman and porter both got a little tipsy. Our fellows roamed through the train searching for girls, but the parlour car closed at midnight and somehow they herded us to our sleeper and locked the doors at both ends. We had no choice but to go to bed.

The next morning we replenished our beer supplies a couple of times when we had a station wait. It was fine in Oregon but in California the tavern laws were different. We could buy all the beer we wanted but had to drink it on the premises. We had a twenty minute stop in Redding. A tavern was across the street. Moon Mullins and I ordered half-a-dozen pints of beer. The bartender put the bottles on the counter and started to take off the tops.

"Leave the tops on. We have to catch the train." I said.

"You can't take anything out of the tavern, soldier. Opened or not opened," he said as he opened all the bottles. "That will be a buck fifty."

"We gotta be on that train in ten minutes," I said.

"We're going to take them anyway," said Moon grabbing the six bottles.

"Oh no, you're not!" said a broad shouldered man with his back to me.

"Who says so?" Moon piqued.

The broad shoulders turned to face me. "I did. You'll either drink it here or leave it."

"And who are you," I asked.

He turned full around. The silver star sparkled on his chest and he patted the six-shooter in his holster. "I'm the Sheriff of this town, Sonny. This here's my badge and this is my persuader."

I turned and looked across the street. Moon was on the station platform with the beer cradled in his arms.

"Sheriff, I have to catch that train and I've finished all my beer. 'Bye now!"

We had a sober trip through California and arrived in San Francisco early Friday morning in good shape. We were picked up and driven across the Bay bridge to the Alameda Naval Air Station. Ensign Porter met us in front of the administration building. "Welcome aboard Canada, nice to have you with us. I will be in charge of your familiarization. Chief Petty Officer Muster has arranged quarters. We'll begin our sessions Monday at 08:00 hours in hangar No2. I don't want to see you until then. Enjoy your weekend!"

On the station we had separate rooms for which we paid fifty cents a day and ate in the station canteen and paid for our meals. The food was excellent and cheap. We were able to use the officers' club with its good dining room. But on the weekend we wanted to see the Golden City's sights.

Six of us took a taxi into San Francisco and got rooms in the Wheaton Hotel at the corner of Market Street and Pine, a block away from the cable car turntable. Of course, being Canadians, if we were going to have a weekend in town we had to lay in a supply of booze. We were surprised at how cheap liquor was. A mickey of rum was eighty-five cents and a quart of Johnnie Walker for four bucks.

We soon discovered people didn't party in hotel rooms. There were bars to drink in. We started in the Wheaton's, took the cable car to the Fairmont's "Patent Leather Room" and ended up in the Mark Hopkin's "Top of the Mark" with its magnificent view of the city and the bay. The Americans had been in the war for only six months and most of them had never heard of the RCAF or seen our blue uniforms. They thought we were Greyhound bus drivers!

On Saturday we did the Fisherman's wharf, Chinatown and the Barbary Coast. We checked out of the Wheaton Hotel Sunday morning and the bottles of booze still sat on the dresser with most of them unopened.

On Monday morning we reported to hangar No.2. The pilots had plenty to do and the wireless operators had to be checked out on all the new radio equipment. We observers had nothing to do until the pilots were flying. When Moon Mullins was ready we took several flights around the Bay area being careful to avoid the restricted areas. We were warned there were some trigger-happy people on the Navy's ack-ack guns. Moon explained the features of the PV 1 aircraft: the arrangement of the fuel tanks and how they were to be used; the automatic pilot and how to set it; the single engine performance with one engine shut off and the prop feathered so the edge of the blade was at right angles to the wings.

By the end of the week we were ready to head home. Nobody liked the idea of having to refund part of our temporary duty pay so we stayed another week. The pilots got some more hours, and we enjoyed the sounds and sights of downtown Frisco. There were officers' hostess clubs in both Alameda and in San Francisco similar to those in Calgary.

We delivered the planes to the base at Pat Bay and the next day we flew back to Alameda in a DC 3 provided by Lockheed to pick up another PV 1.

It all started innocently. When our friends learned the price of unrationed booze in the States, they gave us five or ten dollars and asked us to bring back a bottle or two.

There was voluntary rationing in California. The owners of the privately owned liquor stores would refuse to sell you more than one bottle. Then we found "Annie's Grog Shoppe" in Alameda. A handsome woman in her mid-forties with a load of gold and diamonds on her fingers was the sole owner and proprietor of the store.

"I'd like three bottles of Johnnie Walker's Red Label and ..."

"I'm sorry sir, but I can sell you only one bottle."

"Can I buy another bottle if I come back later today?"

"Well I guess you could if I didn't recognize you."

"Or I can go to another store?"

"Certainly, soldier. How many bottles do you want?"

"Twelve at least."

"Come into the back." She led us into her small warehouse. "I have special arrangements with my best customers. What are you guys doing with this booze?"

"We're flying it back to Canada."

She filled our order and packed it in a case. "You don't need to tell people where you filled your order, and any time you're down again, come and see me. I'll give you the best deal in town."

We delivered our second plane and the booze we'd bought from Annie to Pat Bay. Four days later we were back at Alameda Naval Air Base. We called Annie's Grog Shoppe. "This is your Canadian friend. We were wondering if you could fill our order?"

"I don't take orders over the phone. But if you drop by the store I'll see what I can do. It's nice to hear from you."

We were getting to know our way around the Alameda Navy base and we got a driver from their MT section to drive us over to Annie's in a pickup.

"We've got a two-hundred dollar order this trip. Do you want to fill it?" I asked.

"Sure, but what are you doing with the stuff? Bootlegging it?"

"Not really, there is nothing in it for us. Most of this is for our officer's mess and for some friends."

"I'm sorry I couldn't take your order over the phone but the authorities do check. I have to be careful. Bring your truck to the back door."

I made five trips to Alameda with Moon Mullins and each time our booze orders grew. We were not allowed to fly back to Canada unless the weather was CAVU (ceiling absolute, visibility unlimited). On our fourth trip, a series of low pressure areas coming in from the Pacific kept clouds over Washington and British Columbia, and grounded 149's ferry crews for five days. We had our clothes closet packed to the roof with cases of liquor. By four pm when it was too late to takeoff, we'd crack open a case and have drinks all around.

On the afternoon of the 26th of June I arrived home just as Mary Austin, one of our autocourt friends, was taking Ivy to the hospital. I got there just in time to go with them to the Rest Haven Hospital in

Sidney. Early in the morning of the 27th our daughter Linda was born. Ivy had a tough time.

I used to bring her mint-flavoured calcium wafers from Alameda because they weren't available in Canada. She ate them as if they were chocolate bars. I used to tease her and say the baby would be born wrapped in concrete. There were times during her labour when she was sure the baby was.

Now rumour informed us that Western Air Command was unhappy with the trafficking in spirits by certain ferry crews. A few days later a copy of a memo to the C/O appeared on our DRO's (Daily Routine Orders). I had one trip left and I had collected almost a thousand dollars. I was well on my way to becoming another Al Capone. If we ever got caught we'd be in trouble with both the Air Force and Customs.

Johnny Higham piloted our sixth trip. He was much more cautious and didn't have a dare-devil attitude that Moon Mullins had towards flying and everything else he did, including bootlegging. John was nervous from the start and wouldn't let me get our order filled until the day we were to leave.

I took the order to Annie's Grog Shoppe. "Gee, Gordon, you're getting to be a big time operator."

"This is likely my last trip. I know it will be my last order. We're getting the heat put to us."

"I'll miss you and your business."

"Get this order ready to go on a moment's notice. We're going to load it on the plane just before we takeoff. I'm not flying with Moon this trip."

Two days later we got our CAVU weather and took off with the rear end of the Ventura piled high with cases of booze. When we got south of Seattle and were approaching the US/Canadian border we had to call Air Traffic Control to get International Clearance. Moon Mullins and I had done five trips and never had any trouble.

I watched Johnny as he listened to the tower. Something was wrong. His face flushed and his knuckles whitened as he tightened his grip on the controls. "We have to land to get International Clearance. I wonder what the hell is up. We'll all be in deep shit if they ever inspect this plane."

We parked our plane near the control tower. Three nervous airmen entered the operations room that overflowed with wireless equipment and the chatter of intercoms. We must have looked like three kids who had been smoking and hoped our parents wouldn't smell our breath. John showed him our bill-of-lading.

That guy looks kind of mean. What the hell will I do when he inspects the plane and seizes all that booze? How in hell will I ever pay back the thousand bucks? What will the Air Force do? I may spend the rest of my military career in jail. Serves you right Wagner for trying to make a good fellow of yourself. Be different if you were making a wad of dough. For cripes sake John quit shaking !

To our relief the Custom's Officer hardly looked up to see who we were. He scribbled an entry in his log, pulled a sheet from the five-copy bill-of-lading and bid us good day.

We got permission to take off and started down the runway. We'd used half the runway and we weren't gaining speed. *Jesus, John, if you don't get our airspeed up you'll dump us in the drink. Can't you see the bloody sea wall at the end of the runway. Let's just get this damn tub airborne. Oh my God! You've got the bloody prop in course pitch. Don't pull another Sergeant Bloxham on us. That ocean is a hell of a lot deeper than Lethbridge's irrigation ditch. We got by bloody customs. Come on John, get this machine flying!*

John banged the pitch levers forward. We lurched right. John struggled with the controls pulling the lumbering plane back on to the runway. The ocean loomed ahead. The blurred-ground of the vanishing runway changed to ocean-green. *The props are almost cutting through the whitecaps. The undercarriage will hit the salt chuck. What a hell of a place to buy a bill of goods: me sitting on my "Mae West", a thousand bucks of booze on board, and Ivy with a new baby and tiny Keith. Damn poor way to win a war. I should have stayed in the Medical Branch teaching horny airmen how to use a prophylactic douche. I wonder what it's like in McLeod today.*

I watched as John's thin-lined lips etched determination across his blood-drained face. The Ventura shuddered. The engines growled. John wrestled the joy-stick. Slowly the plane's nose climbed into the horizon as John nursed us into the sky and the sea of threatening whitecaps disappeared below and the scalloped outlined of Vancouver

Island peeped over the horizon. Salt Spring's sugar-loaf mountain never looked so good as Johnny headed towards Pat Bay's runways and landed PV 1 2200 and ended its and my rum-running careers.

I became addicted at the Brentwood Autocourt. I'd heard tales of the great salmon fishing in Brentwood Bay and Saanich Arm. I'd seen the signs near Brentwood wharf saying "Gilbert's, Boats and Tackle For Rent."

On a cool January day an old man with an oil-stained Indian sweater hugging his ample belly and a matching toque perched on top of his balding head put me in a clinker boat, slightly dirtier than his sweater. He started the rusty one-cylinder engine and handed me a green hand-line. "Just go out there and go back and forth in front of that island. That's a Tom Mack you got and it will catch fish if there are any out there."

I had been fishing about an hour when a fir bough got caught in my line. I pulled my line to clear the bough and discovered I had caught a fish. I had dragged it so long that it had drowned. I caught two more that afternoon. I was hooked. Life would never be the same again. I drove by Brentwood Bay recently and the Gilberts are still renting boats and fishing tackle.

We first heard the rumour in the Bengal Room of the Empress Hotel — 149 Squadron was going to Alaska. My logbook says that on the 16th of July, I navigated F/L Williamson and Ventura 2193 to an air base on Annette Island at the southern-most tip of the Alaska Panhandle, about eighty miles west of Prince Rupert.

The Americans had needed an airport as a staging post for the planes supplying their forces in the Aleutians. The southern end of Annette Island was one huge muskeg swamp. With their great ability to get things done they blasted off the side of a mountain and took the rock and dumped it into the muskeg until they had a runway a mile long and six-hundred feet wide. If a bulldozer or a truck fell into the muskeg they left it there and covered it with rock.

Off the south end of the runway a one-way road of crushed rock led to a cluster of Quonset huts set on pilings driven into the muskeg. Three large Quonset huts, joined to form an H, served as our mess, cookhouse and shower room. From the mess single-file wooden sidewalks floated on the spongy muskeg, wandering haphazardly through the scrubby spruce like the branches of a river to find smaller Quonset huts that were our bedrooms. You needed a flashlight to find

The Americans' "muskeg" runway on Annette Island.

your way at night. If you stepped off the sidewalk you'd sink up to your crotch in the icy waters of the muskeg.

Our windowless huts, with doors front and back, were divided by doorless partitions into four rooms. A small platform butted off the back and served as a latrine. In our hut, rules said you could pee if you took at least one pace from the door all other ablutions required a trip to the shower room.

I shared a hut with Denny Swiffen, a fellow observer, the squadron's dentist, Captain Jake Jacobson and one of the MOs F/L John Angus. I remember Jacobson for the lectures he used to give John about his love life and his expression that "some people keep there assholes cleaner than their mouths." John McAngus, a big man, flabby fat and the only son of a wealthy family had been in McGill's Medical College so long that they finally gave him an MD just to get rid of him. He was desperately in love with a divorcee and his family threatened to disinherit him if he married her. When the family changed its mind, John got a week's leave and caught a flight to Vancouver. The light of his life was to fly out from Montreal. John returned ten days later still single and terribly hungover. He had gotten a ride on a plane to

Seattle, got in on a party in Seattle and never did get to Vancouver. His family must have been happy and it didn't seem to bother John.

We never did do very much flying. The weather was bloody awful and maintenance was having trouble working the kinks out of our airplanes. We spent the days in the flight rooms and there was always activity around the hangars. We marvelled at the US Air Force's DC 3 pilots. They were civilians retired from the service or from the airlines who volunteered to help the war effort. Annette Island, like Prince Rupert, got over a hundred inches of rain a year. The skies were seldom clear and day after day the ceiling was less than two hundred feet. Our planes would be grounded because of the low ceiling. We'd hear a plane in the clouds above us as the pilot did his let-down and we'd wonder if he'd ever find the runway. Then he'd burst through the clouds over the end of the runway, land his DC 3 and taxi to the hangar. Even on a clear day those pilots followed their let-down procedure never looking at the ground.

But we had trouble learning to live together. In the evenings there was a movie-run to the theatre on the American base. The Roman Catholic sky-pilot played whisky poker (all you could lose was ten bucks) and Padre Henderson helped the Protestants at the bar. A bridge game continued night after night and a couple of cribbage boards played for big stakes. After a few drinks somebody would start a sing song and we'd try to out do each other with our repartee of smutty songs.

It was the same night after night and after a couple of months everybody got a little "bushed." Then the pilots from a squadron of Hurricanes joined our mess. Our mess lounge bulged with bodies. Nerves grew ragged and tempers flared. Fighter pilots and bomber crews often fought each other when they lacked a common foe. There was a cocky young pilot who knew he needled me. We started to push, shove and swear at each other. I was ready to clean his clock when Jimmy Shaw grabbed my arm.

"Calm down, Saskie. That smart ass gets on everybody's nerves, but we got to learn to live with him. We may have another couple of years in this bloody place. You got to learn to live with these guys whether you like it or not."

A week later fighter pilot was low flying his Hurricane up the Skeena River and failed to see some power cables strung across the river. They never did find all the pieces. A sadness stirred my soul as if somehow I might have death-wished that kid away.

Whether it was on a train, in Alaska, or in the desert American troops always enjoyed the best. Our mess was on US rations and we dined like kings. But we had one cufuffle or snafu (situation normal all f——d up was the word the Americans used). We had butter that had been mixed with paraffin for use in the tropics. In Alaska's cold climate you couldn't spread it, and it gathered dust as it sat unused day after day.

The C/O of the station spent a lot of time in the mess. There was no place else to go. W/C Diamond was the C/O when we arrived. Not a bad guy as far as "wingcos" go. But he was a drugstore cowboy and played the guitar and yodelled a little. The ambitious porch climbers hung around and gave him an adoring audience night after night. I thought he stunk!

In late October some drunken fisherman thought he had seen a submarine in Dixon Entrance just south of Annette. Flight Sergeant Marshall and his crew went to check it out. All day the wind had been blowing up a south-easter and by the time Marshall was airborne horizontal rain slashed across the runway. He never should have taken off. It blew for two days before we could begin to look for their aircraft. We never found a trace! After the war was over we learned that they had crash-landed in the bush less than fifty miles from our base and had lived for several days before they died.

We spent a forty-eight in Ketchikan, an Alaskan fishing town of five-thousand people. The Americans took us there in a converted fish-trawler that sloshed its way over the stormy waters. If you didn't get seasick going to Ketchikan you sure as hell got sick coming back.

In the rain-soaked town we enjoyed being with people again, especially women. After three months in the bush you forget what an ordinary woman looks like. You begin to think they all look like Marilyn Monroe and you're surprised to see them walking on the rain-sheltered streets of Ketchikan. Six of us headed for the cocktail lounge in the Pioneer Hotel and spent the afternoon casing the few dames that dropped by the bar.

It was time to eat and we asked the bartender, "Where can a guy get a good steak in this town?"

"I'd recommend Casey's Steak House, if it's a good steak of meat you want."

A cab was sitting in front of the hotel and the six of us squeezed in. "Take us to Casey's Steak House," someone ordered.

The driver hugged the curb as he eased his cab around the corner, went another fifty feet. "Here's Casey's," he said, "and that will be five bucks."

"What you mean five bucks," Doug Marshall cried, "You just took us around the corner to the side door of the hotel."

"That's right, soldier. You read the sign in my cab. It says a five dollar minimum."

"That's the shortest and most expensive cab ride I've ever had," Doug complained.

"We only have two miles of road in this town, soldier. I gotta make a living just like anybody else."

We spent the evening in the Pioneer's bar. It closed at midnight and we went to a small cafe for a sandwich and coffee before we went to bed. There were a fellow and two girls sitting in a booth near ours. When they left one of the girls handed me a piece of paper as she passed our table.

I unfolded it and read. "Follow me to 777 Sitka St."

"Look at this you guys," I said as I passed the note around the table.

"Are you going to go, Saskie," asked Marshall.

I had to show my "macho." "Why not?"

She stopped at a house not far from the cafe and I watched as she said good night to her friends. The front door was against the wooden sidewalk. "Come in, airman," she said and took me through a side door into a neatly furnished living room.

"How about a cup of coffee? Let me take your great coat."

"I just finished coffee. But why the note?"

"I'm lonely and I like your curly black hair," and she reached over and turned off the light. We had just started to get comfortable when I heard men's voices and there was a loud rap on the front door. In the foggy shadows from a street light I could see the white gob-hats of two American sailors.

"Oh my gosh! Quick. Hide in the bedroom."

"I'm not going into any bedroom," as I grabbed my great coat. "Is there a back door to this place?"

"Yes. Through that door to the kitchen."

I found the door. In the foggy silence I waited. I heard the front close and voices coming from the house.

I often wondered just what kind of a place I'd been in. I never did find out. Early the next morning we took the rough boat trip back to Annette Island.

A short time later W/C Fenter Douglas, a permanent airforce career type who had some time on Hudson aircraft on the east coast, replaced W/C Diamond as squadron C/O. He knew bugger-all about our Venturas.

We were slated to go to Terrace to occupy a new base as soon as it was ready. W/C Douglas had been given a cockpit check of the Ventura by one of our flight commanders and did a few circuits and bumps. My log says it was the 17th of November. The mad- month's rains had drained our leaded clouds to reveal some blue for the first time in weeks. I was in the flight room behaving myself and almost hidden from view reading a sexy novel.

"W/C Douglas wants a navigator and a radio operator for a trip to Terrace. Wagner and McColloch, how would you like to go?" S/L Bolduc announced.

"If you say so, sir, but I'm at an interesting part of this book. Do you mean the C/O is going to solo that machine and we have to go with him?"

"Somebody has to go. You're it. He'll be ready in fifteen minutes. Don't keep him waiting."

He got the machine started and airborne over the waters of Dixon Entrance. We could almost see Prince Rupert when he levelled-out.

"Give me a course to Terrace," he said.

"You can see Prince Rupert straight ahead, sir, We usually just follow the Skeena River up to Terrace."

"I want a compass course to fly."

"Yes, sir." I slapped my protractor on the map. "095, sir."

He turned to 095 and headed for the four-thousand-foot mountains that seemed to jump out of the sea just south of the mouth of the Skeena. We were cruising at 2500 feet and I stood behind him waiting for him to pull up the nose, giving the engines more throttle, and begin to climb over the bloody hills. *What's the matter with the stupid bastard! He must be going to fly straight into that bloody pile of rock. I'm putting on my parachute. I don't give a damn what Fenter Douglas thinks.*

He never touched the throttles as he pulled up the nose of the aircraft and we skimmed up the mountain just a hundred feet above the tree tops. I was afraid we were going to stall as we staggered up the mountain and he leveled off still headed 095 degrees. McCulloch and I both had our chutes buckled on but we were too low to jump.

Then he spotted the Skeena River below us and side-slipped down into the river valley and did a tight turn of 360 degrees. I almost messed my pants as we nearly scraped the plane's belly against a perpendicular rock face. Mac had a sickly grin on his face and shook his head. We levelled off and headed up the river.

I checked the gauges on the main fuel tanks. Both were showing empty. I poked Fenter in the ribs and pointed to the needles. I knew he was supposed to switch to the wing tanks after using the mains. There was also a cabin tank that served as the navigator's desk. You used the cabin tank only as a last resort. *For cripes sakes! He is switching to the cabin tank. I'm no pilot but I know you never fly on the cabin and never, never, ever use it to land or take off. This damn Wingco will prang us. He doesn't know whether he's punched or bored.*

At Terrace we landed and took off on the cabin tank. I tried to dissuade him from landing on the steel-matted emergency runway on the beach at Rose Spit, on the Queen Charlotte Islands and just across

Dixon Entrance from our base on Annette. But he wouldn't listen. Again he used the cabin tank. *I hope to hell there's enough fuel to get us home. There's no way to tell how much fuel is left in the cabin tank. This guy is worse than S/L Wilson. I wonder how he's lived long enough to be a Wing Commander.*

We landed at Annette and ran out of fuel taxiing to the hangar. When I climbed out of the aircraft I bowed to the east and to the west, then north and south to make sure I didn't miss any of the "Gods of Flight" who got me through Fenter Douglas's first Ventura flight.

We did finally get operational and flew anti-submarine patrols over the Pacific Ocean but we fought the weather more than the Japanese subs. With wartime radio silence we had no weather reports of storms moving towards our coast. The Venturas could patrol for eight hours or longer if the pilot carefully nursed the fuel. We knew the winds at an altitude of 1500 to 2000 feet were the same on the surface and we got good at estimating their speed by "counting the number of whitecaps per acre." We could tell the wind's direction from the streak of foam that slid down the wave and into the wind.

Jimmy Shaw was our pilot. Jimmy had a time on that workhorse-flying-boat, the Stranrear, and knew the hazards of west-coast weather. "There's no use flying through those storms coming in from the Pacific, Saskie. You can't see bugger-all when you're in them. If you get through you're stuck with coming back through them.

"Jim said the only way to fly was with an old fashioned collar-button built into your seat and fitted into your rectum. When flying got dicey you could always pucker up and hold on. Often saved you from messing up a good pair of pants."

Three RCAF types had crashed a float plane near Annette and killed themselves. S/L Bolduc picked me to help him fly the corpses to Vancouver. The weather was lousy. We should never have left the ground. Bolduc must have had a date or was badly in need of an oil change, or maybe the corpses wouldn't keep.

There was a break in the clouds over the waters of Dixon Entrance and I managed to get a wind. We had to fly at five thousand feet to make sure we were above the hills on the Queen Charlotte Islands. I had an ETA for Cape Scott on the north end of Vancouver Island. We flew through clouds and never once saw the ground. If we missed Cape Scott we'd have to climb another two- thousand feet to make sure we didn't hit one of those clouds hard-centred by Vancouver Island's Beaufort Mountains.

Right on time and through a small break in the cloud we saw Cape Scott. We dropped down and flew below the five-hundred-foot ceiling. I had never seen the ocean so whipped with whitecaps. There was no way to estimate the gale that threatened to push us backwards. From landmarks, I calculated our head wind to be a hundred-and-thirty miles per hour.

We had to fly over the Beauforts to get to Victoria. I began to tighten up on the collar button. Radio reception on the west coast was never good and often impossible. We were still in the southeast gale when we passed Estevan Point; Tofino was sixty miles to the south.

"Saskie, I just raised Tofino on the radio," said McColloch. "The sun is shining there and the ceiling is absolute."

"It can't be. What's the wind at Tofino?"

"It's calm."

Mac's weather report was correct. At Tofino we broke into clear skies and calm seas. We hopped over the mountains and landed at Pat Bay. A check with their weather office confirmed the 130 mph winds at Estevan Point. The west coast weather could changed faster than the mind of a fickle lover.

In mid-November the squadron moved to Terrace, a small town eighty miles up the Skeena River. The airport, built on a terrace of land a hundred feet above the river and about five miles from the village, was still under construction when we arrived.

Terrace had been planned to be the ultimate base for our defence against Japan. We were to have a skating rink, a swimming pool, a theatre and married quarters. But the plans were cufuffled by the weather. We had thirty airplanes at Terrace but couldn't get them in the air. Warm air from the Pacific came up the valley of the Skeena and flowed up over Terrace. The warm air chilled as it elevated and turned to fog. The sun shone on the village, while at the airport fog kept our planes grounded. During our first month thirty aircraft logged only twenty-nine hours of air-time.

What a hell of a place to build an airdrome. I wonder what sort of genius planned this bloody place. I suppose some politician owned the land. They have a thousand soldiers in the camp adjacent to the town. They sure as hell don't need a thousand airmen. I wonder if we'll ever win this war. I haven't done much to help in the year I've been in aircrew. But then I'm an expendable commodity likely a hell of lot cheaper than the Beaufort Wilson pranged. Now we are a hundred fifty miles farther from the area we are supposed to patrol and we can't get the damn planes off the ground. Some place to win the war. If I don't have to fly, especially with Fenter Douglas, I'll live through this show.

Shortly after we arrived I was sent to Vancouver to attend a workshop in "Air Traffic Control." I was glad to get away from Terrace. Living in half-finished rooms, sloshing through the construction mud, not flying and missing the American rations got on everyone's nerves. The accommodations available in the village were terrible and I never considered bringing Ivy, Keith and Linda to Terrace. When I left Pat Bay Ivy had moved to Courtenay and was living with her sister, Mae Field.

I caught a flight to Vancouver but I had to return by train. The trip from Vancouver to Jasper and from Jasper to Terrace took two days. A week later I had to go to Vancouver to give testimony about a vehicle accident I had witnessed. This time I had to take the train both ways. I got back to Terrace a week before Christmas.

Jim Shaw picked me up at the Terrace railway station. "Welcome back, Saskie, you'll be happy to know that our crew is getting five day's leave for Christmas. Half the squadron gets Christmas and the other half gets New Year's."

"You mean I have to take that train ride again — twice in five days?"

I'd have exactly twelve hours to spend with Ivy and the kids if the trains, the ferries and the buses ran on time. But I was broke. The two trips to Vancouver had depleted my finances. Jimmy lent me enough money to get me there and back, but I hadn't counted on buying a twenty-six of rye whisky — a Christmas ration. I would take it to Courtenay for some holiday cheer.

The CNR (Canadian National Railway) train put us in Vancouver early on the 24th. I had exactly seventy five cents. I waited until the beer parlours opened at eleven am and took a seat in the Devonshire where I could watch the door. If I waited long enough I was bound to meet someone from 149 — it was the squadron's favourite watering hole. I had to borrow enough to get the CPR ferry to Nanaimo and bus fare from Nanaimo to Courtenay. Ten bucks would do it.

Beer was ten cents a glass. I had to save two-bits for a phone call if I got stranded. If worse came to worse I could always sell my bottle of rye. Bootleggers charged thirty-two bucks for a twenty-six.

I nursed five beers and never saw a soul I knew. I had to catch the four pm ferry. I got into the front seat of a Yellow Cab parked in the front of hotel. "I got a twenty-six of rye. What will you give me for it?"

"I'm a cabby, soldier. I don't bootleg."

"I don't either." I felt my conscience prick me as Payne Field and Johnny Higham flashed through my mind. "But I have to catch the ferry to Nanaimo to get home for Christmas."

"I'll give you ten bucks."

"Ten bucks! They're selling twenty-sixes for thirty dollars!"

"I'm not in the bootlegging business, mister."

"Will you throw in a ride to the ferry?"

"I'll take you to the CPR dock. Here's your ten bucks. Have a Merry Christmas."

It was nine before I got to Courtenay. The children had gone to bed, and Ivy, Mae and her husband, Rex, were decorating the Christmas tree.

"I'd offer you a drink, Gordon, but I forgot to go to the liquor store to pick up my Christmas ration," Rex said.

We had a very dry Christmas.

Smithers, a small town a hundred miles further up the Skeena from Terrace, had a landing strip with a control tower, a small hangar and living quarters. With the zero flying hours at Terrace, three planes were sent to Smithers to get some flying time. Jimmy Shaw was made acting C/O, I ran the control tower and McColloch attended to the radio.

The first time three aircraft landed, Smithers' friendly citizens held a dance to welcome us. We curled in their bonspiel. We attended parties in their homes. We helped scrounge unused liquor permits. Smithers was a divisional point for the CNR, and the twenty-four hour widows reminded me of Sudbury. They would check with the dispatcher to find out when their husbands would be home. It started to get out of hand.

The town had a big dance on Valentine's Day. Jimmy Shaw set up a hospitality room in the Hudson Hotel to treat the city fathers and all the other citizens who had been so good to us. During the midnight intermission I took three of the city fathers back to the hotel for a drink. The door to our room was closed, but it wasn't locked. I switched on the light. The sergeant of our MT section and of one Smither's respected twenty-four-hour widows were in bed sound asleep, with their clothes draped neatly over the chairs.

I turned off the lights and closed the door but the damage had been done. The mayor turned to me. "I know we have some horny wives. Every railway town does. But for God's sake, be careful. One of your airmen will end up with an ass full of bird-shot one of these days, or worse."

Jimmy Shaw, CB'ed (confined to barracks) the station for a week. But our days in Smithers were numbered, and we didn't hear it first in the Hudson Hotel beer parlour. 149's C/O, W/C Dennis phoned to tell us that 149 was to be shut down as of the end of March and all personnel would be relocated. Later we learned that 147 BR Squadron was being recalled from Alaska and that it would most likely be shut down.

Everybody wanted to go overseas. It reminded me of Rivers. I hadn't grown any braver and I had managed to survive for nearly four years. I had a wife and two children but I had never really lived at home. If I had my choice I'd like to go back to Pat Bay and live with Ivy, Keith and Linda at Brentwood Autocourt. The pay was good and I had learned to keep out of trouble and make sure I did all the right things without polishing apples or browning my nose.

In the end I didn't have a choice. I had to go wherever I was sent. Most of 149's aircrews were posted overseas. John Higham, Al Watts and Jimmy Shaw went to Air Canada. I was to be in Lachine, Quebec on the 15th of May.

Ivy came to Vancouver and we stayed at the Devonshire Hotel and spent five love-filled days together. The gentle laziness of spring, the new, soft grass-carpet of Stanley Park, the bees busy in blooming maples lengthened our time together and made the future feel remote. We said good bye at the bottom of the gangplank of the Princess Elaine. I told my diary "She looked beautiful as I watched her walk up the gangplank. A lump stuck in my throat and my eyes filled with tears. Our happiness must continue. I will be back."

Overseas to England

I was impressed with the efficiency of Lachine. It seemed to lack the "Air Force Cufuffle." We had a series of shots and a lecture on the prostitutes of Montreal. Dr Lafeaux, with his French- Canadian accent gave us a lecture on venereal disease.

"Day say ders ways to tes for de gonorrhea. Sum ob dem says hif hit tastes saltee, hit his no goud. Sum guy day says to use de coin, and hif hit turans green dem hit his no goud. But der his honly one ways to tell. You have to look in der. And who de hell want to put der eye in der." Despite the lecture and all the warnings a couple of 149'ers missed our overseas draft.

On the 25th of May, after a bumpy and crowded ride from Montreal to Halifax, we boarded the Empress of Scotland (formerly the Empress of Japan). It took us eight days to get from Halifax to Glasgow, eight days sharing a two-hundred bed boudoir, eight days of lining up to wash and shave, eight days of living on two meals a day, eight days with seven thousand other souls trying to find a place to sit or even stand, and eight days of sea, sea and more sea.

We ran into a storm three days out. Forty-foot waves crashed against our bow. The ship rolled, shook and shuddered as she fought against the sea. Fear gripped our guts as we hugged our life-jackets and wondered how mad the waves could get. We felt like rag dolls being tossed around by a mad dog.

My stomach stood the test. With half the ship seasick seats were easy to find, and in the mess with half the benches empty we had extra bread and cheese.

The sea settled and the green tinges faded from people's faces and seats were once more at a premium. Five of us found a cubby hole on the leeward side of ship's deck always sheltered from the chill of the north-west wind. With the roll of the ship the dull-grey skies dipped to meet the pewter grey of the rolling sea. The lifeboats hanging from the davits swung with slow, hypnotic rhythm like a pendulum. The horizon appeared and disappeared above the ships railing. We stared silently, each in his own reverie.

I wonder what Ivy and the kids are doing beyond this world of grey? How far will this lumbering ship take me into the grey uncertainty of this bloody war? Will I ever find my way back? Or am I on a one way trip? Come on, Gordon, somewhere the sun must be shining. You can't live in the distant past nor in the imagined future. You got a bottle of rye in your kit bag. Why not share it with your friends and live in the here and now? You might even find some sunshine in this dreary world of grey.

I filled my issue-tissue canteen (water bottle) with a mixture of Seagram's VO and water and passed it back and forth and we felt it warm our guts and chase the greys away.

"That really hit the spot, Saskie," Walter Kennedy said as he sucked the last drop from the canteen. "Too bad we don't have another. Next time I travel on a troop ship I'll make damn sure it has a wet bar."

"I'll bet there is a bootlegger amongst the thousand of people on this ship. I'll try the crew." I didn't have to go far. The first member of the ship's crew I asked took me below and filled the canteen.

We passed the canteen back and forth, growing louder and happier and even raised some sunshine as breaks of blue appeared and the sun pendulated in between the clouds. People promenading around the deck stopped to stare and wonder where we had found our good cheer.

We drained the canteen for the second time, and they sent me to see if I could find some more. It took me longer to find the second bottle, and when I returned the gang had gone for their afternoon meal. By this time I wasn't feeling any pain. I wandered around the ship looking for the gang. Every time I would meet somebody I knew or wanted to know, I offered them a drink. I was everybody's friend and had the doubtful distinction of being the only one of the seven thousand passengers to get drunk. I wandered all over the ship, got lost and ended up in the galley where I poured the cook a drink and he gave me a roasted chicken.

The next day we hit another storm. I didn't get seasick but I nursed a granddaddy of a headache and at times was quite prepared to die.

On the first day of June, we awoke to find the Empress of Canada riding at anchor in the Firth of Clyde with the shoreline of Glasgow barely visible through the Scotch mist. We waited all day watching the tenders ferry loads of men and equipment to the docks. Our turn came in the late afternoon.

We were welcomed by the warm hospitality of Scotland. The Scottish women, with their rosy-cheeked complexion, served us tea and cakes. I will never forget the lovely blue-eyed girl who smiled and said, "What will it be, Love, a cuppa tea?" I had never been called Love before and with my puritanical upbringing the word "love" was used sparingly with almost a sacred connotation. You might like a lot of people but you loved very few.

We spent the night on an English train and I found it comfortable and much smoother than our Canadian trains. Next morning we were unloaded and taken to the reception centre at Innsworth, a small village near Gloucester.

Two thousand Canadian aircrew officers were stationed in Innsworth waiting for posting. We lived in huts with single cots and dressers lined against both walls. We had bat women to make our beds, look after our clothes and scrounge the odd bucket of coal for the small heater. It got damn chilly some nights.

Britain was on double-day-light saving time and in the long days of June it was nearly midnight before the stars began to shine. Night's veil of darkness enhanced by a starry sky or a full moon has always been associated with the procreation of the human race. Double-daylight-saving time and the Armed Forces' curfew might deny young people the benefit of darkness but never deny the passions of youth. On a late evening stroll I saw at least six couples wrestling on the ground partly hidden in the long grass of a roadside hay field.

Women in Britain were different from Canadian women. Maybe it was the war, with its four years of fear of air raids, bombs and invasion, that made them live in the "here and now." Their promiscuity wasn't cheap. They didn't require a long and beautiful friendship, they didn't save their lovemaking for an "imagined future." I was standing at the mess bar when Canada's ace pilot, Buzz Buerling, came in. The barmaid with a suggestive wiggle said, "Blimey me! Ain't he handsome? I'd lift me piny for that bloke any day."

It didn't take us long to find the Royal Anne, a stately old hotel in

Cheltenham, and it became our favourite watering hole. The bar had a daily ration. If you got there early enough, you might get a beer. Whisky and gin went next, followed by the brandy ration, and we finished with sherry. The bar closed at ten but emptied as soon as all the sherry was gone.

If you were still thirsty, you could go to a private club where you could get a one-night membership for half a crown if they had an empty chair (you had to sit to drink). You could get most anything you wanted, including sawdust sausage rolls. The clubs closed at midnight. You had to find your way back to Innsworth in the black-out. We sat there on the night of the 5th of June and listened to the continuous throb of aircraft engines. The long awaited invasion of Europe was underway.

Well, we're all getting close to the action. We're overseas whether we like it or not. I'll have to get down to London and find out where some of my friends are. Sure are lots of service men in this area. There seems to be a hell of a lot of organized confusion around this place.

We got signed in and all settled and they gave us a week's leave. Kennedy, Switzer and Alstetder and I decided to spend our seven days in Scotland. I particularly wanted to visit Markinch, the Scottish namesake of our home town in Saskatchewan, and the place where they made "Haig and Haig" scotch whisky.

The Red Cross in Edinburgh sent us to private homes in Sterling. Walt Kennedy and I stayed with Jock Smith, a retired teacher and his wife. Norm Altstedter and Bill Switzer bunked down in Lady Wallace's castle. We visited the site of the Battle of Bannockburn and relived the story of Robert Bruce, when in the despair after six defeats of his own he watched a spider complete its web on the seventh try. The spider inspired Bruce to try again and he drove the English out of Scotland in the seventh Battle of Bannockburn. Lady Wallace had us to tea. Her castle seemed cold, hard and unfriendly. We were served tea and cakes on the sunny patio of the main entrance, and I will never forget her remark when we were introduced as Canadians. "You colonials are doing a wonderful job."

We took a bus trip to Loch Lomond. We didn't see the Loch-Ness monster. Peggy Lee's voice echoed across the blue waters and I could hear her sing, "On the bonny, bonny banks of Loch Lomond."

Because of double-daylight-saving time and Scotland's northern latitude, the sun was still high in the sky, when at eight o'clock Walt and I entered Sterling's Golden Lion to try their beer. The pub closed at ten. It was still bright daylight when we stepped out onto the sidewalk.

"Walt, I could use a bite to eat. Let's ask somebody where we can find a restaurant."

"Good idea, Saskie."

"Excuse me, sir. Can you tell us where we can find a restaurant?" I asked a couple of fellows who had followed us from the bar.

"Is it a meal you'll be wanting?"

"Perhaps there's a place we can get a sandwich and a cup of tea."

"Just follow us, we'll show you the way."

We followed them for three or four blocks before they stopped at the entrance of a covered alley. "It's a wee bit dark in here, so stay close behind us."

The alley was about fifteen feet wide, with solid brick walls on either side. There were no lights and no windows. *A damn funny place for a restaurant. Maybe we should get the hell out of here. Must be nearly seventy feet back to the street.*

We were right behind them. I wondered if we might get knocked on the head. "Watch it, mate," one of them said. "There's a turn here."

I heard a door open and the click of a switch. A dull light glowed at the top of a long, narrow flight of stairs. We had to go single file. I was bringing up the rear, and I left the door open. *There's no restaurant up here. More likely to be a whore house or maybe a bootlegger. By gosh, there is daylight up there!*

The stairway lead into a kitchen, and we gathered around the kitchen table sizing one another up. "I am John and this is my friend Alex."

"Hello, John. Hello, Alex. I'm Gordon, and this is my friend, Walt. But this doesn't look like a restaurant to me."

"No. It's John's home. Our wives and families are out to a carnival on the common. So we were out for a quiet pint at the Lion. The women and the kids should be home soon."

"What would you like to eat?" asked John.

"Don't suppose you have any eggs. I haven't had an egg since I left Canada."

"How would you like some bacon and eggs?"

"You mean we can have **two eggs**!"

"John and I own the butcher shop just below this suite. We buy directly from the farmers, so we bend the ration regulations once in a while."

Whenever I hear and smell the sizzling of bacon and eggs, the image of those friendly Scots floats over the pan.

We had just finished our meal when the two wives and their four children returned. The women joined us in a cup of tea. Then John asked if he could pour us a wee brandy. "Mary," he half commanded, "would you get the brandy and glasses ready."

"Aye, John," she replied, opening the door to the parlour. I listened to the tinkle of glass, curious to see the inside of the parlour. "It's all ready, gentleman. Do come in and make yourselves comfortable."

We entered a small, seldom-used parlour, furnished with fine old furniture. Carefully arranged on a small table stood four brandy sniffers, and a decanter wearing a silver necklace labelled "Brandy." I had expected the women would be joining us.

"Thanks, Mary, we'll do nicely now. Please shut the door when you leave."

When the decanter was empty, it was almost midnight and we said good bye. Mary and her children had gone to bed and Alex's wife and kids had gone home. Alex led us down the narrow stairs and out onto the street. As we found our way to our billets there was still enough light to read the road signs.

On our return to Edinburgh we stayed at the Shelbourne Hotel just off Princess Street where we were introduced to rum and ginger — white rum mixed with a ginger cordial. It was the first and last time I tasted it. It was good!

I took my trip to Markinch, a small tidy town on the bank of a small coastal river. On the wall of the grammar school library, pressed, framed and under glass, I found the prairie crocus our Canadian Markinch school had sent to Scotland in 1925.

I wonder what happened to the heather they sent us. I can still see that sprig of purple flowers hanging in its picture frame on our school hall. The last time I was in Markinch our old school was closed. Saskatchewan had had a bumper crop and the four rooms and the basement were full of wheat. As a ten-year-old child I wondered what these Markinch people looked like, if they played dibs and how many marbles they had to give to get a cat's-eye agate. If they knew that it wasn't storks that brought babies and if they lifted the girls skirts and tried to see what was underneath their bloomers. It took a bloody war to get me here. I wonder what it will take to get me back? Maybe I should get a sprig of heather and take it with me. It might bring me good luck. I don't believe in good luck charms. I carried the left hind foot of a jack rabbit but it didn't do much to help me through the "dirty thirties."

I found a sprig of heather and a wee bottle of Haig and Haig whisky. The heather, now crisp and faded with just a hint of faded purple, lies with my diary's 15th of June, 1944 entry — my thirtieth birthday. The now-well-aged, wee bottle of whisky, with its yellowed Haig and Haig label, sits in our china cabinet.

Edinburgh introduced us to afternoon dancing. The Place Royale, a large dance hall on the lower side of Princess Street, opened at three and closed at six. A beautiful young woman frisked you as you entered. You could buy soft drinks but no alcohol. A revolving stage provided the music of two orchestras. The dance floor was jammed with sailors, soldiers and airmen and lots of girls. Russian sailors dressed in their whites had trouble talking but not dancing. They stole the show!

Back at Innsworth we were kept busy with a defence course, lectures on escape procedures, more parade square drill and exercise classes. I volunteered to help a local farmer harvest his hay crop and got a couple of good meals and all the apple cider I could drink. The days dragged by. People were posted out and new officers arrived, fresh from Canada; some of them were still in their teens. By the looks of these peach-fuzzed officers the Commonwealth Training plan must be scraping the bottom of the barrel. Some of these kids weren't old enough to shave!

London, 1944.

Norm Altstedter, Doug Marshall and I spent a forty-eight in London. We arrived at the Paddington railway station to find the platform swarming with people, mostly children who were being evacuated because of the buzz-bombs. Suddenly the mass of people stood silent. Above the panting of the engine and the angry hiss of steam we listened to the "Ruhrrrrrrr, Ruhrrrrrrr, Ruhrrrrrrr" of a buzz bomb as it grew louder and louder. It roared overhead. The sound stopped. We waited. Not for long. BANG! A gust of wind rattled the station windows. Then the people noise swelled again and the mob pushed towards the train.

We stayed at the Regent Place, visited the Tower, Buckingham Palace, the Wind Mill and helped close the hotel's bar.

The next morning we were gathered in Marshall's room pouring a drink for the women who were doing up the room. We heard it coming. The Ruhrrrrrrr, Ruhrrrrrrr, Ruhrrrrrrr got closer and louder. Then stopped.

"There's its bloody shadow," yelled Marshall.

"**BANG! Vroommmmuff!**" The window glass splattered over the floor. Debris flew past the window followed by a cloud of dust and the smell of cordite. Doug and I had dropped to the floor. The cleaning woman laughed and took a sip of her drink. "You should'a been here during the blitz. Them buzz bombs ain't nothing compared to Jerry's big ones."

After the dust had settled we walked down the street to see the damage. The buzz-bomb had hit the front of a three-story house and blown the front rooms open but had caused less damage than I had imagined. A middle-aged woman covered with the brown dust of the brick emerged from the rubble. She was dazed but had managed to pull herself free.

During the night several more bombs droned over London but they were far away from the hotel. The next day the Paddington station was still crowded. On the train we had to stand in the corridors all the way to Gloucester.

To India

Excitement ran through the barracks. For weeks rumor had it that the RCAF's 149 Squadron was on its way to India. Now it was actually happening. Tomorrow we'd draw our tropical kits and get our shots, catch a train to London the next day, and have a forty-eight hour pass for one last fling in Picadilly. Then we had to report at Swindon's Lyneham airport at noon on Sunday ready for duty — and sober.

After spending three months at Innsworth Reception Depot, which was plugged full with two thousand aircrew, we were anxious to get going. Thrilled with the thought of duty in mysterious India, we were prepared for elephants and tigers, cobras and fakirs. Our squadron's aircraft had patrolled the west coast of Canada until the Yanks put the run to the enemy in the Pacific, so we were especially prepared for the Japanese in Burma. We'd been needled for half-a-dozen diseases, vaccinated for smallpox, and our aircraft sprayed with DDT. After my year in the Air Force Medical Branch I knew about doctors and hospitals, chiropractors and osteopaths, and I had read about Christian Science and Helen Eddy, but I had never heard about doctors who practice naturopathy treating diseases with natural agencies and rejecting the use of drugs and medicines.

They loaded ten of us into a York — a Lancaster bomber converted to a transport plane. We settled down amongst our kit bags, and the converted bomber's four in-line Merlin engines pulled us up into England's cloud-leaded skies just as the evening dusk surrendered to the blacked-out countryside.

The engines settled into a comfortable cruising throb and the intercom crackled. "This is your Captain speaking. Welcome aboard our cozy Mediterranean cruise. Cuddle up around your luggage. We are headed for Morocco. Ordinarily, we fly over Spain but tonight Jerry has some patrols in the Bay of Biscay. So we'll fly around Portugal at eight thousand feet. Should be smooth all the way and we'll be into Rabat, Morocco about midnight, nighty-night you lucky people."

The dark steel-blue of Rabat's midnight sky sparkled with stars close enough to touch. The night air, delicately scented with an exotic flower, welcomed us to the balmy cool of the Moroccan desert. We shed our woollen tunics and found a lunch counter where a sleepy native vendor sold soggy tomato sandwiches and weak, lukewarm coffee. An hour later, after refueling the York and stretching our legs, we were airborne again and bound for Tripoli, flying high over the Sahara.

After flying seven hours we landed at the Castel Benito airbase close to Tripoli, the capital of Libya. When we stepped from the York we stood on our own shadows as the midday sun bored into our skulls. The scars of Monty and Rommel's battle for the desert graffitied the airdrome. The corrugated-steel hangar looked like a tin can John Wayne might have used for target practice. The ruins of the bombed-out buildings poked their jagged, shell-torn skeletons through the rippled drifts of Sahara sand. The British, who "muddle through" the hard way, used tents for offices, mess halls and cookhouses.

The hundred-degree temperature brought out our newly-issued tropical clothes. The tunics fit like muu-muus and the too-long khaki shorts hid pale, knobby knees. We looked like patients on leave from a maternity ward as the ever-present native peddlers flocked to their new crop of sitting ducks.

The York, with its glycol-cooled engines, couldn't take off in the desert heat, so we spent the day following the shade around the hangar. In the evening we watched a movie on the outdoor screen set up on the smooth desert sand. The show over, and the intense heat of the day having cooled enough to allow the heat- senstive Merlin to takeoff, we changed back into blues, cuddled once more amongst our kit bags and flew on to Egypt.

The light of a new day greyed the eastern sky. The lights of Cairo rolled over the horizon; the dawn jewelled the turquoise of the Nile and sparkled along her emerald banks as it meandered to the pyramids.

"We'll land at the American base," blared the intercom. "Bloody RAF still haven't fixed the holes Rommel left in the runways."

"After seven hours in the air you guys must be hungry," the American duty-sergeant said, when our pilot parked our York and signed us in. "There's a restaurant in the far hangar. Opens at six. They serve great bacon and eggs."

"A restaurant? You got a real restaurant — with bacon and eggs?" It was typical of the Americans. Their service men had everything.

Cairo introduced us to the mystic East. Streets teamed with hawkers and street-boys who swarmed around us, attracted to our brand-new maternity suits, our lily-white skin and our gullibility.

A street urchin smeared fresh horse droppings on my highly-polished leather shoes. "Ha! Sir, I clean your shoes. Okay? Just one piastre for you, Sir."

He squatted in front of me and before I knew it, he'd pulled polish and a brush from his wooden shoe-shine box, grabbed my foot and had lifted it onto his box. With one swipe of his hand he removed the manure, cleaned his dirtied left hand on his shirt tail, and proceeded vigorously to slap my shoes with Nugget, polishing them to mirror-brightness. I watched this young entrepreneur, fascinated by his spunk and the deftness of his movements.

"Okey-dokey Mister, shoes just like new. One piastre, please."

We had just left our bus and I had no Egyptian money. The heavy sidewalk-traffic pushed past us on the crowded street. All the money I had was an English pound note. "Can you change this?" I asked offering him the note.

"Oh yes, Mister, my friend he can change."

He snatched the bill and turned and ran down the street. I started to run after him but he ducked down an alley and disappeared. I looked back to see another shoe-shine boy running in the opposite direction with two shoe-shine boxes.

We visited the world-famous Sheppard's Hotel, admiring the beautiful black-haired Egyptian women and

Tony Mason at the Pyramids.

the posh decor, and challenged their world-renowned bartender Sam. If he didn't know how to mix your favourite cocktail the drink was on the house. We paid for all our drinks.

In an ancient Oldsmobile, a Cairo taxi driver gave us the tourist treatment of the pyramids. We had our pictures taken on a camel. Back at the American base we treated ourselves to T-bone steaks smothered in mushrooms and washed it down with Pabst's beer. In the starlight theatre we sat on the desert sand and watched Eddie Cantor in "Show Business."

When the desert cooled, our York's Merlin engines once more pulled us into the sky and we slept again amongst our luggage.

Early the next morning we landed at Shaibah in the Iraqi desert, and taxied to a small hangar that looked like a phone booth stranded in a sea of sand. It was not yet eight o'clock, and desert winds had not started to shift Shaibah's sand across Iraq's landscape. But it was hot, hot enough for a four-foot long lizard to seek the cool wing-shadow of our aircraft. He stood there, defiant, his awkward wide-spread legs looking like he'd just finished doing his push-ups. When we crawled from our York, he scooted across the tarmac to disappear behind the shady side of the hangar.

We loaded our gear into a truck and followed a narrow sand-drifted trail, marked only by four-gallon square gas cans set every fifty feet, across the ocean of sand. The road would occasionally disappear, entirely buried in the drifted sand, and without those cans to guide us we could have wandered into the desert and got lost in a sand storm

150

within shouting distance of the base.

Our driver took us to the officer's mess—a long, thatched- roofed, adobe building with a goat-skin water cooler hanging near the entrance. We had a breakfast of bacon and eggs and bread fried in bacon grease. The bare-foot, turbaned mess boy pestered us with his sing-song plea, "You likee dites, Sahib, nice sweet dites?"

Our pilot joined us and stood by our table twirling his weather-beaten cap. With a cheshire grin, his Yorkshire accent almost meowed. "You lucky blokes are going to have a holiday. The outside-port engine has blown a rod and a new one has to come from England. Might take a week or two. The mess steward will show you to your quarters. Bloody lucky to hit Shaibah at the peak of the tourist season."

We all got separate tents, each six-by-eight, double flapped and stoutly anchored to the desert floor, and each with a folding canvas cot and regulation gray wool blankets. We moved in and stored our gear. By nine, the morning wind began to blow and the sand swirled across the desert, reducing the outside visibility to a hundred feet and filling the mess with a dusty fog.

By four in the afternoon the wind died and the temperature hit a hundred and ten. Banks of dust were piled everywhere, inside as well as out — on windowsills, beneath the doors, and on our tent-protected beds. It was like a prairie blizzard with sand instead of snow.

"How often do you have dust storms like this?" I asked the driver of a transport truck as he brushed away the dust piled against the windshield.

"Every day," he replied. "Because of the sand storms we work in split shifts starting at four in the morning and ending at eight. Then we start again at four in the afternoon and work till eight at night. Bloody hot right now but it will soon cool off."

"How long have you been here?"

He looked at his watch. "Two years, six months, ten days and fifteen hours. I've got five months, nineteens days and about nine hours to go. I'll sure as hell be glad to see the last of this damn place."

Sitting in the mess that first evening watching the chameleons dart up and down the walls and across the ceiling, we heard a scraping noise coming from near my chair. "That's a ruddy scorpion! He must be right under your chair!" said a burly, red-headed RAF officer with a huge handle-bar mustache. "Get up out of your chair, Canada, and we'll have a boo."

He lifted the heavy chair and there was the scorpion dragging its claws across the concrete. "I'll get him, mate. Jim, you get the wash tub."

The scorpion was about six or seven inches long. As they tried to pick him up with a dust pan, he curled his tail over his back, preparing to strike. Big Red scooped him up and dropped him into a full-sized wash tub in the centre of the room.

"Wonder if there's another one around? We could have them fight it out," said Jim, a small, wiry, black-haired pilot with the DSO and bar pinned beneath his wings.

"Why the hell don't you just throw him back into the desert? Jim, you bloody Spitfire types wanta shoot up everything you see. Ruddy Scorpio never did anybody any harm. Let the poor bastard go," said Charles, the wingless station adjutant.

"Charles, you earth-bound admin types give me a pain in the ass. Why don't you go and get some hours?" said Jim. "We haven't had any action around since God knows when."

"Red, I caught a camel spider today. Bloody beast's body is big as a half crown. Do you suppose he'd be any match for the scorpion?"

"Danny, me boy, your bloody spider won't stand a chance. I'll put a quid on me scorpion. Go get your camel and let'em have it out," said big Red.

"You're on you red-headed Australian bastard. But I want odds. Gimme me two to one. Eh?"

"You bloody Canadians always want odds. Well, Danny boy, you got yourself a bet. Where's your ruddy spider?"

The spider covered the bottom of a two-quart glass jar and when Danny dumped him into the washtub he stretched each of his eight legs like a prize fighter, took a run to the centre of the tub, hesitated, ran back, tried unsuccessfully to crawl up the sides, then rested and preened his hairy coat with his front legs. His double-sectioned body was the size of a quarter floated atop his eight spine-covered legs. Stretched out, he spanned nearly five inches.

Scorpio, with his back to the wall, shuffled his six legs, waved his antenna, clicked his claws and waited. "Kick the side of the tub, Red. Looks like they're both bloody doped," said an excited Jim.

"Boom!" Scorpio's tail curved up and over his back and his pincers raised from the floor ready for the attack. Spider's legs stiffened and he shuffled forward. Suddenly they became aware of each other. Spider darted to the centre of the tub. Scorpio slowly waddled forward pincer and tail at the ready. Spider saw the movement and raced in for the kill. Scorpio tried to grab him with his pincer and arched his tail, aiming his deadly stinger at Spider's hairy body. He missed and Spider scooted out of the way. Scorpio sat and waited.

"No way will your bloody spider ever win, Danny. Old Scorpio will wait and Mr. Spider will come too close to Scorpio's tail and it will be lights for your spider," boomed big Red.

Spider attacked again and again. "Get'em from the side, Spider. Watch out for those bloody pincers!" Danny yelled moving from side to side like a fighter shadow boxing.

Scorpio forayed forth like a slow moving panzer-tank. He caught Spider between his claws and again arched his tail ready for the strike. "You got him now, Scorpio. Let him have it. Spear him." But the deadly tail missed as Spider ducked under Scorpio's pinchers.

Spider ran back and forth, trying to strike broadside. Then, as if they'd decided to call it a draw, they rested.

"Give the ruddy tub a kick," said Spider's owner.

"Let'em have a rest. They've fought damn well. Leave'm be for a spell."

"BOOM !" went the tub and Spider dashed in. Scorpio grabbed and hung on.

"You got the bastard now, Scorpio. Drive your stinger into his guts. Kill'im, Scorpio. Kill'im," screamed the fighter pilot.

Scorpio slashed out—the hairy body in range. Spider sidestepped the jab, reared back, leaving a hunk of leg in Scorpio's claw.

153

He rolled to his feet and tackled Scorpio from the side. He straddled the armour-plated Scorpio, and sank his barbed beak into Scorpio's armour-naked neck. Scorpio's tail curled for the fatal blow. Spider stood on end, driving his beak deeper. The arched tail never struck. Scorpio's tail uncurled, his six legs collapsed, and he sank to the bath-tub canvas. He'd never fight again!

"Well I'll be goddamned," groaned Red. "Here's your bloody quid, Danny boy. Keep your Mr. Spider healthy and we'll have another go some day."

"Shows you guys that it isn't size that counts. Speed and maneuverability is what a fighter needs. Better call your spider Spitfire, and I'll give him a bit of my DSO," said an excited Jim.

"Damn good fight, Danny, but heh, why don't you let him go? He won didn't he? Just a little harmless fun, really."

"You're right Charlie, but it helped to blow off some steam. People get cantankerous living in this hellish place. Jim and you came damn close to trading punches the other night. Watching a washtub brawl is a helluva lot better than fisticuffs."

We spent five days in Shaibah's dust bowl until we hitched a ride on a DC 3 — those workhorse-airplanes didn't care how hot the desert got. The noon-day sun sizzled the shade to 110 degrees and raised the DC's cockpit thermometer to 145 Fahrenheit. As we sat on Shaibah's runway waiting for the pilot to complete his check, I remembered the old hymn and realized how Daniel must have felt "when he was tried in the fiery furnace."

Once airborne we levelled off into the heavenly coolness at five thousand feet, headed down the Persian Gulf and landed on the Island of Bahrein. The airport, the military quarters and the oil wells belonged to the Sheik of Bahrein. The hundred-and-ten degree temperature of an August afternoon and the ninety percent humidity belonged to the devil. But the Sheik had a pool and we muu-muued, bleached Canadians were welcome to use it.

To escape from Bahrein's sauna-like heat we spent the afternoon in the pool. Twenty by thirty feet, shaded by a thatched roof, the pool sat above ground like an oversized bathtub. An artesian well fed it with deliciously cool water. We had the pool to ourselves and soaked in its goodness for three hours.

As we walked from the pool Joe Zwingler suddenly stopped, grabbed the seat of his shorts. "Damn it, I got gyppo-gut." We'd never heard the expression, but Joe had already done a tour in the African campaign. "I've messed my pants," and we watched a trickle of yellow ran down his bare leg.

In the coming months we'd all become familiar with the discomforts of gyppo-gut. It was the expression the troops used to describe dysentery.

Bahrein's heat and humidity made sleep difficult and the M/O(Medical Officer) issued sleeping pills to all who wanted one. We were on a desert island, but at night the air chilled and condensed the moisture in the island's super-saturated air. The slate floors had to be mopped every morning. Clothes had to be hung in the sun every day or they would mildew. It seemed incredible.

The next morning before daylight we crawled out of damp sheets, pulled on our damp clothes and after a breakfast featuring stewed dates, we fled Bahrein's hot sogginess and set course for Karachi, Pakistan.

Half-way there our DC 3 needed food and so did we. Below us, Juwanii, a Royal Airforce Ferry Command base in eastern Iran, simmered. A few bleached buildings, lonely and shadowless in the noon-day sun, crowded together like abandoned toys in a great sand box. A tired windsock flopped lazily through the desert heat waves. By the time we landed and a red-headed, sunburnt attendant had parked our aircraft, the cockpit thermometer smoldered at 130 degrees.

"How long have you been in the desert?" I asked the red head.

"Almost two years."

"Does that sunburn ever turn to tan?"

"No, Sir, I'll put my shirt on in an hour and that'll have to do me for a week."

"Where's the mess?"

"It's the last building on the left, Sir."

We walked across the blistering sand. "This is the hottest place we've hit," said Bill Switzer. "Even hotter than Tripoli, Saskie."

"Do you see those fellows in front of the tent? Reminds me of the song George Formby sings about — *'Maddogs and Englishmen who go out in the mid-day sun. . . .'*" said Tony Mason.

We passed four desiccated-looking officers, wearing pith helmets, dark glasses and faded khaki uniforms sitting in the blazing sun having "a cuppa" while their servant waited patiently in the shade of the veranda. The song still jingled through my mind — a scene from *Lawrence of Arabia.* We found fuel and food and another boy with stewed dates, and by two o'clock, after another roast in the hell-like cockpit, we cooled at five thousand feet and set course for Karachi.

Date	Hour	Aircraft Type and No.	Pilot	Duty	Remarks (Including results of bombing, gunnery, exercises, etc.)	Fly Day
					Time carried forward:—	4394½
			Posted	to 229	Group India	
Aug-21-44	1000	York MW118	S/L Barkley	Passenger	Lynham-UK — Rabat F.N.	7:00
Aug-22-44	0600	MW118	S/L Barkley	Passenger	Rabat — Castel Benito. Lybia	7:15
Aug-22-44	2300	MW118	F/L Niven	Passenger	Castel Benito — Cairo.	7:00
Aug-23-44	2330	MW118 Dakota	F/L Niven.	Passenger	Cairo- Shaibah. Iraq.	7:10
Aug-26-44	0930	KW749	F/O Robertson	Passenger.	Shaibah- Bahrein-	2:05
Aug-27-44	0600	KW749	F/O Robertson	Passenger	Bahrein — Jurvanei	5:00
Aug-27-44	1400	KW749	F/O Robertson	Passenger	Jurvanei — Karachi	2:00
					Total Time for August	87:30
			Posted	to R.A.F.	Station Chaklala Sept. 12 1944	

India

In their campaign to chase the Japanese out of Burma, the British army needed aircraft to transport supplies and paratroops into the jungles of north-western Burma. The Royal Air Force received the army's request and asked the Royal Canadian Air Force to supply the aircrews. The RAF would fly us to India, providing the planes and the base. The RCAF would form two new squadrons, train the crews and take the squadrons into Burma. At least that was the plan, a good one really.

But Karachi turned out to be a disaster! In London, the headquarters of the RAF and the RCAF were fifteen minutes apart by London taxi or twenty minutes by the underground. With a typical military cufuffle, a hundred and fifty Canadian aircrew were flown to India; but nobody knew we were coming. So, having no advance notice, an Indian contractor pitched a British-square of two-man tents on the desert sands on the outskirts of Karachi, dug a two-man latrine on each of the four sides, called it Camp Mauripur, hung out the welcome sign and the Canadians moved in. Fortunately, the British seemed to have an inexhaustible supply of tents.

Our plane was a week late and Mauripur had no vacancy, so they trucked us into downtown Karachi to the Bristol Hotel. We drove through miles of open desert where huge, ugly, red-necked vultures fed on stinking carcasses of donkeys, fighting for their share with wild dogs and hyenas. We passed through a long stretch of corrugated iron and packing-box hovels where people teemed like ants and rushed to greet our trucks with outstretched hands crying plaintively, "Bakhshish Sahib, Bakhshish!" *My God! Is this India? Do I have to spend three years here?* Like the airman we had encountered earlier at Shaibah, I began to count the days.

The shanty town gave way to homes, shops, and streets blocked by rickshaws and oxcarts piled high with sugar cane. Tiny donkeys carried bales of hay three times their size; two men sat on the back of one that must have weighed less than its riders. Tongas, two-wheeled carts pulled by gaunt rib-slabbed horses with the driver perched on a small seat just behind the whipple tree, helped plug the traffic. Our truck slowed in the heavy traffic and stopped several times to let one of India's sacred cows amble across the street. We passed a shop with "Sun Life of Canada" blazoned across its store-front. On the veranda guarding the entrance a big old cow calmly chewed her cud.

While we waited for space at Mauripur, we were billeted in Karachi's Bristol Hotel, a comfortable place with plenty of servants and good food. After our evening meal we relaxed in the lobby and watched as pink chameleons darted over the pink walls, flicking their long tongues to grab their evening prey and scurrying back to their hiding places. In the early morning light I caught blood-filled bed bugs crawling up my mosquito net.

The first morning we climbed aboard a tonga to do the town. It carried four, sitting back to back. "How far to the bazaar?" we asked the driver.

"Not far, Sahib. Maybe one mile. You want to go to the big bazaar?"

"How much do you charge?"

"We see, Sahib."

The Indian rupee was worth thirty-three cents. "A rupee is just like a quarter. If we each give him a rupee that should do. You don't get much of a taxi ride for a buck," said Tony.

"I hope I can find a pocket knife. Somebody must have stolen mine in England. I can't live without a pocket knife," said Bill Switzer.

"Sahib want good knife? I show you good shop,Sahib."

The bazaar hummed with humanity. It was "beggar's day." Begging is a way of life in India and one day a week beggars are allowed on the streets. India has a washer-like coin called a "pice" minted especially for begging, worth a quarter of a cent.

After the rationed-starved shelves of Canada and Britain Karachi's bazaar amazed us. Canadian whiskey, rationed at home, sold for half the price of our "bottle-a-month." Ketchup, sugar cubes and peanut butter, which had all disappeared from our stores early in the war, abounded in Karachi's bazaars.

There was lots of Coca Cola and it reminded me of the soap-box orator I heard in Hyde Park. He shouted "The British conquered the world with the Bible and Scotch Whiskey. Now the Americans are using Spam and Coca Cola."

Bill found a fine pearl-handled knife. "Look Saskie, it's made in Sheffield and it's only three rupees."

We spent the morning in the bazaar. Each time we emerged from a shop our tonga driver was waiting. "Tonga, Sahib, tonga?" he wailed. He was still following us when we decided we would walk back to the Bristol. Later we learned that we had paid our tonga wallah ten times his regular fare.

Beggars blocked the sidewalks. A blind man with pus for eyes sat in the shade of a building attended by a small boy rattling a few coins in a tin cup. A dog-boy, his arms and legs broken and twisted by his parents when he was a baby to make him more pathetic, walked on all-fours, laughing as he whined, "No Momma, no Papa, no conna (food). Bakhshish, Sahib, Bakhshish." At the street corner, four men sitting on their heels played a game of cards. People slept on the sidewalk, their loose-fitting clothes covering their heads to keep off the flies. The butcher shop nearly turned us off steaks forever as the vendors tried to shoo the flies from meat piled on the counters. Big rats scurried back and forth in the gutters beneath the planked floor.

Teeth for sale in Karachi.

"Let's get the hell out of here, Bill."

"Do you suppose this is where the Bristol Hotel gets those good steaks we had last night? I hope not. Let's go Saskie."

"There seems to be plenty of food in the market, but did you notice how thin everybody is? Why there isn't a fat person anywhere. Look at their legs. They're no bigger than my forearm!"

"Saskie, I read a bit about India before we left England and they say that ninety-five percent of the Indian people never know what it's like not to be hungry from the day they are born until the day they die. They can't afford the food in their own markets!"

Back at the Bristol Bill said, "I've wanted to shorten the straps on my suitcase ever since I left England. This Sheffield steel seems sharp enough." The usually calm Bill exploded. "Dammit, Saskie, look at this!" He showed me his new pearl-handled knife with its shiny blade bent at right angles. As he tried to straighten it, the blade snapped.

In Terrace I had roomed with Bill and I had never seen him lose

160

his temper nor heard him swear. He had been a banker on civvy street, as honest and forthright as they come and he didn't appreciate being cheated. With a sigh of exasperation he said, "Saskie, I'm like that airman in Shaibah. I've started counting the days until we get the hell out of India."

We had four days at the Bristol before we moved to Camp Mauripur, where Red Meyers and I shared a tent closely packed amongst a maze of anchoring ropes. A mess hall had been built alongside the acre of tents but the screens for the windows and the doors hadn't arrived. We had to eat with one hand while we used the other to shoo the flies off our food.

By the time we arrived in Mauripur, all the Canadians there had gyppo-gut, and we got it a few days later. I remember how Joe Zwingler had introduced us to "gyppo-gut" in Bahrein. The camp didn't supply toilet paper so newspapers and even glossy magazines were in great demand. In emergencies some fellows used the big English pound notes or the smaller Indian rupees. If there was a line-up at the latrine and you just couldn't wait, you took twenty paces into the desert and made damn sure you buried it. At night, in the unlit campsite, people rushing to the latrines, often stumbled over tent ropes and messed their pants before they found the latrine or reached the desert sands.

Alongside Muaripur the Indian government was building a new road, and in the hours we idled away we watched its construction. It was all done by hand — the workers didn't even have a wheelbarrow.

With a mattock, men hoed the dirt from the ditch, shovelled it into wash basins, put the loaded basin on the head of a woman and she carried the dirt to the road-bed.

Indian women seemed to do all the hard work, their small children always with them. Their naked kids played by the roadside, building sand castles and romping with their playmates. When their children had to poop, the mothers wiped them with their fingers and then cleaned their hands with sand.

At Mauripur I saw two workers use a regular round-mouthed shovel to mix gravel and cement — one man on the handle while his helper pulled on a rope tied just above the spade. At lunch time they ate their Indian chapattis — a rolled pancake stuffed with curried rice. After lunch the women sat and picked the nits out of each other's hair. They seemed to be happy people and their language had a musical ring as they talked and laughed most of the day.

Indian women did the menial jobs. Young girls collected cow dung for fuel, because wood and coal were expensive. One afternoon we stopped our bikes as a couple of cows ambled across the road. The recent monsoons had greened the grass and the cows' loose stool splattered as it hit the pavement. We had to wait while two young girls rushed in, scooped up the steaming mess with their hands, loaded it into a basin which they put on their heads, and followed the cows. Some of the muck trickled over the sides of the basin into their hair, but they seemed to take no notice.

At home the women hand-mixed the dung with hay or straw, shaped it into pancakes the size of dinner plates and slapped them on the sunny side of buildings to dry. There were two million people in Karachi, and India is not noted for its winds. The air is still. At five thousand feet in Canada winds blow at thirty to forty knots; in India they blow at five to ten. The air hung heavy over Karachi, trapping the smoke and odour of the burning dung. As Karachi's millions cooked their chapattis and rice, the stench of the smouldering manure pile saturated the air we breathed, tainted the food we ate and would be with us all the days of our Indian tour. In their musings, travel magazines stress the beauty of the Taj Mahal for the prospective traveller but they never mention India's pungent, pervasive aroma.

We spent two weeks in Mauripur struggling with gyppo-gut and basking in the hot Indian sun. The Indian contractor eventually got the screens on the mess hall and most of us got control of our bowels. We had all been excited about our Indian posting. Now we tried to visualize how long a three-year tour would take and if we would live long enough to go home. I thought we had come to fight the Japs, not gyppo-gut, prickly heat, malaria and jaundice. How much longer would we have to sit in this bloody desert waiting for the "Brass" to untangle their cufuffle?

We flew to Chaklala, an airbase adjacent to the town of Rawal-

Rawalpindi's main street.

pindi. "Pindi", a hundred miles from the Khyber Pass and the border of Afghanistan, was the headquarters of the British Army. With bulldog tenacity, and by exploitation of India's cheap labour, the British had transplanted a bit of England to Pindi.

A captain in the British army employed seven or eight servants and lived in a compound of single family bungalows surrounded by manicured gardens. He had a gardener, a sweeper, a water boy, a laundry wallah, a cook, a nanny, a valet and a butler. There were no trade unions in India but centuries of tradition and the over- supply of labour made sure there were as many jobs as possible. A sweeper couldn't touch the laundry, nor could the cook sweep the floor.

At Chaklala, Red and I hired a bearer (servant) — he sort of came with the tent. He stood at attention in front of the open- flapped tent, wearing a tattle-tale grey turban, a knee-length black overcoat and the baggy pants of all Mohammedan men. The Islamic belief is that Mohammed, when he returns to earth, will be born of man, a man who has made his pilgrimage to Mecca. Some of us joked that there had to be room in the pants for the arrival.

"Shalom, Sahib! My name is Ashab. For you I am to be your bearer. Here I have very good chitties (letters of references) from Army Sahibs. Please read Sahib."

We had never had a servant but we ranked the same as an army captain. "How much do you want and what do you do?" asked Red.

"See, Sahib, this chitty from British officer. He pay five rupees for one month. He only one in tent. You Canadian officers pay ten rupees and Ashab do first class for you."

"Okay, Ashab, we'll pay you five rupees every two weeks. I think we can afford it, don't you, Red? It's nearly seven bucks a month. I wonder what he does for that money?"

Ashab woke us each morning with a cup of tea, and had our basin filled with hot water for washing and shaving. He laid out clean clothes, with socks turned to slide onto the foot. He served us breakfast in the mess, made our beds, sent our dirty clothes to the laundry and tidied up our tent. He brought us tea at the morning class-break and served us at lunch time. Before tea-time he had our bath ready (we bathed in galvanized tubs behind our tents) and laid out a change of clothes. After our bath he served us tea and cakes. Later, in the mess, he brought us drinks and waited on us at dinner, and if we wished he would stay and serve drinks all evening. He never asked for overtime nor missed a day's work.

The British complained that we Canadians were over-paying our bearers and upsetting the country's economy but when the Americans arrived they doubled the bearers' wages.

I often wished I could wrap up Ashab and send him home to help Ivy with our two small children. In those days of war time scarcities, it took Ivy ten months and a case of beer to get a washing machine.

We never kept Ashab for the evening. "Sahib, you use bicycle tonight? I go see my missus tonight. Too far for me to walk, Sahib."

I lent him my bike most nights. We all used bikes to get around the base and to peddle into Pindi. When I rented mine from the station's bicycle wallah, he put new red tubes in both tires. But every time I wanted to use my bike it had a flat tire and I'd ask Ashab to have it fixed.

One day I had a flat tire right in front of the bicycle shop. I watched them fix the flat. The new, red inner-tube that had been put in the tire when I rented the bike had been replaced by a multi-patched black tube — little wonder the tires were always flat. Had Ashab stolen the red tubes? I doubted he had. Bearers might steal — it was part of living. But he would never steal from his master.

"Ashab, what happened to the bike's red inner tubes?"

"I don't know, Sahib. I never see red tubes. Always black tubes. You see my chitties, Sahib. If I take red tubes, Ashab lose chitties and never get bearer job again."

After that Ashab walked to see his missus, and I never had another flat tire.

At Chaklala airbase the RCAF formed two new Transport Squadrons, 435 and 436, and the thirty crews began operational training on DC3's. We were being trained to drop paratroops and supplies in the campaign to liberate Burma. The wireless operator dispatched the paratroopers from the DC 3's (we called them Dakotas) and he had to make at least one jump. Anybody in the squadron could jump if they wished, but I never had the desire — especially after watching a "roman candle" by one of the instructors. Paratroopers carried two chutes, one on the back, released by a static line attached to the aircraft, the other on the chest, which released by pulling the ripcord. We watched in horror as both the instructor's chutes unfurled without opening. He tried all the tricks he had taught his students as he spun to his death like a burnt-out roman candle.

The first time I saw the short, stocky and slant-eyed soldiers wearing an Australian bush hat with the left brim turned up, I thought they were Chinese with a extra good tan. But they were Gurkhas from Nepal and from the same part of the country as the sherpas of Mount Everest. Their regiments had been part of the British army for almost two hundred years. They were in Chaklala to train as paratroopers and were bivouacked across the road from us.

Fearless warriors, Gurkhas sought no quarter and gave none. They took no prisoners. Cecil Law, author of Chinthe, the story of 435 in Burma, tells how at Imphal a Gurkha patrol was ordered to take some

Japanese prisoners for interrogation. Reluctantly, and with some loss of face they returned with seven officers. After the British had completed their interrogation, the Gurkhas were ordered to march them to the prisoner's compound. The seven Japanese officers were never seen again . . . nor their bodies found.

While we were at Chaklala the Gurkhas celebrated "Dussera" and here is how Joe Manley told the story in Law's Chinthe.

The body of the ox after decapitation.

The ring of blood around the sacrificial post.

The Festival or Dussera lasts for three days. On the last day the beheading ceremonies take place. Gurkhas are very hospitable and guests are served with cigarettes and fruit.

Gurkhas dressed as women perform a native dance to open the ceremony. The first act is the slicing of a melon with a khukri, followed by the beheading of several goats. The big event of the day is the decapitation of a full grown bullock. For this a special khukri is used, which is about three feet long and is wielded by one of the best men of the battalion. It is considered quite an honoured and he spends three days fasting and praying in preparation for it. The whole festival revolves around the importance of only one stroke being required to behead the beast. If this is fulfilled, good fortune and success in battle will favour the battalion for the ensuing year. Otherwise, it is a bad omen. After the head has fallen, while the blood is still flowing, the carcass is drawn around the sacrificial posts, describing a circle of blood.

Rice is then mixed with the blood to form a paste. The paste is spread in a layer over the forehead of each Gurkha as he steps within the sacred circle. The sign of the rice and blood on the forehead is an indication that the omen is good; that both man and the land will be fertile.

Joe Manley

When dispatching paratroops the object is to get the troops on the

Gurkka Soldier and a Khukri

ground in the closest formation. In the jungle two or three seconds could be two or three hundred impassable yards. One second was the maximum. If a jumper hesitated the dispatcher pushed him out. Despite their unquestionable courage in combat, it was often the Gurkhas who had to be kicked out.

Despite the ever-present consciousness of the fearful realities of war and combat we were training for, we enjoyed our days at Chaklala. We had great instructors who made the classes interesting as they "genned" us on the war in Burma. We read the weekly intelligence reports coming out of Burma, and the only fear I had was that I might be taken prisoner by the Japanese—the reports from their prisoner-of-war camps horrified us.

The British had been in the North West Frontier for nearly a hundred years, gradually transporting all the amenities and comforts of the old country to India, including beer. Rawalpindi boasted the only brewery in India, for there never was a soldier nor an airman who didn't love his suds. I don't suppose we drank anymore or any harder than miners did in Levack. Time hung heavy and the bar provided companionship.

The "pukka" (by the book) British army officers did not fully appreciate the rough and tumble Canadian officers. We were a bunch of kids plucked from small towns and cities, from farms, factories and mines, and, because we had learned to fly, we were given commissions. When you had two years of service, you automatically became a flight lieutenant, while a British officer could spend a life-time to get a similar rank. Our Canadian pay was higher than the British, and for some unknown reason the Indian government paid us an additional hundred dollars a month just for being in India. A Canadian flight lieutenant made as much as a RAF air commodore.

Flashman Club, Rawalpindi

168

Cucumber sandwiches by the pool.
Red Meyers on right.

As officers we enjoyed the privileges of the "Flashman Club." We swam in their pool and had afternoon tea with cucumber sandwiches served at poolside tables. Indian kitehawks perching in the nearby trees would swoop down and grab a sandwich from any plate left uncovered. If you took a bite of a sandwich and held the remainder, the big birds would snatch it out of your hand, wing feathers lashing your face.

The club's elegant dining room served eight course meals of soup, fish, fowl and meat, with pancakes, pudding and cake for dessert and finished with a savory — a sardine on a sliver of toast — leaving a hell of a taste in your mouth. We attended the club dances and twirled the Commanding Officer's wife around the floor with the unbridled vigour of spring colts. The Colonel would have kicked us out, but the women loved "those wild Canadians." One night they even shut down the bar, and our Commanding Officer threatened to put the club out of bounds if we didn't behave ourselves.

After the dance the tonga drivers waited in dark shadows of the dimly-lit street, bleatingly calling "Tonga, Sahib, tonga." As we climbed into their rigs they asked, "Sahib, like jiggy jig? I know for you nice girl, Sahib. You need jiggy jig, Sahib?"

The red light district was strictly out of bounds and well patrolled by the military police so we hired the tongas to take us back to Chaklala. Often we would each put a rupee in the kitty and race back to camp. The winning driver got the pot — more than he made in a week.

We found Sam's restaurant. Sam served great steaks. In India we never knew whether the steaks were beef or camel, but they tasted good. Like my dad always said, "Gordon, there are no poor steaks — some are just a little tougher than others." Sam's boasted a cocktail bar, and we would have a couple of drinks before our meal, sometimes staying for drinks after dinner.

One evening we found a white woman sitting alone in the lounge. We soon learned she was a nurse on leave from the Burma front. We hadn't seen or talked to a woman for nearly two months. She was older than we were, old enough to be the mother of some of the younger fellows, but we swarmed around her table, hungry for the sound of a woman's voice, for the luxury of the smell of cologne, longing to touch the softness of her fresh-washed hair. We bought her drinks, then Sam set a large table and we all sat around and wined and dined her. On her way to England for a well- earned leave, she flew out the next morning. She was one of three European women I talked to in my eight months in India.

Another evening after dinner at Sam's, Red, Bill and I decided we would walk back to Chaklala. We had been well fed and a balmy laziness floating in the jasmine-scented air calmed our homesick souls. "Do you hear that music? It sounds just like the Hildebrand orchestra. Gosh! It could be coming from Markinch's town hall."

"Sure sounds like Canadian small-town jazz, Saskie," said Bill.

"Sounds like the music is coming from down the next side street," said Red.

We found the hall with the double doors open to the evening coolness. We could see the bouncing dancers as the rhythm of *Sweet Georgia Brown* pulsed in the evening air, stirring a warm nostalgia in our secretly homesick hearts. "They're really jiving. Come on, let's have a boo," said Red.

The dance floor trembled to the tune, comfortably crowded with Indian couples, mostly people our age. The older people sat on folding chairs surrounding the dance floor. "You know Bill, this could be Markinch, except that everybody has a real good tan. See that tall girl in the white dress? She's not from this country. She's too dark and her hair's kinky, but she sure knows how to dance."

"Why don't you ask her for a dance, Saskie?"

"She'll probably turn me down. I'll just watch for a while."

The music stopped and the girls all gathered at the front of the hall near the five-piece band. The men congregated around the door. The place hummed with a sing-song chatter and the aroma of sweaty bodies. Hair tonic and cologne smelled friendly and sent tunes and sexy ideas racing through my mind. It seemed like months since I'd held a woman in my arms.

Melanie

She stood tall amongst the girls, her slim figure sheathed in a white-eyelet dress revealing her soft, smooth light-ebony skin. Her short kinky hair was gathered in a little pony-tail tied with a whiff of red wool.

The saxophone lilted into the opening bars of *Harbour Lights*. I headed for the girls as couples moved onto the floor. I was almost there. I caught her eye, smiled and she smiled back as I mouthed the words, *May I have this dance?*

Then some other fellow stepped between us and asked her to dance. "I'm sorry I have it taken," she said, taking my outstretched hand and following me onto the dance floor. If music is man's universal language, then the dance expresses the joy people feel for each other, and it too is universal. Here I was, halfway around the world, and my partner followed me as though we had been dancing forever. She felt so good. So close. She smelled so womanly. Her kinky hair was soft against my cheek.

"You're a lovely dancer."

"Thank you. You're easy to follow." Her voice had a come-hither tone, mellow and smooth like rich ice cream.

"Do you come here often?"

"Most every Friday night. I love to dance."

We had the next dance and when the music finished the band started to play the "Home Waltz." "Are you here with anybody?" I asked with visions of moonlit stroll in the jasmine-scented evening.

"No, I'm not. I came with my mother and father. In my country girls must always have a chaperon. But we would like you to come home with us."

Then I recalled our stay at the Bristol hotel in Karachi. An Indian woman and her daughter had also been guests. In the evenings an American soldier came to visit. The three of them sat on the veranda well-spaced around a coffee table. The young couple were never alone.

"Shall we dance?"

"I'd love to."

"In Canada when you dance the 'Home Waltz' with someone, you are supposed to take her home. May I take you home?"

"I'd enjoy being alone with you. Women in your country have so much freedom. I envy them. Girls in India are considered a burden on our families and we must do nothing that might hinder a successful marriage."

We surrendered ourselves to the waltz. She nestled her cheek against mine and I held her close. The red woollen tie in her hair tickled my nose. The music died and as we finished our last whirl, I held both her hands and bowed. "Thank you for a lovely evening. It's been a pleasure to dance with you and I'd like to know your name. Mine's Gordon."

"Thank you, Gordon, I've enjoyed dancing with you. I am called Melanie. Now, I'd like you to meet my parents."

She led me across the hall and introduced me to her mother and father and her younger sister. We made our way out of the hall and onto the street where Bill and Red were waiting.

"Would you like to come home with us for a cup of tea?" Melanie asked.

"Not tonight, thank you. Perhaps another time."

"Good night, Gordon." She took my hand in hers. Its softness and its gentle squeeze sent a flood of feeling to my lonely heart. "We'll be here next Friday night."

"Good night, Melanie, it's been a pleasure. I'll see you next Friday."

I should've accepted her parents' invitation. It would be interesting to be in an Indian home. But Melanie obviously isn't their daughter and I don't wanted to get involved with her family. After all, I am a married man. But Melanie fascinates me. I wonder if it's because she's black. I smelt her perfume on my tunic this morning. It stirred my soul and gave me goose pimples. I'd better sit down and write a sexy letter to Ivy. Maybe I'll get some mail today that will help. I didn't get to the dance the following Friday. But I got two letters from Ivy and a parcel.

We continued our training with more lectures and flying cross-country exercises. Early one morning we did a low-level cross-country flight. All pilots love to fly low. At a hundred feet the sensation of speed is real. The ground streaks by. Buildings and trees leap out of the ground. Our pilot Frank Smith was in his glory.

We took off at daybreak and my log book shows we flew for two hours. We flew out for an hour at 3000 feet and did a three-leg return to Chaklala at naught feet. As we skimmed across the Indian countryside we stampeded animals, and in the villages we startled people sleeping on the flat roofs of their houses. We watched with devilish glee as they sat up in bed, jumped up and ran down the stairs or jumped off the roof. One brave man stood and shook his fist as we flashed by.

I had not yet recovered from the diarrhea I got at Camp Mauripur. I had several stool tests but they could never find any amoeba. Since they treated only the severest forms of dysentery, amoebic dysentery, I like everybody else, was supposed to recover from ordinary gyppo-gut on my own.

I got so that I would just have to "go" no matter where I was. Bicycling on country roads, I just did as the Indians did — used the side of the road. But in the towns toilet facilities were hard to find, and often I had to duck down a lane or try to hide behind or beside a building. I was losing weight and feeling wretched. Finally in late October, Chaklala's M/O prescribed a sulfa drug, but it didn't help, so they put me in the hospital and I came down with jaundice.

Above, coolie with rice
and below, with a load of coal.

By the time I got rid of my yellow complexion I had lost forty pounds and was sent to a RAF rest camp near the mountain town of Muree. The town nestled in the foothills of the Himalayas thirty miles from Rawalpindi and 7000 feet higher. A macadamized (blacktopped) road, lined for most of its length with coniferous trees and vegetation similar to that of our British Columbia forests, corkscrewed up the mountainside to the town. The steep valley walls, terraced almost to the summit, looked like the stairways an Indian Paul Bunyan might use to add sparkle to the stars, to get green cheese from the moon or to dance around the sun.

The rest camp perched on the summit of a hill five miles past Muree and two-hundred feet higher, was aptly named Topa. There was no road for the last quarter of a mile. We followed footpaths and stairs, puffing our way through the thin air to our new quarters.

Later we learned that all the building materials and the furniture, including the piano, had been carried up on the backs of the mountain coolies (see photos). The coolie in the black overcoat is carrying a sack of rice weighing over two hundred pounds. The other coolie has a load of coal. These coolies were the only people in India who didn't have spindly legs.

I often wondered what it must be like to be a human

Indian Sawmill

beast-of-burden. Life was cheap in India. During one of our walks in the woods around Topa we found their version of a sawmill. At Chakala we watched the construction of a new runway. The only piece of equipment used was a steam roller. People worked like ants. Mattocks scraped the dirt into piles. Two-man shovels loaded it into basins. Straight-backed, slim women balanced the basins on their heads, carrying the fill onto the runway. Quarried rock arrived strapped to the backs of wobbly-kneed donkeys, and stone masons broke the jagged rock into gravel. Women wearing wooden yokes transported cans of oil to the piles of new gravel where two-handed shovellers mixed the blacktop. With the grace of ballet dancers women balanced basins of this blacktop on their heads, and then spread it on the growing runway where the wheezing steam roller ironed it smooth and level.

One day shortly after my arrival, on a five-mile hike from Topa to Muree, Bill Switzer, Jack Barker and I were enjoying our walk along the pine-shaded road when we saw a neat pile of pea-gravel two feet wide and a foot on the road side. We followed it for a mile or more and we came to an Indian worker sitting comfortably on his heels, while with a small hammer he broke egg-sized gravel into smaller pea-size pieces. We stopped to watch and tried to find out what hours he worked and how much he was paid, but his English was poor and our Hindustani was no better. As we walked on we saw that his supply of egg-sized gravel continued for at least two miles — he would be busy for awhile yet.

Farther along the road a family of baboons sitting on a bank ten feet above the road started to scream and throw hunks of wood and small rocks at us. The size of German Shepherd dogs, they snarled bearing their fangs, threatening sorties down the bank. We had been warned not to aggravate them and that they usually ran from a loud noise. We yelled "Bang!" at the top of our voices. They stopped screaming, turned and ran, flashing their red backsides as they disappeared into the forest.

Our long, low, veranda-fronted brick building over-looked a wide valley. The view from the veranda jumped over the nearby badminton court and tumbled down the terraced mountainside into the valley, then climbed the tiny terraced stairs to the top of the other side. In the background a jungle of mountains fought for space as the snow-clad summits of the Himalayas scalloped the blue horizon.

The building was divided into eight separate cell-like rooms, each with a small window and a narrow glass-paneled door opening on the veranda. Each had a fireplace in one corner and was furnished with a rope charpoy (bed), a small table and chair . When I arrived in Muree I moved in with a dozen fellows from Chaklala including Bill Switzer, Gordon Weatherbee, Jay Ronalds and Tommy Thompson from 149 squadron. Most of us were recovering from jaundice. We revelled in the temperate climate, soaking up the mountain sunshine, more comfortable in our blue uniforms than our tropical khakis. With good food and plenty of rest we convalesced rapidly. Jay Ronalds, a stout pilot, suffered from prickly heat. The insides of his thighs from his knees to his groin were a raw oozing sore when we arrived, but after two or three days in Muree they healed.

We had our Chaklala medical records with us when we met our naturopath. Flight Lieutenant Dr. Witherhead boasted about the lucrative Hartley Street practice he had given up in London to join the airforce and explained how he would use natural remedies to help us regain our health. He held a commission in the Royal Air Force and was responsible for the rest camp's health. I learned later that during the war, because of the shortage of medical doctors, the service recruited naturopaths and chiropractors and used them in rehabilitation centres and camps like Topa.

"You've had a rough time, Wagner, but we'll soon have you healthy and back to your squadron. I want you to take this powder and dissolve it in a bottle of water — a quart beer bottle will do nicely. Take a tablespoon three times a day. In twenty-four hours you'll feel better and in forty-eight you'll be a new man! Do plenty of walking, drink no alcoholic beverages, and come back to see me in a week."

In late November we wandered through mossy hills near the camp or walked into the small village of Jhakagali where we found a small restaurant that served a good mixed grill. We learned to bargain in the bazaars for small pieces of Indian brass, including jewel boxes with five sliding panels which had to be moved in a sequence before the lid would open. I found a boutonniere commemorating the coronation of Edward VIII. In the afternoons we lay in the sun or played badminton. After four years in the service we had all become experts at killing time.

We all had bearers; my Mohammed had red hair and bright blue eyes. Alexander the Great had advanced as far as Muree and they claim the blue-eyed natives are descendants of his troops. There may be some doubt regarding the blue-eyed men in Alexander's army, but plenty of blue-eyed British soldiers have roamed the hills of Muree in the last century of colonialism. The November nights were chilly and we burned large pine cones the size of cantaloupe in our fireplaces. We bought the cones from enterprising young boys for a couples on annas a sack. The cones were full of pitch and gave a quick hot heat but they burnt too quickly.

I was just beginning to feel better when I developed a boil on the back of my neck. I went to see Dr. Witherhead. "Yes, young man, you do have a nasty boil. I'll give you six of these little packets of an old Chinese remedy. You are to put the powder on your tongue and let it dissolve. Don't wash it down with water; just let it mix well with your saliva before you swallow it. In twenty-fours hours you'll get relief and in forty-eight you'll be a new man."

My neck got worse. Two days later my naturopathic doctor told me I had a carbuncle and gave me some more powders to take. "Mix a tablespoon of this in a cup of lukewarm water and take it before each meal and before you go to bed. You have bad a infection there but this should fix it."

My damn neck got so sore that I couldn't sleep and red lines of infection reached to my forehead's hairline. I found a can of Thermafuge at the Jhakigali bazaar. It came in a pea-green can. I remembered my mother using it for poultices when I was a small boy. I took the can to the treatment room.

"Jock, I found this Thermafuge in the bazaar and I'd like you to help me poultice this damn carbuncle. Those powders Hartley Street's gift to medicine prescribed aren't doing a bit of good."

Jock MacLean, a rosy-cheeked, tubby Scotch corporal said, "I don't fancy those weird concoctions the M/O hands out. I remember my mother using this green stuff when I was a boy. I'll get it good and hot and tape it to your neck. Probably it'll hurt like hell but we got to get that boil open and draining."

He got it hot all right. It damn near sent me through the roof. He applied fresh poultices three times a day. By the third day the inflammation had gone down, the sore was draining, and I was able to sleep at night. But we never told the naturopathic doctor.

By mid-December the weather cooled. It often rained and one night we had a couple of inches of snow. The British fireplaces were no better in the camp than those in chimney-potted London. In London you could get coal or feed shillings into a gas heater, but all the coal that came up to Topa on the backs of coolies was for the kitchen, the officer's mess or the staff quarters. The pitchy pine cones burned madly for a few minutes, but we never had enough cones to heat our cell-like rooms. My bearer, Mohammed, brought me tea and warm wash-water every morning. If I wasn't feeling too well, he brought me my breakfast.

Meanwhile the squadron had moved forward and was on operations on the India-Burma border in the vicinity of Imphal. I was all set to go back to the squadron when my carbuncle flared up again. More powders from Doctor Witherhead to mix and take three times a day with the usual assurance—twenty-four to feel better and forty-eight to be a new man—and he said I'd be in Topa for another two weeks. Jock and I went back to the Thermafuge poultices and sucked some more guck out of the back of my neck. Christmas was nearly on us and Bill Switzer, Gordon Weatherbee and I were still recuperating and Jack Barker, Stu McBain and Cece Law had joined us.

The hierarchy of the military never impressed me. I had learned to tolerate the racist colonial British attitude to the Indians, but in Rawalpindi I refused to go to the head of the line when waiting to get on a bus. The British soldiers and their memsahibs got on the bus first while the natives waited—it was their country and I took my turn despite requests from the Indian bus driver to come aboard.

One day I did come close to using my rank. I was about to enter the medical treatment room and at the entrance an English corporal had three Indian airmen he was escorting to sick parade. In his irritating cockney accent he berated, cursed, and described their ancestors in the most derogative, foul-mouth language I have ever heard. Oh, how I wanted to give that little corporal a dose of his own medicine!

Who the hell do you think you are? This is their country you're living in, and these people are paying you. I suppose you think they're colonials. You bloody bastards would treat us Canadians the same way if you thought you could get away with it. You ignorant son of a bitch, for two cents I'd throw my rank and put you on charge.

Calm down, Gordon, there is really nothing you can do. Gandhi, Nehru and Jinnah will soon kick the smart-ass the hell out of India. You don't want to get involved in a court martial.

It reminds me of a day when I was five years old and discovered I was a German, of the day just before I joined the service when one of my so-called Anglo-Saxon friends accused me being a member of the "German Bund", of the day that Lady Wallace in strutting in her cold-hearted castle called me a colonial, of the days I spent living on American bases in Alameda and Annette Island where it didn't matter whether your name ended in a "ski" or started with a "Mac" you were bloody well an American and damn proud of it. I'm not even a Canadian. There is no such think as a Canadian citizen. I'm a goddamned British subject and so are my kids and they're the sixth generation born in Canada. If I live through this glorified cufuffle I'll bloody well change that. We'll get our own flag too. Put a beaver or a maple leaf on it. I don't want my kids learning about the crosses of Saint George, Andrew and Patrick. And most of all I don't want them to have fight a war to save the British Isles or any other European country. It also reminds me that it is mail time.

Unless you've been in the service you never realize the importance of mail day. Our mail came through regularly when our 435 and 436 squadrons were still at Chaklala. It came up on the duty run, so we'd watch for the truck and head for the orderly room. Once the squadron moved into the Burma campaign, the delivery of my mail became irregular. The airforce had its own postal service and Ivy received my almost daily letters in four days and often in three; parcels took a little longer. Just before Christmas I received five or six parcels. Ivy's always contained some canned meat and in one parcel she'd packed raisins and soap. I appreciated the meat in England, but we got plenty of meat in India and I didn't relish soapy raisins.

"Mohammed, have some raisins. My memsahib sent them from Canada. They taste a little like soap but if you like them you may take them home."

"Raisins taste fine to me, Sahib. My missus and children will like. Thank you, Sahib."

"Would you like a can of Spam?"

"Thanks not, Sahib, we cannot eat pork."

"How many children do you have, Mohammed?"

"Six were born, Sahib, but only three live now, two girls and one boy."

"Do you live in Jhakgali?"

"No Sahib, I live on the road to Srinagar. Maybe three miles from this place."

"Could I come and see your place?"

"I would be honoured to have Sahib visit. You come tomorrow, Sahib?"

"What time, Mohammed, and how will we find your place?"

"Do not come before three o'clock, Sahib. You follow road to Srinagar for three miles, maybe more. I will be waiting for you by the road. You bring your friend, okay Sahib?"

The next day Barker and I followed the Srinagar road as it twisted along the terraced mountain side. We found Mohammed waiting on the road side with his children. One was a girl about nine, the other probably six, and their baby brother was a year old. Mohammed led us down the steep mountain side, the older girl carrying the baby on her hip. We zigzagged along a goat trail dropping from terrace to terrace. I marvelled at the agility of the girl carrying the baby as she switched the baby from one hip to the other while we eased around boulders and stepped from rock to rock. Two hundred feet down the mountain Mohammed led us on to a level terrace. "Welcome to our home, Sahib."

The quarter-moon-shaped terrace, about 150 feet long and 50 feet wide, teemed with life. Chickens scratched in the dusty soil, cackling chicken-talk to each other. A small black kid butted its mother's udder. At the far end a water buffalo chewed its cud. From behind a pile of rocks three boys, ranging in age from sixteen to six, joined the circus.

The terrace above, held in place by a six-foot stone wall, was the roof of Mohammed's home. A three-by-five foot framed entrance led into a cave-like room. There were neither windows nor chimney. Down the middle of the twelve-by-twenty foot room ran a log which separated the people on one side from the livestock on the other. The furniture consisted of only four rope beds.

Mohammed invited us inside. In the middle of the room two women squatted at a brazier cooking chapattis over an open dung-fuelled fire. The smoke clung to the ceiling and stung our eyes. The women turned, and we got a quick look at their faces before they hid behind their purdahs.

"How would you like to live in here, Saskie?"

"I would probably be a damn sight warmer than in those over-ventilated cells we have at Topa."

"Mohammed, what do you use for a door?" I asked.

"Depends, Sahib. Sometimes we hang just mosquito net, sometimes bed sheet or blanket. We are never cold. Besides, Sahib, no wood, no pine cones and no coal here. Only English have fireplace and send all the heat up the chimney."

"Do you have two wives, Mohammed?"

"No. Mohammed can't keep two women. Only rich men can. The other woman is our neighbour and these boys are her children."

"Can I take a picture of the women?"

"Please no, Sahib."

"How about you and the children?"

"Please yes, Sahib."

The children, Mohammed, and even the animals enjoyed having their photos taken and I half-hoped to get one of the women but they didn't come out of the house.

"Sahib like some tea?"

The author visits with his bearer Mohammed, his children and livestock.

"Oh no, Mohammed! No thanks. We can only drink tea made in our mess. It's the doctor's orders."

"I understand, Sahib."

Mohammed and the five children led us back to the road and we thanked him and promised to give him copies of the photos.

I enjoyed our visit with Mohammed and particularly the opportunity to see his home. He was not part of the staff at Topa. I had hired him and paid his wages. The visit was a privilege not usually experienced by the military.

There were five RAF staff officers in our mess, a couple of RAF types convalescing and an ass-kissing American who somehow had landed in Topa. We Canadians kept to ourselves. We ate in the officers' mess but rarely used the bar. On cold rainy evenings we would gather around the mess fireplace to keep warm or go to bed in our uniforms.

On the warm afternoon of Christmas Eve, Bill Switzer, Weatherbee, Barker and I walked into Jhakigali, did a little shopping and stopped for char (tea) and cakes. On the way home we found a holly tree loaded with red berries and took some cuttings to decorate our rooms.

"Gosh, Saskie, it's beginning to feel like Christmas," said Bill.

"Little warm for you boys who are used to Christmas on the prairies," Weatherbee chuckled.

"Weatherbee, you Easterners shouldn't talk. I spent last Christmas in the manning depot in Toronto and damn near froze my balls." said Barker who came from Spy Hill, Saskatchewan.

"I suppose they'll have a pukka-pukka deal in the mess to night. I think I'll break down and have me a beer. It's been a couple of months since I've had a drink."

"Good idea, Saskie. I haven't had the buttons shined on my tunic since we got here. Let's all meet in the mess about six-thirty. I won't have a beer but I'll try their Scotch," said Bill.

We picked some poinsettias from the hedge around the camp and were feeling real Christmassy by the time we reached the camp.

Six of us gathered in the mess, all spit and polish, and ready to celebrate Christmas half-a-world from home. We exchanged Christmas greetings and showed our respect for each other in the only way that men know how — the firm and earnest handshake.

"Come on, men, step up to the bar and the hell with what our naturopathic sawbones has to say. Khidmatgar, I'll have a beer," I said.

"Sorry, Sahib, no beer tonight."

"What do you mean, no beer tonight?" wailed Barker. "I saw the coolie bring some in this afternoon."

"I am very sorry, Sahib, but no beer tonight. Beer only for staff tonight, Sahib."

"Who the hell gave you those orders?" barked Barker, his crew-cut blonde hair bristling.

"Sahib, the Commanding Officer told me today," said the khidmatgar as he nervously wiped the bar.

"Give me a beer, you bloody wog, before I climb this bar and help myself."

"Take it easy, Barker, it really isn't his fault. But it is a helluva poor Christmas spirit! Can you imagine not sharing at Christmas? I don't know what that goddamn C/O did before they put those flight-looey stripes on his sleeves," said the usually calm Bill Switzer.

"Probably pimped in Picadilly. I can't stand his accent and I get bloody tired of getting up every time he enters the mess. He sure likes to throw his weight around. Reminds me of the cockney corporal I nearly put on charge in Pindi," I said.

"He's a proper bastard," replied Weatherbee. "I'm an RC and six of us wanted to attend midnight mass in Muree. The MT (motor transport) officer okayed it and an RC driver volunteered to drive the van, but the old man wouldn't approve the run."

"I spent one Christmas in a mining camp in the backwoods of Ontario, and I was on hospital duty Christmas Day at No.2 Wireless School in Calgary, but I had a good day both times. Can you imagine having Christmas Eve dinner together and not sharing your good cheer! The Christmas I spent in Levack we ran out of beer and money, but Bruno gave us a case of twenty-four on the cuff and we split our last half-dozen between eight guys. These bloody Englishmen are something else!"

"Come on, Saskie, let's sit down and relax," said the ever calm Switzer.

"To hell, let's go and sit in the dining room and get the khidmatgar to serve us. Damned if I'll wait for that bastard of a C/O! Come you guys, let's see if we can get something to eat."

"Lead the way, Weatherbee!" we all chorused.

We sat at a table and rattled spoons against our cups to get the khidmatgar's attention. The white-turbaned, red-sashed waiter almost sparkled as he came to our table. "Very sorry Sahibs, but no food can be served until the Commanding Officer gives us permission. I would be happy if Sahibs would wait in the lounge until Flight Lieutenant Morgenthorpe is ready to eat."

"We want to eat now," bristled Barker. "I'm damn hungry."

"Sahibs will make it very difficult for me if they don't remove themselves to the lounge."

"Don't worry, Khidmatgar, we won't get you into trouble. But we are damn well going to stay!" said Barker.

From the dining room we watched the five staff members, the two RAF convalescences and the ass-kissing American gather in the lounge and linger over their drinks. They took their time, and about eight o'clock they wandered in for dinner with their drinks in hand.

"Don't you guys get up. Let's see if he's got guts enough to put us on charge!" Barker bristled.

There were two tables with room for eight people on each side. We six were sitting side by side, facing the C/O's table. They approached their table, positioning themselves on either side of the C/O, and gently placed their glasses on the table. The old man drew himself up to his five-foot-eight and slowly stared at each of us in turn. You could see his mustache bristle as he drilled each of us with his eyes. I found it damn hard to stay seated. I felt Switzer's leg move and thought he was going to stand. I gave his tunic a little tug. None of us stood up.

"Haarummmuppp!" the C/O grunted.

Well, you old bastard, you' d sure like to throw your rank around and put these smart-ass Canadians in their place. If you ordered us to stand, I guess we' d have to stand up. I think you' re afraid we might draw-and-quarter you. Come on, you old turkey, show us you got some guts!

For a moment I thought he would do just that. His face flushed and little beads of sweat oozed onto his forehead. He squared his shoulders, ramrodded his back, took a look at the bearer standing in the door way with a tray full of food, cleared his throat and calmly said, "Gentlemen, please be seated."

After the meal we gathered in two separate groups in the lounge and tried not to notice each other. There is a custom in the services that on Christmas Eve the officers visit the Sergeants' Mess and on Christmas Day the sergeants return the visit. We knew a couple of the sergeants, and they had asked us to their mess. I had said I'd be there. Ordinarily the C/O would have asked us to go with him, but we could hardly expect that — not after the dinner mutiny!

It was sad and kind of funny as they sneaked away in two's and three's to the sergeants' mess like kids swiping candy. We were happy to see them go as we threw some more fuel on the fireplace and talked of what Christmas might be like at home.

Christmas morning we all took breakfast in our cell-like rooms. The day warmed in the Christmas morning sun. Bill Switzer, Weatherbee and I strolled peacefully over the mountain knolls, then sat on a moss covered log and looked across the valley. We filled our souls with the silence of memories and eased our homesick heartaches with the comfort of being together. How long we sat in that studied silence I don't recall, but we rose together and turned to one another.

"Merry Christmas, Saskie," said Bill, "I just hope we don't have to spend another in this God-forsaken land. Merry Christmas to you, Weatherbee."

We exchanged greetings and held our firm handshake just a little longer than men consider proper while the warm feeling of comradeship cruised through our beings. We'd need each other before this day was over or this bloody war was won!

We visited the mess on the way back. The sergeants were there and well into their cups. It's forty-four years since the three of us walked into that group of men and it's still hard to believe that not one of them so much as looked at us or wished us a Merry Christmas!

But Stu McBean saved the day!

We were sunning ourselves and trying to decide whether to play a game of badminton or go for a walk when Stu McBean rounded the corner of our row of cells.

"Merry Christmas, you bloody mutineers. I hope you enjoyed the friendly gathering with the sergeants this morning. We're throwing an afternoon tea and would like you fellows to join us."

"Hope it's strictly Canadian," said Barker, "I'm not much for afternoon teas but as long as those bloody limies won't be there, I'll come."

"I suppose you guys have Christmas cards from home. We'd like to borrow them for decorations."

We gathered up our cards and gave Stu the holly we had found. "We'll be receiving from four o'clock on, and dress is optional. Eh what, old boy!"

I tried to read but couldn't concentrate. I climbed up the knoll and sat on that same log and watched the light change the shadows on the mountainsides. A veil of loneliness crept up the terraced slopes. Lovely Ivy, skinny Keith and chubby Linda were half round the world and thirteen time zones away. Their Christmas day was just beginning. The misty veil topped the knoll and a great love wrenched my soul. They were there, hazy in the valley's shadows, gathered around their Christmas tree. I reached out to draw my loves nearer. Three-year-old Keith ran his new car across the floor and baby Linda rocked her new mama doll to sleep, while Ivy, beautiful in her pink dressing gown, smiled her come-hither look as she brushed her soft hair aside and tried to speak to me. My body tensed and my heart began to pound as I reached out to touch her. I tried to stand but I couldn't get off the log. Then I heard Keith say, "Mummy is Daddy ... still gone bye-byes?"

"I'm right here, Keith," I shouted.

"I'm right here, Keith," the echo answered. "I'm right here, Keith," mocked the echo as it faded into the hills. The veil lifted from the valley and vultures circled in the sky. I stood and wiped my eyes and watched the shadows lengthen. As I walked towards the sinking sun, a warm glow soothed my aching heart. **I'd been home for Christmas!**

I wasn't too anxious to go to Stu's tea, but after a shower and change of clothes I felt better. Stu, Em Taylor and Cece had a large room, at one time probably used as married quarters. I've been to many Christmas parties in my seventy-four years, but I'll never forget Stu McBean's afternoon tea on Christmas Day, 1944!

The room's white-washed walls were ringed with cedar and pine boughs. A spray of berried holly nested in poinsettia branches graced the fireplace. Our collection of Christmas cards hung in attractive clusters on the wall. Somebody had found some red and green ribbons in the bazaar, and bows were everywhere. They'd found a table and centred it with a small Christmas tree. The table groaned with goodies: a Christmas cake from Canada, an assortment of cookies and sweets from the shop in Jhakigali, a couple of bottles of Indian wine and a bottle of Indian whiskey.

"Merry Christmas, Stu! You've done one helluva a job and really made Christmas come alive. Just walking into this little bit of Canada has made my day. I was feeling damn low as I walked down here. You've saved the day for all of us!"

"Thank you, Saskie. Cece, Em and I had been talking about a party for awhile and after that fiasco last night and again today, we decided to put this together. Thanks for coming and a Merry Christmas!"

We lit the fireplace and took turns throwing the large pine cones into the fire, watching the flames paint pictures of Christmases past, wondering what the future would bring or when we would see our loved ones again in Spy Hill, Mississauga, Saskatoon or Markinch.

We tried to barbecue Spam on forks tied to sticks. We mostly singed or burned it, but it was hot and tasted great between slices of bread. We munched on cake and cookies and washed them down with bitter sips of Indian wine. As the shadows lengthened, the flaming cones bounced our shadows off the white-washed walls. As the wine and whiskey warmed our souls, we sat in silent deference to each other's thoughts and loves. It was a Christmas to be remembered.

I felt miserable for a few days after Christmas — too much Indian wine, I thought. Then I suspected I was getting jaundice again. Doc Witherhead prescribed more powders to mix and suck and assured a forty-eight hour cure. By New Year's I was staying in bed with my clothes on and shivering under extra blankets. The next day a stab-like pain ripped through the left side of my chest and my right shoulder each time I drew a breath. Mohammed fed and washed me. Witherhead brought me more of his bloody powders. Again Stu McBean saved the day. Stu was a druggist on "civvy" street and he gave me one of those giant-sized bottles of Bayer aspirins to ease the pain.

But the pain worsened. Each time my heart beat, the stabbing pain would rip through my left chest, shoulder and arm. I chewed aspirin, swallowed Witherhead's herbs and piled on more blankets.

The weather turned cold. On the 4th of January it snowed all day. Mohammed was snow bound. The supply of pine cones for the fireplace lay buried. Jack Barker scrounged more blankets and brought food I couldn't eat.

"Saskie, you look bloody awful this morning. I'd better get the nature quack to take a look at you. When did you see him last?" asked a worried Barker.

"I saw him on sick parade two days ago, but he just gave me more of his damn powders. I chew these aspirin and they help some."

Witherhead stamped the snow from his boots as he entered my dingy room. "How long have you been in bed?"

"The last two days. It's the only place I can keep warm."

"Have you been taking the medicine I prescribed?"

"Yes, but it doesn't seem to help."

"How many of these aspirin have you taken?"

"Plenty, they're the only things that help."

"Those aspirins will kill you. You'd better let me take them."

"You leave those goddamn aspirin where they are, and you'd better get me the hell out of here before those bloody herbs you hand out put me under."

"Wagner, that is no way to address the Senior Medical Officer, but you're not yourself today. I'll arrange to have you sent to BMH (British Military Hospital) in Rawalpindi tomorrow. It's too late to go today. I'll send Corporal Maclean over to give you a wash, and do try to leave the aspirin alone. I'll send a new treatment with the corporal. Do try it, it should help."

By the next morning Topa lay under two feet of snow and I was still chewing aspirin. Scotty loaded me onto a stretcher and they carried me down the hill to where an open-aired ambulance waited. They buried me in blankets and we headed down the winding, snow-covered road for Rawalpindi. We got stuck in the snow several times on the trip and I had to help push us out of the snow banks.

When I arrived at Rawalpindi's BMH, my temperature was a 104.5. They put me in a bed with real sheets, gave me a bed bath and fresh smelling pyjamas. My diary says, "BMH looks good after that dirty room in Topa."

The next day they probed, poked, sampled and X-rayed me and stood me in front of a fluoroscope. Then Dr Feinstein, a woman doctor who had fled Austria when the Germans arrived, stood beside my bed.

"I see you had dysentery for a long time. Have you had any attacks lately?"

"No. Just the odd day but nothing like I had before."

"Your liver is almost twice its normal size and, although I'm waiting for the results of one test, you have an advanced case of amoebic hepatitis with multiple abscesses in your liver. Some of the abscesses have formed adhesions to the diaphragm, so that each time you breathe or your heart beats it stretches the adhesion. That is what is giving you the pain."

"Have I had amoebic dysentery? They could never find any amoeba in my stool samples."

"That happens some times. We are reluctant to use the emetin treatment unless we find amoeba."

"What happens now?"

"You'll have daily injections of emetin for at least ten days. You'll have to stay in bed and be quiet. You'll gradually improve and I hope we can get that liver back to its right size. Now just relax and take it easy. I'll see you tomorrow."

For the first few days I wasn't interested in what was happening around me. As long as I lay still the pain wasn't too bad. A young army doctor and one of the two English nurses made the rounds each morning, and I got a jab in the arm with a dull needle every day.

I have a hazy memory of the third night. At first it seemed unreal, like a bad dream. I awoke and heard loud voices in the far corner of the ward. I didn't realize they were having a party until the orderly brought in another large enamel jug full of beer. They were gathered around Ben's bed. He had wrenched his knee when he fell from a horse and was able to get around on crutches. I finally asked them to calm down. They did for a short while and went to bed when they ran out of beer.

After a week of treatment I began to feel better and take notice of my surroundings. There were ten beds in the ward, five on each side with the entrance at one end and the ever-present fireplace at the other. There were two Canadians with infantile paralysis. I never did get to know them before they were taken to another hospital.

In the bed next to me was an Indian officer who kept to himself blew his nose on the bed sheets and enjoyed visits from his two wives. During their visits they drew the curtains around his bed and sat in silence. I caught sight of them one day on either side of his bed, their hands under the covers — and they weren't rubbing his chest.

Across from me, Jock Sutherland, a Scottish captain in the 14th Army, with his forearm, elbow and upper arm in a right-angle cast, lay with the arm suspended from a frame above his bed. Jock Sutherland had more guts and good humour packed into his small body than is decent for one man to have.

Jock had come to Chaklala for parachute training. In a hangar they winched the trainees up to the roof of the hangar and let them down gradually so they would learn how to land when they hit the ground. Jock was at the hangar roof when the pin holding the pulley broke and he fell thirty feet to the concrete floor. He landed on his right elbow, shattering it and driving splintered bones through his forearm and his upper arm. He had had two operations to repair his arm before I arrived and had one more while I was there. I spent fifty-five days in that ward and never once did I hear Jock complain. He was still there when I left. After the war we corresponded for a while, and he told me they did get his elbow back to eighty percent of normal. He wanted to come to Canada, but the last I heard he had his old job as an engineer, had married and settled down to life in Scotland.

They kept me in bed for a month. It was a lonely time, without any mail and without any visitors. The pain was gone and I started to put on some weight. I awoke one afternoon to see Terry Nugent standing beside my bed. Was I glad to see him! We were both Air Observers and had been with 149 Squadron from its beginning.

"Saskie, what the hell are you doing in here? You look like you're ready for the box."

"Nug, it's great to see you. What are you doing in this God-forsaken country?"

"That son-of-bitch Wingco Fenter Douglas tried to court martial Burns and me for the shambles we made of the sergeants' mess in Terrace, so we missed the draft you guys were on. We've been a couple of months behind you. We were supposed to go to 435, but now they're sending us to a bloody RAF squadron."

"You'll love that!"

"Oh, rathah! Saskie, do you like peanuts?"

"I love them. Is that what's in that bag? I thought I could smell them."

Every time I shell a peanut I think of Terry Nugent and the lonely void he filled in both my appetite and my heart.

My diary says it was February the first when Dr. Feinstein stopped by my bed. She took my hand, felt my pulse and, in her charming beside manner, this lovely women held my hand and said, "Wagner, our emetin treatment has got rid of your amoebic hepatitis but your liver is still enlarged. I'm recommending that you be sent back to Canada or at least to England. Once you get away from this climate, your liver will likely recover. We don't want to risk another infection."

"How soon will I get out of here?"

"You can get up today, but take it easy. You'll have to have a medical board authorize your return to England. I'll order that today and you should be on your way in a month."

The orderly found my uniform and I got up that afternoon. I was a little woozy, but in a few days I was an up-patient and had to make my bed and help around the ward. You had to be careful not to do anything that was assigned to the Indian staff.

I had been in bed for a month and had watched the sweeper clean the floor. He wore tattered clothes and a sloppily wound turban that matched his unkempt matted beard. In a large bucket he carried a bundle of rags that matched his clothes. A long rope was tied to the bundle, and he would stand in the middle of the ward, flinging this dampened mop across the floor. He could throw it under the beds and make a pass at the corners. He repeated this routine day after day, but he never rinsed or cleaned the rags and never reached the corners. It was all I could do to contain myself, especially after my training as a nursing orderly from the Nursing Sister with her white gloves. I wanted to dig the dirt out of those corners.

By mid-February I was taking my meals in the hospital mess and had managed to get to Pindi for a steak at Sam's. Sitting in the warm sun one afternoon I looked out to see Joe Ballentyne with my kit bag by his side.

"Hi, Saskie, I moved in to your quarters when you left Topa. I packed all your things into your kit bag. I meant to bring your stuff down long ago."

"Thanks, Joe. Damn good of you. How is everything in Topa?"

"Much the same. Everybody from 435 and 436 has gone to Burma. You're looking well, Saskie, for a guy whose supposed to be dead."

"Dead!"

"Yeah. Doc Witherhead said, Wagner will never get out of BMH. That man has no will to live. We'll likely have to ship his stuff back to Canada."

"That son-of-bitch! Him and his goddamn powders! They should ship him back to Blighty before he kills someone."

"Take it easy, Saskie."

"I'm sorry, Joe, couldn't help it. But I'm on my way home. Supposed to go to Bombay about the end of February. Thanks for looking after my gear."

"You're welcome old man. Have a good trip home. Wish I was going with you."

I have often wondered how close Dr. Witherhead had come to killing me. We had been prepared for the elephants and the tigers, cobras and the fakirs and for the Japanese in Burma, but nobody had warned us about the naturopaths.

I had gained a few pounds and felt better each day. I spent my time sunbathing, visiting the bazaars, taking tea and cucumber sandwiches at Flashman's and steaks at Sam's. But I didn't get any mail.

Then in early February I got a cablegram, one of those standard messages that have a number, and to save time the number is cabled. It read "Baby girl. Both well." That's all it said! It wasn't till I got back to London in April that I learned our new girl's name was Shirley, and that she had been born on the 27th of January.

I did get a letter from our pilot, Smitty, at the Imphal valley base. "Gus Reid has taken your place as the crew's navigator," he wrote. "Some parcels of cigarettes and some mail have come for you. I distributed the smokes amongst the crew and forwarded your mail." The mail never did arrive. I found it two months later in the post office in London.

Smitty's letter also said that Whitey Holton was missing. You never get used to news like that. Whitey was a special sort of a guy. Handsome, with his almost white blonde hair and deep blue eyes. Cheerful, in a quiet way. Ready to help or lend a sympathetic ear to people's troubles while keeping his own to himself. He and Nugent had trained and joined 149 together, so I had to tell Terry.

I biked out to Chaklala and found Nugent's tent. Leave it to the English — they had tents with fireplaces! The February nights got cold, fire wood was hard to find, and there were no pine cones. But somewhere Nugent and his tent-mates Burns and Webb had found some old ten-foot-long telephone poles. They didn't have an axe or saw to cut them, so they would get the fire going and then keep pushing the logs into the fireplace as they burned.

I arrived at noon. The tent looked like a smoke house. When I opened the tent flap smoke billowed out. Three poles, tucked under the tent flaps, lay across the floor, their smouldering ends a couple of feet from the hearth. *These guys could kill themselves with this smoke. They might be dead already,* I thought. But Burns and Webb were snoring and Nugent's eye blinked. On a gimpy card table sat a "morning after" array of an empty Canadian Club bottle, three glasses, a jug of water, two empty cans of pork and beans and one of Spam.

"Wakey, wakey," I called in my best limey imitation.

"Oh, bugger off!"

"Come on, Nug. Wake up and get the hell out of this smoke house before you choke to death."

They had been flying all night, so they had the day off, but I got them up. "I had letter from Smitty this morning."

"How are things in Imphal?" Nugent asked.

"Whitey Holton bought himself a bill of goods. The plane is missing. Why the hell do all the good types go? Poor Whitey, I wonder if he ever got things patched up with his wife? Remember at Terrace how depressed he was? He had gone home on an unexpected leave and caught his wife in bed with some guy. His wife believed she was in love with this yokel. Whitey couldn't understand that, but he was prepared to forgive her."

We put the fire out and the four of us cycled into Pindi to have a steak at Sam's. We lifted our glasses. "Whitey," we said and sat silently, each with his own memories and wondering: wondering why him and not me, wondering what this bloody war was all about, wondering what there was to save in India, wondering if we would make it home and wondering if our wives were sleeping with someone else. F—- the goddamn war.

The Saddar Bazaar was within easy walking distance of the hospital and now that I was stronger I went shopping for small gifts to take home. I knew Jewish merchants believe it is bad luck if you don't make a sale to the day's first customer, and I discovered Indian shopkeepers had the same superstition. As soon as the M/O had made his morning rounds I would head for the bazaar. I enjoyed bargaining with the shopkeepers.

One day Red Finlay and I were wandering through the bazaar, "Isn't that a new shop, Saskie?" asked Red.

"Yeah. It is."

"Let's have a boo. I need a new suitcase. All my stuff got shipped to Imphal."

While he looked for a bag, I spotted a silver ring with a skull and cross bones on it. The young girl behind the counter couldn't have been more than ten years old.

"How much for the ring?" I asked. I didn't intend to buy the ring, but she was a cute little girl and I had to wait for Red.

"One moment, Sahib. I will ask my father."

She was back in a minute with a smile enhancing the twinkle in her black eyes and the gloss of her coal-black braids. "The ring is fifteen rupees, Sahib. But because this is the first day he has opened his new shop, the ring for you will be ten rupees, Sahib."

"Nay nay, five rupees."

"I will ask my father." She returned. "He says nine rupees, Sahib. It is nice ring for you, Sahib. All sterling silver, Sahib."

"Nay, five rupees." I didn't want the ring but I was enjoying the game. We bartered back and forth until Red was ready to go. By that time the price had dropped to six rupees.

"Nay, little memsahib. Only five rupees." I turned and followed Red out to the street.

We hadn't gone a dozen steps when she grabbed my tunic and cried, "Sahib, my father says five rupees will be okay. Please come back, Sahib. It is the first time I sell anything in my father's store. It will be bad luck for me if Sahib does not buy the ring. Please, Sahib." Tears glistened in her big black eyes.

I bought the ring and still wear it.

One morning I thought I saw Melanie in a jewellery store — a tall, slim black girl with the red piece of wool bobbing on the top of her head. I hadn't seen her for nearly six months. It must be her, because there weren't many black women in Rawalpidi. My heart beat a little faster as I entered the store; it might be Melanie.

But she had disappeared. She must have gone through the back door into the storeroom. I browsed around the shop hoping she would reappear.

"Good morning, Sahib. Sahib is interested in a beautiful ring, maybe?"

"Not really. Does a girl called Melanie work here?"

"No, Sahib, no girls work in my store."

"I saw a girl go into the back of your shop. I thought I recognized her."

"Sorry Sahib. No girls here. Would Sahib like to see nice star sapphire ring? I have for you today a good price."

"She is a black girl—looks like a Negro, her last name is Gilchrist."

"Very sorry, Sahib. Look Sahib, beautiful star in blue sapphire. The ring is pure platinum, Sahib."

"Thank you. Not today."

I called back to the store several times that day and on the following days, but no Melanie. I'd have to wait till Friday and go to the dance.

Em Taylor and I had finished a great steak at Sam's, "Em, have you ever been to the dances at the Telegraph Club?"

"No, but I've heard about them."

"Would you like to go? It's not far from here. I met a black girl there and I'd like to see her again."

"I'm not much for dances, but I'll tag along."

The tropical lack of twilight had inked the sky, an orange full moon peeped over the tree tops, and the mauve perfume of lilacs danced on the balmy evening breeze. The strains of *In The Mood* drifting through the calm summer night, stirred my soul. **Melanie had to be there.**

I spotted her at once. She looked more beautiful than I remembered. She wore a pink sleeveless dress, with a full frilly skirt, pink pumps to match and her hair pulled to the top and tied with a small pink bow. We danced, dance after dance, enjoying the rhythm of "big band" jazz.

"It's wonderful to see you again. It's almost five months since we last danced," I said.

"It has been a long time. I always hoped I would see you again.

Are you still at Chaklala?"

"I'm at the British Military Hospital here in Rawalpindi. I thought I saw you in a jewellery store in the Saddar Bazaar on Tuesday."

"You did, and I saw you."

"Why didn't you come out? The owner said there was nobody else in the shop."

"He's my uncle. I keep his books but he won't let me work in the store."

"Why did he say you weren't there?"

"It's a long story and I don't want to think about it. Let's just dance."

After each dance she joined the girls at the front of the hall while I moved to the back with the men. Once during a pause in the music we stopped near her parents and she led me over to say hello.

"Mother and Dad, you remember Gordon Wagner."

"Indeed we do."

"Good evening Mr. and Mrs. Gilchrist. Nice to see you again."

"What brings you to Rawalpindi? I heard your squadron had gone to Imphal."

"I've had a long stay in hospital, but I'm fine now. It is a pleasure to dance with your lovely daughter."

"I'm certain the pleasure is mutual. Would you care to join us for tea after the dance, Mr. Wagner?"

"Thank you, Mrs. Gilchrist, I'll have to check with my friend."

The band started and I led Melanie onto the floor and finished the dance.

"You've got quite a crush on that black girl, Saskie. You make quite a couple," said Em.

"Switzer, Red Meyers and I were here just before I got the jaundice. She's a great dancer! You've been dancing with that good-looking Eurasian girl a lot. The home waltz is coming up but you won't be able to take her home unless you go with her parents,"

I warned.

The tenor saxophone led the band into Wayne King's *Home Waltz*. The lights dimmed as we lost ourselves to the music and to each other. She raised her face to mine and with her eyes and her soft sensuous voice asked, "Gordon, will come home with us for tea?"

I would have enjoyed having tea with her family. But during our four days at the Bristol in Karachi we had watched an American soldier court an Indian girl. She and her mother were staying at the Bristol. Each evening the GI would arrive at tea time. They had tea on the veranda, dinner in the dining room and spend the evening sitting in a cozy threesome just outside our window.

I didn't want to get involved with Melanie's family. **I wanted to see Melanie alone!**

"Thanks, Melanie, but not tonight. But I do want to see you and see you soon. Can I take you to Flashman's for lunch or perhaps for afternoon tea?"

"I wouldn't be welcome in Flashman's. I'm black. Remember? I'd love to have lunch or tea with you, but it won't be easy."

"I'm going back to Canada soon. I want to see you before I leave."

"Do you know where Gaye's Cafe is? I'll be there at two-thirty Tuesday afternoon. If anything happens that I can't make it I'll send you a telegram," Melanie said.

"I know Gaye's. I'll be there."

We surrendered ourselves to the dance and became one as I held her in my arms and felt her firm breasts against me, the little pink ribbon tickling my nose. I gave her one last whirl as the waltz faded. While the band played "The King" we held hands and felt the vibrations flow between us.

I waited impatiently till Tuesday, wondering about this ebony girl and how she fitted in mystic India, about her Indian parents and the over-protective uncle. Did I really want to know?

The morning passed without the telegram. I arrived early enough to get a table in a quiet corner on the cafe's patio that overlooked a rose garden. She came gracefully and regally through the garden, walking towards me.

She wore the white eyelet dress she had worn the night I met her. "Hello, Melanie, you look stunning! I always think of you in white. But today you have a white ribbon in your hair. I like it."

"I wore it especially for you."

I took both her hands. They were warm and soft and I wanted to take her in my arms, but I kissed her hands and we settled in the high-backed wicker chairs and ordered cucumber sandwiches and tea.

"I'm ever so happy to see you again, Gordon. You look like you've lost some weight. Can you tell me where you've been or is that a military secret?"

I told her about my sickness, that I was on my way back to Canada and that I would be leaving Rawalpindi in a few days. "Tell me about yourself. What is a black girl doing in Rawalpindi? Are the people you live with your real mother and father?"

"No, they are my guardians, though I think of them as my mother and father. They had a prosperous business in East Africa and were good friends of my real father. But when I was two years old my parents were killed in a terrible rebellion. All the Indians had to flee the country. Somehow I escaped the massacre and my guardians brought me to India and gave me a home."

"Do you find it difficult being black in India?"

"It's never easy being black. You Canadians should know."

"Don't mistake us for Americans. But we do have our prejudices. Why is your family so protective? I can understand your parents being concerned, but why would your uncle be so difficult?"

"Apparently I am the key, a sort of hostage, to the business and monies that belonged to both my real and my adopted parents. They believe that if some day peace is restored to my country and if I'm my family's only survivor I will inherit whatever is left of the family fortune. I may even be a princess. The family is worried something might happen to me. My uncle thought you might be an undercover agent. They watch me closely.

"But that is enough about me. Tell me about Canada. Do you live near the Rockies or Banff?"

Our tea-time passed quickly. "I must go," she said. "They will wonder where I am. So you might go before Friday? I'll be at the dance and hope you'll be there. This has been a delightful afternoon, Gordon. Thanks so much. I'll remember it forever!"

"So will I, Melanie. You're a beautiful and wonderful woman!"

We stood, I took both her hands. She leaned forward and quickly kissed my lips. Then, plucking the white ribbon from her hair and laying it on the table, she turned and walked sedately through the rose garden and out of my life. The white ribbon marks the 20th of April, 1944, in my diary. Friday evening I caught the Bombay Express.

We seldom realize how much just being with people really means. I had not looked at photos I have for years and now all those memories of my days at Rawalpindi's BMH came back to haunt me. Bill Wilkes and his crew of Art Kilgour, Em Taylor and Red Finlay, Jock Sutherland, Cowboy Ben and Nursing Sister Brown had lived together for two months. One thing both Jimmy Shaw and the service had taught me was to be tolerant and enjoy the people you have to live with. When you say goodbye you realize how much they have been part of you and helped in your recovery.

I had my belongings packed, ready to catch the Bombay Express, and only a few minutes left to say good bye. I had seen Nursing Sister Brown almost every day but never had a real talk with her. Just knowing you would see a lovely women once a day meant a lot in our world of men. She was alone in her office writing reports. "I want to thank you for all the tender loving care you've given me. I'm going to miss your cheery smile."

"We'll miss you, Gordon. I hope things go well with you, and that you get that liver down to size."

"Could I have your address? I'd like to send you something when I get back to Canada. Would you like some nylons?"

"That's very thoughtful. I'd rather have lipstick. I haven't had any for over a year. Some Revlon's Misty Rose would be nice, but it doesn't matter as long as it's lipstick and it's red."

"I didn't realize lipstick was so hard to get."

"They say Madame Chiang Kai-Shek had a plane-full flown over the Hump; that's why there is none here."

She stood and walked around her desk, handed me a note with her address on it then reached up and kissed my cheek. "Goodbye, Gordon, good luck and God bless!"

We held a farewell tea around Jock Sutherland's bed, for he had had another operation on his elbow and his arm was in suspension again. "Goodbye, you no-good Scotsman. Take care of yourself. It's been great to know you, and I hope it's not too long before you're catching the Bombay Express."

"Goodbye Saskie, I'm going to miss you. Remember if you ever get up to Edinburgh, be sure to look up my folks. They'll be happy to see you."

I shook his left hand and he grinned and blinked back a tear and I had to sniffle mine. "I'll write you from London."

"Say hello to the girls on Piccadilly. Bon voyage, man!"

I was on my way home. When you "go to war" you know it could be a one-way trip. You go where they send you; you don't have any choice. So a devil-may-care attitude prevails and impatience to get the most out of life because you may not pass this way again.

I had turned the corner. I was headed home. I would leave some good friends behind, most of whom I hoped to see again. Others, their images carved in vivid memories, would never age.

Lorne Taylor. With a belly full of beer, on a midnight flight over Lethbridge's bombing range, dropping practice bombs into the pickle

Right to left standing, Red Finley, unknown, unknown, Nursing sister Brown, Em Taylor, Cowboy Ben, sitting, Art Kilgour, Bill Wilkes, and the author.

Lorne Taylor

and young son were our Brentwood neighbours.

And Whitey Holton. Rotting in the Burmese jungle.

How the hell did I get into this bloody war? Did I really have a choice? Wouldn't I have done more to win this cufuffle if I stayed underground and worked for Inco? Our politicians can always find the resources to fight a war. Why couldn't they look after us in the hungry thirties? We got the wrong people on the battlefields. That's where the generals, the armament

barrel from 5000 feet ... then buying "a bill-of-goods" on his first trip over Germany.

Paul Soder. Tall, gangly, redheaded. Coaxing boogie-woogie from the canteen piano at Edmonton's Air Observers' School. Waiting to return to Canada after flying sixty missions. Volunteering to do one more ... His mother lost three sons, one in the Army, one in the Navy, and then Paul.

Kenny Sage. Tall, quiet, efficient. A born fighter pilot, so sure of himself in the Hurricanes at Pat Bay. Shot down in his Typhoon on D-Day. He and his wife

Paul Soder on left.

manufacturers, the bankers and some of the preachers should be. Maybe they could decide what side God was on. Well, I' ve survived despite Dr. Witherhead, my macho ego, wiggling microscopic amoeba, the bugs of jaundice and carbuncle holes in my neck. I' m on my way home. Hurrah for me. I may get through this show after all.

My train was to leave Rawalpindi at seven pm. At the station a porter unloaded my tin steamer-trunk, a stuffed kit bag and large suitcase before I could get out of the tonga. "I will take Sahib's luggage and find nice compartment for Sahib," he grinned, showing teeth stained red from betel nuts.

"You can't carry all that luggage."

"Yes, Sahib, I carry."

He balanced the trunk on his turbaned head then knelt down while another porter put the kit bag and suitcase on top of the trunk. *He' ll never stand up and if he does the kit bag will fall off.*

But he did and it didn't, and he led me up the stairs to an over-the-track bridge to my train on another platform.

He put my bags aboard and I handed him a rupee — five times the usual tip but I had enjoyed the show.

"Thank you, Sahib, Canada give good baksheesh."

The British had brought their railway system to India. Trains ran on time. But the Bombay Express featured none of the amenities of the Orient Express. With military privilege I shared a luggage-jammed compartment with an English captain. Teeming hordes of people piled into the coaches. Children sat on their parents' knees. People sat on people. People packed the aisles. Bodies were packed in layers like sardines. As the train began to move non-paying people climbed on the roofs. Others stood on the narrow ledge skirting the bottom of the coach, linking their arms around the posts of the open window. As the train rounded a curve, I could see people plastered on the roof and sides from the engine to the last coach.

A man in a bright blue coat, with a small child in his arms, rushed towards the moving train. He pushed the child through the open window into the arms of a woman. As the train gained speed, he ran alongside, trying to grab the window frame. He jumped. Got his hands on the window, but his feet dragged along the ground. If he let go he'd be under the wheels. He finally got one foot on the ledge, pulled himself up, hooked his arm around the window post and reached through the open window to calm his child. *I wonder how far they were going ...*

I turned to see who my travelling companion was and introduced myself to an English captain. "I'm Gordon Wagner. Going to Bombay."

"Charles Smitheringale. I'll be with you as far as Delhi."

"This is my first train trip in India," I said. "I brought my blankets, but where do we sleep?"

"You curl up on your wooden bench and I'll use the one on this side. You have to raise that trap door to use the honey bucket."

"What do we do for meals?"

"You can buy tea and cakes at any stop. If you want a meal you order it at one station. Your order's telegraphed ahead and you get your food at the next stop. You'll have plenty of time to eat before you get to another station where they pick up the dirty dishes! Works well and the food is rather good."

The short tropical twilight gave way to a moonless night. The brightness of a single light in the ceiling of our compartment varied with the speed of the train, making reading difficult, so we went to bed early. I spread my blankets over the slatted seat, and rolled my tunic around my boots for a pillow and crawled in. I slept well. Once I thought I heard the door open but decided I was dreaming and went back to sleep.

I woke briefly as dawn highlighted the windows. *Was that a noise by the door? Must have been outside.* I rolled over and went back to sleep.

"What the hell are you doing in here, you bloody wog?" Smitheringale's loud yell jarred me awake.

He towered over an Indian huddled against the door, threatening him with his swagger stick. "Open that door and get the hell out here."

"Please no, Sahib. Please wait until train stops. I die if you push me from fast train!"

I spoke quickly. "I heard him come in during the night, John. Let him be. He hasn't done any harm, and jumping from a moving train could kill him."

"What's one wog more or less? We should turn him over to the police."

"Please no, Sahib. See, I have chittie from British officer," and he handed Smitheringale a carefully wrapped letter.

"Well I'll be damned!" exclaimed the captain. "I know your master. He was with our outfit in Rawalpindi. You can stay on till the next stop."

When we pulled into a station we let our man off. The train was still covered with people. On the side of the train away from the platform people squatted to relieve themselves in the open-air privy. I looked for the man in the bright blue coat. He was still hooked to the window post.

We ordered breakfast, and it was served an hour later in Lahore. All day we rolled through the Indian countryside, arriving in Delhi for supper. Smitheringale left, but the man in the blue coat hung on. He was still there as the Bombay Express clickity-clacked over the rails into another moonless night.

The next morning we were in a bleak, desert-like countryside. The blue-coated man was gone and so were most of the outdoor passengers.

All day we travelled through desolate plains. I found it difficult to believe that this great emptiness could exist in a country of four-hundred million people. But Indian's population lives near her great rivers. Today, India has more than eight- hundred million people cramped around her rivers. The plains remain desolate.

Next morning we arrived in Bombay and were taken to an embarkation depot called Worli to wait our turn for a ship bound for Blighty. Worli was one the holding-areas that the Air Force used to cramp as many bodies as possible into the smallest space possible. You lived with rumours about when the next ship would sail, killing time as best you could.

We slept under mosquito nets on rope charpoys jammed side by side. The rope beds were full of bedbugs. You had to get your charpoy out into the sun every day to control the blood-sucking little buggers. I missed a couple of days. One morning, just as the light of dawn crept into the barracks, half a dozen blood-filled sandy-coloured bugs struggled up the mosquito netting. I got four confirmed and one probable before they found refuge in the upper seams.

I looked forward to seeing Max Faibish. He had written me from Bombay saying he had seen my records go through their office. I had his Bombay address.

I had known Max all my life. Played with him as a child. I went through school with him. Worked summers on Billie MacLean's farm with him. We both attended the University of Saskatchewan from '35 to '38. He followed me to the mines in Sudbury, where we roomed together. Unbeknownst to one another, we both joined the Air Force. We were stationed and met in Calgary, Lethbridge and London, he in accounts and I in aircrew.

I phoned Air Force Pay-Accounts, got in touch with Max, and arranged to meet him for dinner. I found his barracks and asked "Do you have a Max Faibish here?"

"Yah, he's in the shower I think. Hey Faibish, there's someone here to see you."

"Send him down to my room. I'll be right there."

He had a white towel wrapped around his middle. His wet mop of coal-black hair almost hid his squinting eyes.

"Hello, Max, it's Gordon Wagner."

"Hi, Gordon. It will be great to see you again as soon as I find those damn glasses. I'm almost blind without them. Ah, here they are. So you're on your way home. Wish I was."

"Wonderful to see you, Max. Rumour has it that we are to sail on the 12th of March. How long have you been in Bombay?"

"Nearly a year now. I hate the bloody place. I wear civvies in the evening. I detest uniforms."

"I see there's a new scar on the sleeve of your uniform."

"Oh yes. I lost my temper and told the C/O off and he knocked me down from sergeant to corporal. But that's not new. There is a restaurant nearby that serves great steaks, and if we're lucky we might get a quart of Australian beer."

"Sounds great."

"I have a friend who will join us. He is in the barracks across the way. Let's go."

We picked up George, Max's friend and found the restaurant. We ordered steaks and the waiter found us a quart bottle of Australian beer. We had to pay ten rupees, but we enjoyed the nippy ale. At three dollars and thirty cents a quart, you had to. The food was good, especially the steaks. There was no more beer so we sat supping Canadian rye and reminiscing.

"You'll have to excuse me, fellows," said George, "I'm supposed to be the fourth at bridge. I'll be seeing you tomorrow, Max. Goodbye Gordon, it's nice to meet you. You'll be around for awhile. We'll see you again."

"Probably not," I replied, "I want to be on the next troop ship out of here. It's been a pleasure to know you."

He started to leave but turned at the door and said, "Don't you think it is great how we Jews stick together?" and headed for the exit.

"That's a new one, Max. Remember the time we played in a baseball tournament on the Moscowpetin Indian reserve? In the gathering dark we got lost and I stopped to get directions from some Indians. They told me how to get off the reserve and then asked me what Indian reserve I was from. Another time in Sudbury's Little Italy, I was taken for an Italian. One afternoon while I was waiting for a bus in downtown Calgary a little old lady said my curly black hair reminded her of a spaniel. But that's the first time I have ever been taken for a Jew."

"George is right though, we do stick together. That is how we survived. I've met a few Jewish families here in Bombay. I've been asked to spend Sunday at a Jewish home. How would you like to come with me? The Levroys will make you feel right at home and they have a great cook. Levroy is Max Factor's representative for the Far East. They got out of Singapore just ahead of the Japanese."

"I'd enjoy that. He should be able to tell me where I can get some lipstick. I promised I'd send some to the nurses who looked after me in Pindi."

"Let's have another rye. I think there's a dance hall not too far away. You get awfully lonely for women in this country."

We finished our drinks and found ourselves a tonga. "Take us to a dance hall, driver."

"Sorry, Sahib, but dance hall only for Indian people".

"Never mind. Just take us," said Max.

"Maybe Sahibs like some jiggy jig?"

"Never mind the jiggy jig. Just take us to the dance hall."

We found the dance hall, and sounds of Sammy Kay's "Swing and Sway" seeped through warm evening air. But they wouldn't let us in.

"Climb aboard and I'll have the driver take us to the red light district. You have to see it to believe it."

We travelled up a winding road. It got narrower, steeper and darker. On both sides of the street, narrow, single-storied buildings pushed each other for elbow room. Squeezed between the walls heavy iron-barred doors, padlocked from the inside with stout chains, barred the entrances. Hard by the doors five-by-five foot windows, glassless and also heavily barred, stared like black pupil-less eyes into the narrow street. The moon, high above the horizon, half-waned and haloed by a veil of high clouds, cast a ghostly glow off the white-washed walls.

"Come on, Gordon, let's get out and walk along the street."

"Looks too damn spooky for me, Max. But let's have a boo."

We followed our weak shadows along the eerie street. The first door and window shouted black silence. From the next barred window we heard movement and caught, in the reflection of diluted moonlight, a bearded face pushed against the bars as a voice grated. "Sahib, I have nice young girl for jiggy jig. For you, Sahib, tonight only ten rupees. The door is unlock, Sahib. Come in, come in. Have good time tonight."

His head turned as we walked by. The dull light reflected the white of his eyes and bounced moonbeams off his gold teeth when he smiled.

Further along the sound of struggling bodies slipped with a sultry silence from the black void as the groans and moans of ecstasy aroused the male in us.

"Let's get the hell out of here, Max, before I have an accident."

Two doors down a sexy voice called from the black shadows. "Your attention for one moment, Sahib. Let me show Sahib what waits behind the curtain." A rustling sound and soft light slowly undressed the darkness, revealing a woman caressing her half-clad body with the suggestive moves of coitus.

"I am getting on the tonga, Max. Tonga! Tonga!" I called. "You'd better climb aboard. The next thing you know you'll be ten rupees poorer and lord knows what else you'll have."

"Don't worry, Gordon, I'd never get drunk enough to go in one of those hell-holes. I wanted you to see it. Driver, do you know where "Ruby's" is on Spencer Street?"

"Oh yes, Sahib, I know Ruby's place. Much better place for Sahib. Jiggy jig no good here for Sahib. Maybe get sick here. No good for Sahib. Ruby's place good. Nice and clean, Ruby been many years on Spencer Street." He slashed his whip across the skinny horse's angular rump and we took off at a brisk pace for Ruby's.

I can still see that red-carpeted, green-walled stairway that led to the scarlet door with its yellow rimmed peek-hole. Single-eye let us in, and the big Chinese bouncer showed us into Ruby's parlour. I can still smell the poignant mixture of tobacco smoke, cheap perfume and lysol. I can still feel the pudgy hand offered by the bejewelled, bulging, well-stacked, deep-cleaved, mascara-eyed, peroxide blonde. I can still hear the whiskey rasp of the mannish voice saying, "Welcome to Ruby's, Canada. All my girls are busy right now. Make yourself at home. Would you like a drink? I have some Canadian Club."

"I'd enjoy some with water. Easy on the water and no ice," said Max.

"Make it two," I echoed.

The good-sized room was divided by back to back chesterfields. Bright lights shone off white walls. Red and blue easy-chairs rested against three of the walls and brightly-painted straight backed chairs lined the other. The line of chairs was divided by a green curtain.

Max and I sat in a love seat across from the green curtain. Two slightly rotund Chinese businessmen, dressed in immaculate white, talked in a mixture of Chinese and English. A pair of American soldiers, their chests covered with ribbons, nursed coke bottles. A coloured soldier, wearing the patches of South Africa, took long drags on a cigarette, shifting uncomfortably from foot to foot. A husky, square-built Malaysian, dressed in the uniform of the French Navy, stood almost at attention, glaring at the green curtain.

Ruby brought our drinks. Then the green curtain parted and five girls entered the room. They were an assortment of Eurasian girls and were dressed in loose-fitting but revealing gowns. The Chinese business men wasted no time. They took the closest two girls and disappeared behind the green curtain. The sailor almost saluted as he stood in front of a girl with Chinese features. He took her hand, bowed once, and she led him through the green curtain. The American offered to buy two girls a drink. They declined, saying they weren't allowed to drink during working hours. With half-finished cokes, they were swallowed by the hungry green curtain. We watched the South African hesitate, then make a dash for the curtain. He grabbed a girl on the way, and pushed her through the green curtain.

Men emerged from the curtain and left. But a small, dissipated, well-dressed Chinese man settled into an easy chair. In a short while three girls emerged from the curtain. The dapper Chinese man wasted no time. He took the nearest girl and headed through the curtain for a second time.

"That guy must be some relation to Peter Rabbit. I wouldn't be surprised if it was his third," said Max. "I kinda like that girl with her hair tied in a pony tail." He finished his drink and led Pony-tail through the green curtain.

I sipped on my rye and water watching the rather plain looking girl that was left. "What the matter, Canada? Looks like you're hanging at half-past-six. Why don't you let me get it up to twelve o'clock."

"I don't think you could do anything about it. Besides I've been in hospital for almost six months. I'm on my way home to my wife and family and I don't need anything you have. Be it good or bad."

She sat down beside me and tried to arouse me, but I stayed at half-past six. When Max came back I walked down those red-carpeted green-walled stairs as pure as I had come up.

"How would you like to go to the races on Saturday, Gordon? I go every week. The track is a little ways past Worli."

"Sure. Why not?"

"I'll come to your quarters at Worli and catch a bus from there."

"Sounds good."

"I'll be there about noon. Good night, Gordon."

"Goodnight, Max. See you on Saturday."

Max came to my Worli quarters about noon on Saturday and we caught a trolley to take to the race track. We had been on the trolley for about half an hour when Max said, "See those vultures circling over that low hill? That's where the Parsees burial ground is."

"The hill over to the right with towers that look like the frame work of windmills?"

"Right. The Parsees believe that flesh pollutes the sacred elements, and will neither burn, bury nor cast their dead into the sea. They put their dead on those towers and the bodies are eaten by vultures and the bones drop into pits below."

"Sounds gruesome. Can't fancy myself being pulled to pieces by a vulture. The airport must be near here."

"Yes, it's about a mile north of the burial hill."

"I remember our pilots talking about the vulture warning in the Bombay Airport's landing procedure."

"The Parsees are amongst the wealthiest people in India. They dominate international trade in the city, are well-educated and politically active. The practice of using vultures to dispose of their dead is both economical and sanitary. The Hindus burn their corpses. It sends a horrible odour of burning flesh into India's calm air. It takes a lot of wood for cremation. Wood is expensive and also in short supply."

"Here is the race track. They have another efficient way of stripping. They don't use vultures."

The Bombay racetrack crawled with crowded humanity. Because of the caste system, the spectator's areas were divided into three compounds, each surrounded by high wire fences. Two of the areas had grandstands. The smaller and more posh, with fancy boxes, were for the Brahmins and the uppity-up British. The other was for Indian tradesmen and people like Max and me, although as an officer of His Majesty's Armed Forces I could have sat with the brass.

The third area was for the "depressed class" — the workers. The mehtar (the sweeper), the dohbi walla (the laundry man), or the pani wallah (the water man) had neither grandstand nor bleachers but milled around in the high-fenced compound like caged animals at a zoo. They had no access to the tote board, for they might get too close to a Brahmin. The untouchables in the "bull pen" could defile a Brahmin from a distance of thirty paces.

The milling mob placed their bets with that wizard of communication and mathematics, the hand-signalling bookie. During the excitement of the race, they crowded against the fence, climbing onto the backs of one another. As the winner crossed the finish line, the howling mass collapsed into a squirming lump of struggling bodies, like fish worms from an overturned can.

My diary tells me I made a few rupees and Max hit one long-shot and insisted on paying for the steak dinner we had at Chef George's.

I managed to find a vacant charpoy for Max and he spent the night with me in the Worli barracks. I looked forward to tomorrow's visit with Max's Jewish friends. I hadn't seen the inside of a house since our disembarkation leave in Scotland when the Red Cross arranged a week-end stay in Sterling with Jock Smith, a retired teacher and his wife.

On Sunday Max took me to the home of Mr. and Mrs. Levroy. They lived in the penthouse of a ten-story apartment adjacent to the sea. Lazy ceiling fans mixed the gentle seabreeze with the Levory's genuine hospitality. The soft hiss of the barefooted-servants on the deep-piled Persian rugs as they served us drinks, lunch and dinner made me forget I was a hemisphere away from home.

"Max tells me you are with Max Factor. I understand you got out of Singapore just before the Japanese captured the city."

"Yes, we were on the last ship to leave. Our best friends were to leave the next day but they never made it. They and their six- year old son are in a detention camp. We get reports through the underground. I'm afraid they are having a rough time."

"I used to read the intelligence reports coming out of the prison camps in Burma. It is difficult to believe that the Japanese are a civilized people. Some of the things they do to prisoners are barbaric."

"The allies have Hitler on the run. The war in Europe won't last much longer and we'll give Hirohito our full attention."

"I wonder if you could help me. I spent two months in the hospital in Rawalpindi. There were only two nursing sisters on staff and when I left I asked what they would like me to send them once I got back to Canada. They chose lipstick over nylons. Is there any place to get lipstick in Bombay?"

"I'm sure we can manage that. Here's my card. Call the office number and ask for Rose. I'll tell her you're going to call. She'll look after you."

"Thank you. Lord knows when I'll get home. The war may be over by then. Tell me something. Pilots flying 'The Hump' claim there was a plane load of cosmetics flown into China for Madam Chiang. I thought they were flying over the Himalayas to help the Chinese war effort. Is that why you can't buy lipstick in India? You can buy Heinz ketchup, peanut butter and Crown Royal whiskey here, but you can't buy them in Canada."

I've heard the same story. I don't know if it's true, but I wouldn't be surprised if it were. I'll speak to Rose in the morning."

We thanked our hosts and on the way home Max told me that he was investigating the possibility of opening an import-export business when he got out of the service. Mr Levroy had indicated that he would help him get started.

Max did just that. But that is another story.

The early March weather in Bombay was ideal. The daytime temperature hovered around the mid-eighties, cooling slightly during the night. We slept with just a towel draped across our naked bellies. As in Karachi if you forgot to put your charpoy out for its daily sun bath, and you woke early enough, you could get a brace of bedbugs before breakfast.

Rumour still had us leaving on the 12th of March, and it was just a week away. One warm afternoon Em Taylor and I visited the Bombay zoo. The animals were enjoying their siesta during the heat of the day like any sensible person would. We bought some cookies to see if we could entice the animals from their dens. We couldn't get the animals to move, but we gathered a crowd of Indian boys begging for the cookies. They completely surrounded us. We couldn't move. Em Taylor, recovering from a broken leg, carried a cane. It was getting scary.

"Give me your cane, Em, I'll scare these young buggers back," I said, taking a mean swing at the jabbering mob.

"Haha, Sahib. Sahib is angry. We are hungry. Give us the cookies, Sahib. Cookies, Sahib!"

"Give them the cookies, Saskie. Let's get the hell out of here. This little mob could get nasty."

I took the package of Peak-Frean's and threw a "forward pass" over their heads. The package landed on the grass. The boys pounced on the cookies. We headed for the exit.

The days were hot, especially in the afternoons. In the mornings we shopped in Worli's nearby bazaar and went swimming in the afternoons at Breach Kandy, where there was a large salt water pool.

I awoke one morning with a pounding headache. I went on sick parade and ended up in Worli's hospital. *Damn it all. I suppose I'll miss the next boat. Maybe I'm not destined to leave this bloody country.*

The next morning I had a temperature of a hundred and four and the M/O sent me to the British Military Hospital at Calaba, a Bombay suburb. I had pneumonia. The first night in BMH, with the Bombay night temperature near eighty, I slept under six blankets.

I received good care at Calaba. They put me on a sulfa drug and in three or four days I was feeling better. When I had entered BMH, the hole my "Muree carbuncle" had left in my neck was still draining. The sulfa finally healed my neck and cured the pneumonia.

I spent ten days in the hospital. Max and Em Taylor came to visit often. I was eating well and feeling better than I had for a long time. One Friday evening Max dropped in.

"I'm going to the races tomorrow, Gordon. Could you let me have a hundred rupees?"

"Sure."

"I've studied the handicaps closely and here's a list of the horses I've picked for the eight races. I'm going to put ten rupees on the nose in each race. Here, I made a copy for you. There's probably a bookie somewhere in the hospital."

"Here's the hundred, Max. Good luck!"

"Thanks, Gordon. See you tomorrow."

When Max had gone the fellow in the bed next to me said, "I know a bookie that comes to the hospital. What do you say we put a fiver on each of his horses?"

We did. Six of Max's horses won. I could just see Max with his pockets full of rupees. We had done well with our bets. I figured Max would be doubling up and make a killing. I'd get my hundred rupees back. Max would be in clover.

Max came to visit on Sunday looking a little sheepish. He had changed his mind when he got to the track. He had failed to place a bet on any of the six winners he had given us. I took pity on his tough luck and lent him twenty more rupees.

In all, I spent twelve days in Calaba's hospital and went back to Worli on Wednesday, the 21st of March, 1945. The troop ship was in the harbour — we would ship out almost any day.

Our movement orders came the next day. I had lunch with Max — Chez George's biggest steak. We visited Mr. Levroy's office, got the nurses' lipstick, and I mailed it. When I got back to Worli our orders were posted — we would sail on Saturday.

We spent Friday packing, and in the evening I dropped by the mess bar and was enjoying a lemonade when a RAF pilot sat on the stool next to me. He ordered a beer.

"Sorry, Sahib, not beer here," said the khidmatgar.

"Make me gin and lime."

"Yes, Sahib. Right away, Sahib. Does Sahib have a bar chitty?"

"No. I just arrived. I'll pay for the drink."

"Where did you come from?" I asked the pilot.

"I just flew in from Canada. I came from Comox. Finished my course four days ago."

"From Comox! My wife lives in Courtenay! She's building a house on the Lake Trail Road. I don't know exactly where the house is, but it's near the railway tracks. A man by the name of Stewart McQuillan is making her kitchen cupboards."

"I know Stewart McQuillan. I used to date one of his sisters. I know the house."

"You do?"

"We used to pass the little cottage almost every day. I think your wife moved in just before Christmas."

"I've been separated from my squadron since October. I don't know what they're doing with my mail. I've only had half a dozen letters in the last six months."

"The McQuillan girl's first name is Eleanor. When I write I'll tell her about meeting you. It's a small world."

"I've been in hospitals or convalescence homes since last October. Just got out of the hospital a couple of days ago. We're shipping out tomorrow. I'll be happy to see the last of India. Do you know where you're going?"

"No. We ferried a DC 3 all the way from Comox. We thought we might get a spot of Ferry Command. But no such luck. We're waiting for a posting to a RAF squadron. But I did enjoy Comox, that's a lovely valley. I'd like to go back there after this show is over."

"I must get to bed. We're on parade at five-thirty tomorrow morning. My name is Gordon Wagner. What is your's?"

"I'm Tom Stoddart."

"Goodnight, Tom. I'll say hello to Eleanor when I get back to Courtenay."

In 1943, when 149 Squadron was posted to Alaska, Ivy had moved to Courtenay to live with her sister, Mae. Things got a little crowded, with two families in Mae's living quarters in the back of the Tsolum Grocery Store, but Ivy couldn't find a place to rent. The RCAF base in Comox had just opened. Every shack, beach cottage and empty room was filled.

But Clarence Field, Ivy's come-by-marriage uncle, had just opened Field Sawmills. His mill was on the Lake Trail Road where Arden Elementary School now stands. Ivy had some money she had been saving to buy a fur coat, but she thought about it and decided she could do without the coat for a while. She started a new project instead. She could get rough-sawn, unplaned lumber from Field's Sawmill.

During the hungry thirties many of the City of Courtenay's empty lots had reverted to the City for delinquent taxes. The City wanted a hundred dollars for a fifty-foot lot. Ivy offered two hundred and eighty dollars for three adjoining lots. The city accepted the offer and the property's boundaries were relocated by Vilhelm Schjelderup, the city's land surveyor.

She needed a permit. But the War Measures Act didn't allow the city to issue building permits for the construction of a new house. So she got a permit to build a garage and turned it into a house. She borrowed five hundred dollars from Fred Pearce of the Pearce Furniture Store in Courtenay.

I had signed over most of my pay to Ivy before I was posted overseas. When I heard Ivy had started to build a house I bought a couple of Victory Bonds with a monthly deduction from my pay leaving my pay at less than sixty dollars a month — about the same as I got when I first enlisted.

In England, at Innsworth, a small village near Gloucester, five thousand pilots, navigators, wireless operators and air gunners waited for postings. Our pay was good, the food wasn't. The barracks were cold even in August. There was a large cabbage patch near our quarters. We snacked on cabbage and fine cheese we scrounged from the mess.

Our mess had a large billiard table. On pay day a continuous crap game lasted from noon to midnight. The crowd at times was layers deep. Junior Nowlan was one of 149's best crap players. One night he came back to barracks with winnings over two thousand dollars. He couldn't send his winnings home, nor could he take more than ten pounds to India.

I watched Junior as he emptied all his pockets and built a pile of those big British pound notes on his bed. "What am I going to do with all this bread?"

"Why don't you buy my Victory Bonds? My wife is trying to build a house. Two thousand bucks would sure help."

"How are you going to get the money back to Canada?"

"I'm going down to London on a forty-eight day after to-morrow, and I'll see what I can do."

In London I picked the first bank I came to. It was "Barclay's Bank," in Barclay's Square, where Vera Lynn's nightingale sang. I soon discovered that I could send only ten pounds home. I asked to see the manager, and I must have told him a good tale about our house, my wife, our kids and my two thousand dollars, because between Barclay's, Thomas Cook and Sons, RCAF Pay and Accounts and Junior Nowlan I got the money sent to Courtenay.

I often wonder if there is someone leading me. Why did I go to that bar, on that night, talk to a stranger, to discover he had seen and knew the location of the "rose-covered-cottage" of my dreams? Courtenay was half-way around the world from Worli. Had I turned the corner? Was I really on my way home?

I had been in the service for nearly five years. I had never really had a home; I had never realized what it was to be a married man. I knew I had a good woman. Not many guys were going back to a wife who had built a home and mothered three children. I liked the Comox Valley. Somebody else could have my old job in Sudbury's nickel mines.

During the long lonely days and nights I spent in the hospitals, I dreamed of the little rose-covered cottage I would come home to. Now, half way around the world, I had met someone who had seen our house. If all went well I would see our rose-covered cottage, Ivy and our three kids.

It was still dark when we climbed into the transport trucks for the trip to the troopship. The grey light of dawn cast a ghostly glow over the streets of downtown Bombay. The grey sky melded with the grey-walled buildings, the grey streets and the sidewalks. The scene was flat. Shadowless. The stench of dung, rancid ghee and sweat, pressed death-like on the flatness.

The truck slowed. The engine backfired, exploding the grey silence. Grey shrouded bumps moved. The movement revealed the camouflage of people sleeping on the sidewalks. The memory of Bombay's street people, huddled under their grey shawls on their concrete beds, still haunts me.

Above, Commanding Officer and Crew. Flt. Lt. Meyers, Wing Cmdr. Harnett, WO. Foley, Flt. Lt. Johnson.

Below, Flt. Lt. Hempsell, Sq. Ldr. Clements, FO. Moore, Flt. Lt. Clarke.

435 Crews - from Cecil Law's "Chinthe"

Above, Flt. Lt. Hempstock, Flt. Lt. Ashburner, FO. Courts and FO. Gill.

Below, Flt. Lt. Alstedter, FO. Weilde, Flt. Lt. Kennedy, FO. Mason.

435 Crews - from Cecil Law's "Chinthe"

Above, Flt. Lt. McKegney, PO. Singleton, WO. Hutchinson, FO. Johannson.

Below, Flt. Lt. Switzer, Flt. Lt. Boyle, FO. Nolan, Flt. Sgt. Karle.

435 Crews - from Cecil Law's "Chinthe"

Above, PO. Barrett, FO. Hanberry, Flt. Lt. Ronalds.

Below, Flt. Sgt. MacNicol, FO. Barker, FO. Fleming, FO. Foster.

435 Crews - from Cecil Law's "Chinthe"

Above, PO. Smith, Sgt. Shaw, Flt. Lt. Reid, WO. McCullough.

Below, FO. McMichael, Flt. Lt. Rosati, Sq. Ldr. Rue, FO. Saunders.

435 Crews - from Cecil Law's "Chinthe"

Above, FO. West, FO. Lonsdale, Flt. Lt. Duncan, FO. Hill.

Below, Flt. Sgt. MacPherson, FO. Walker, FO. Sproat, WO. Jose.

435 Crews - from Cecil Law's "Chinthe"

Homeward Bound

A blood-red sun rose through the murky inversion hovering over the city as we climbed the gangplank to board the P. & O.'s ship, the *Ranchi*. Fourteen of us were assigned to a cabin on the promenade deck. The *Ranchi* had been one of P & O's flag ships, plying the London-India run before she had been converted into a troopship. We had one of the "posh" cabins. The word "posh" is derived from the expression "port side on the way out (to India) and starboard on the way home." A cabin with seven bunk beds (upper and lower), a couple of chairs and an adequate bathroom was to be our home for the next twenty-six days.

We watched a human conveyer belt carry basins of coal from a huge dock-side barge into the bowels of our ships. The harbour sizzled as the noon-day sun hovered a few degrees off our zenith. With the *Ranchi* filled with coal and a good supper under our belts, a couple of angry tugs mugged us into the middle of the harbour.

Heat clung to the ship's metal. The heat in our fourteen-bed stateroom was sleeplessly hot. It was still hot at breakfast. Our ship spent the morning cruising back and forth in the mouth of the harbour, swinging (adjusting) its compass. At thirteen-hundred hours on the 25th day of March, 1945, we watched Bombay and India sink below the horizon. A fresh breeze off the Indian Ocean cooled our cabin flushing the odour of India from my nostrils forever.

Despite the seven double-bunks in our stateroom we were comfortable and soon settled into a leisurely routine. For five days the bow of the *Ranchi* ploughed through the Arabian Sea sending endless furrows of wake across the glassy-calm sea. Flying fish skipped through the waves and schools of porpoise tried to push the ship off course, frolicking the most turbulent wake. A cooling breeze, created by the speed of the ship, kept the heat of the shadowless noonday sun comfortable. We read, sunbathed, played cards, ate well, slept a lot and enjoyed our luxury cruise.

We got to know our bunk-mates. Earl, a tall bear-like, middle-aged Englishman, with a mop of blond, unruly hair became the unofficial leader. He wore bright green pyjamas and we called him the "Green Hornet." He had been an Intelligence Officer and was on his way back to his professorship at Oxford. He had the bunk next to the washroom, was always up early and tied up the bathroom facilities for almost half an hour every day.

George Young, an RCAF navigator, had the lower part of our double-bunk. He was from Toronto and had been a policeman. Across the room I found Tim, an RCAF pilot, who had worked in the Frood mines in Sudbury. He had a couple of thousand dollars in Indian gems. I wondered if they weren't Birmingham glass. There was the Wing Commander (Wingco) who spent all day every day knitting a sweater that looked too big for anyone to wear. In the next bunk, John, a precocious nineteen-year-old RAF pilot proved to be a refreshing challenge.

One afternoon while we were alone in our stateroom the professor said, "Canada must be a wonderful country."

"I'll be glad to get home."

"You know," he said, "you're an officer in the Air Force, with a university degree and you spent a couple of years working in the mines. If you and Tim had been miners in England you'd be there all your lives."

"I never thought about it," I replied. "I grew up in the worst of the depression, worked my way through university and when I graduated the mines were the only place I could get a job."

"If I was younger I'd like to try life in Canada. I never realized how strong our class system is. We think India is bad!"

Six days out we entered the Red Sea. The temperature moderated with cool evenings. Three days later we entered the Bay of Suez and spent the better part of two days riding at anchor in Port Taufig at the southern entrance of the Suez Canal waiting for our turn.

On the evening of the second day we joined a convoy sailing up the canal. In the cool of the desert evening we leaned on the ship's railing recalling some of the history of the canal and how its 101 miles cut 6500 miles off the trip from Bombay to England. A sandy beach on both sides of the 500-foot-wide "ditch" looked inviting. Just as the sun's golden disk sank into the horizon, the *Ranchi* left the "ditch," pointed her bow at sunset and sailed into a lake of gold that forms part of the canal system. The short twilight of the thirty-degree latitude canopied the lake with touchable stars and the desert-chill drove us indoors. In the morning we were anchored in Port Said.

At Port Taufig, and at Port Said, the harbour was dirty. Big turds and garbage floated in the water around the ship. Vendors with their boats loaded with fezes, fly switches, brass ware and knives bargained over the ship's sides. You lowered a rope, the hawker tied the goods on the rope and you pulled it up the sixty feet to the deck and you sent your money back down. Young men and boys swam in the filthy water begging the passengers to throw them money. It didn't seem to matter where the coin landed — one of the divers got it. They'd wave the coin and beg for more. Somebody threw a large English penny and when the diver surfaced he hollered, "Cheap English, son-of-a-bitch!"

In both harbours the ship loaded cargo and a dozen or more civilians came aboard. At Port Said we had four nurses join us. We never did find out where their quarters were but they added glamour and fantasy to our deck and our mess.

We entered the "Oh so Blue!" waters of the Mediterranean Sea that same evening. The air chilled and we changed into our blue uniforms. Three days out of Port Said, we sighted Pantelleria, a small island between Sicily and Tunisia. In the western Mediterranean we sailed through the warm air of a tropical storm. Rough sea reduced the number of people in the mess hall. During the morning of our seventeenth day, a wild storm tossed us into Gibraltar's harbour. We lingered in sight of "The Rock" for three gloomy days forming a convoy to tackle the submarine-infested Atlantic.

On the 13th of April, our 20th day at sea, in choppy seas somewhere off the coast of Portugal we learned that President Roosevelt had died. The heavy lead-grey skies, the angry dark-grey Atlantic, and the murky collection of dirty-grey ships added gloom to the depressing news. It stunned me, like the day in 1939 when war was declared and the Sunday of Pearl Harbour.

The days in the convoy seemed endless. A quiet anxiety hung over the ship. We lumbered through the heavy seas, watching our escorting Destroyers manoeuvre around the convoy.

During the 24th day a cold drizzle of British weather welcomed us to the Irish Sea. That night explosions of depth charges shook the

Ranchi. There must be German submarines in the area. My guts tightened and the whole ship shuddered with each explosion. *What a hell of a place to be torpedoed. We must be less than day from landing. Those depth charges were damn close. Imagine what it must be like in a submarine with those blasts going off.*

The next morning we sighted the Isle of Arran and worked our way up the Clyde dropping anchor off Greenock at noon. The morning of our 26th day we inched our way up the narrow Clyde River to anchor in Glasgow's busy harbour. We watched as the tenders hustled back and forth, and wondered how long we would have to wait. We'd been at sea for twenty six days and we were anxious to feel solid ground beneath our feet. Finally after ten long, long hours they lowered the gangplank. We still had our sea-legs when we stepped ashore. Those rosy cheeked Scottish girls offering us "a cuppa tea, Love" looked enticing. It had been nearly a year since we'd seen so many white women. But we didn't stop for tea. We were hustled aboard a train on our way to London.

In London I was alone. I found a room at the Dominion Officers' Club in Barclay Square. Next day I found the Canadian Armed Services post office and had fifty-six letters from Ivy. My mail had been going to our squadron in Burma. It had been returned to London. Just another cufuffle. I learned that our new daughter's name was Shirley and that Ivy had moved into her new house just before Shirley was born. My heart ached with loneliness. How much longer would it be before I would see my loved ones?

I was busy reporting to medical boards, locating my luggage, attending interviews with a counsellor at RCAF headquarters. My liver was almost its normal size and they decided to send me back to Canada. But I was lonely. I walked London's crowded streets glancing at every face hoping to recognize someone. But they were all strangers. I couldn't believe with all those thousands and thousands of people I wouldn't see a familiar face.

Ivy's letters and the warmth of spring turned my young man's fancy. On a fine sunny day, in a queue for an afternoon movie, I was squeezed next to a girl with hair that glistened with a silky softness. It looked so clean, so healthy and so inviting I longed to run my hand over the gentle waves. I raised my hand to touch it. The queue moved. I pretended I had an itchy nose. I'd never be that brave again.

I did finally find friends. Ernest Leggett, from my hometown, Markinch, was in Pay Accounts in London. He had been overseas for three years and despite his English ancestry had a belly full of Britain. Porky Clarke and I had worked together in Calgary when I started my military career in the Army Medical Corps. I found him at Warrington, where I waited for a posting home.

In early May I was barracked with POWs (Prisoners of War) who had just been liberated from German camps. An RCAF pilot had spent four years behind barbed wire. He was a Pilot Officer when he bailed out over Hamburg. Now he was a Flight Lieutenant with four years of accumulated pay — a nest-egg of $15,000.

I was posted to an "Embarkation Depot" in Warrington, a town ten miles from Liverpool. We attended parades every day hoping our posting home would be announced. We were all packed and ready to leave.

Through the Red Cross I accepted an invitation to spend a weekend in nearby Chester. The Greene's had a comfortable home on a small acreage near the city. John and his wife Ann were teachers. Their son Charles was waiting for his eighteenth birthday so he could join the AirForce. His sixteen-year-old sister, Queenie, still at school, showed me the wall the Romans built and the double-tiered shop built near the old wall. They made me feel I was part of the family and renewed my respect for the British.

We were on parade on the 8th of May when the announcement of the German surrender blared across the parade grounds. George Young, who had been on the *Ranchi* with me, had been posted to Warrington. We joined the celebrating crowds in Manchester. The Midlands Hotel had a bar a hundred feet long. The crowd against the bar was five or six people deep. If you were lucky you had a mug with a handle. You thrust your mug towards the bar and worked your way forward until you reached the taps. You held onto your mug while the barmaid filled it. Then squirmed back through the mob to find your friend and drink your beer. We carried our mugs from pub to pub.

At the Golden Swan a three piece band was playing "Waltzing Matilda" for some Aussies who had just entered the pub. When they saw Young and me they belted out "When it's Spring Time in the Rockies."

We ended up at a house party with a feed of bacon and eggs.

"Canada, the last bus passes our corner at twelve thirty. It will be along in ten minutes."

We thanked our congenial hosts and sat on the curb waiting for the last bus, a little woozy from booze and food . I never did get used to the traffic driving on the wrong side of the road. The last bus whizzed by but we were sitting on the wrong side of the road. We sat and waited hoping there might be another bus and must have fallen asleep.

"What are you fellows doing here at this time of the night?" asked a policeman.

"Waiting for a bus."

"The last trolley went by here fifteen minutes ago."

"We have to catch a train to Warrington. Can you tell us how to get to the station?"

"Just follow those trolley tracks. You can't miss it."

"How far is it?"

"About eight or nine miles."

It was daylight by the time we reached the station. There was no train for two hours. There was a YMCA across the street, we found an empty bench and stretched out for a couple hours of sleep.

We were packed. Our luggage was shipped. Yet — it was six days before we caught an early train to Greennock and boarded the Ile de France at eight p.m.

We were the first troopship out of England after VE day. Ten thousand men were crammed into the ship. I had just found my bunk when my name blared from the PA system to report to the orderly room. I was "joed" for a guard officer with my first shift from 4:00 to 8:00 hours.

We had a small two-by-four office that once had been a head. Terry Corrigal, wearing the wing of an air-gunner, was my sergeant. We wore MP arm-bands and made a tour of the troop's quarters each shift. We checked the conditions of troops living quarters, tried to stop the gambling, and made sure that smoking was restricted to the designated areas.

I thought we were crowded with two hundred officers in one of the dining saloons. But the men below decks were tiered in narrow bunks, piled five or six high, and set back to back with a foot between the bunks, barely enough room to roll over. Naked light bulbs, caged in heavy wire, cast a deathly glow through the stuffy dungeon. The layers of sleeping bodies looked more like corpses.

The main gangways, three feet wide, ran through each deck and where they intersected, in the dingy light of a caged-forty-watter, small fortunes changed hands in a twenty-four-hour crap game that ran non-stop from Greenock to New York. Terry and I stepped gingerly around the kneeling players to avoid stepping on the piles of English pounds, Canadian and American dollars littering the floor. One winner wore a dozen watches on each arm and had four cameras hanging from his shoulders.

Three days out we hit rough weather and the dungeon decks reeked with the stench of vomit but the crap games continued. A day from New York we crossed the Gulf Stream. The warm moist air turned the dungeon into a sweat shop, but the crap games never stopped.

Terry, a bit of a b.s. artist, had been the tail gunner in a Lancaster bomber that bought a "bill of goods" over Germany. He gave a vivid description of how he climbed out of the rear turret and from his parachute watched the "Lanc" crash and burn. From his tales about life in a German prison camp, I thought he and his crew had been POWs for two or three years.

Terry sat across our small desk doodling. "Terry, could I borrow your pencil for a moment? I need an eraser."

I'll never forget that pencil. White, with a red-lettered ad that read, "Everything for the Builder, Central Builders, Courtenay, B.C."

"Terry, where in the hell did you get this pencil?"

"From my pilot."

"What was his name?"

"Noel McPhee, his old man owns a lumberyard. Why?"

"My wife lives in Courtenay. I know the store but I don't know the McPhees."

"You do!"

"Was Noel Mcphee with you in the POW camp?"

"No. We were on our twenty-ninth trip, one more trip and our tour was finished. Our primary target was Dusseldorf. We'd made it through some heavy flack and were just about ready to start our bombing run, when an ack-ack hit the cockpit. I was the tail gunner and it knocked me unconscious. I came to. I had a helluva time getting out of the turret. By the time my chute opened the front end of the planes was a ball of fire. I was the only one to get out.

"I landed in a tree not far from the crash. I got there before the Germans picked me up. It was a hell of a mess. I hate to think about it."

It was mid-June before I got back to Courtenay. I visited Noel's father, Wallace, and brother Bob in their store on Mill Street. I was surprised to learn that Noel had been missing since March 14, 1945. His father felt sure Noel would walk out of the Russian zone. I did not have the heart to tell him Terry's stories. I don't think Wallace McPhee ever abandoned his hope. Perhaps now that he has found his place amongst the stars his search for Noel has ended.

We crept into New York harbour and slid past the Statue of Liberty with the lady hidden in a veil of fog. We were the first troopship into New York after VE day. We received a noisy welcome as the tiny tug nudged the Ile de France into a pier.

With the inefficiency we Canadians had learned to accept, no arrangements had been made to get us to Canada. By noon we were the only troops still on board. Because there were no sleeping cars available for the over-night trip to Montreal, we were given the choice of spending another night on our aging lady and taking the train to Montreal in the morning; or we could go that night in a day coach. After five years in the service we had learned to sleep anywhere, anytime.

Our crumbled day-coach dumped us onto Lachine's platform on a bright, fresh and sunny Canadian spring morning. A large chestnut tree, wearing her dusty-pink spring calico, shaded the platform. Beds of yellow and red tulips, nodding gently in the morning's first breeze, whispered welcome. High in the chestnut tree, a robin, his red chest brilliant in the new-day's sun, stretched his voice to heaven singing, "Cheerio, cheerio, cheerio."

Hello, Canada! I'm home at last! I walked over to the chestnut tree, pulled the flowers on a lower branch to my lips, and kissed them!

We spent the morning signing in and out of Lachine. I had my ticket to Vancouver and would board the CPR's "Canadian" tomorrow. I wired Ivy. Montreal, Que., 24/5/45. ARRIVE VANCOUVER CPR 8.30 AM 31/5/45 STOP LOVE AND KISSES STOP GORDON.

On our way overseas I had discovered Ben's, a kosher restaurant tucked in behind Montreal's Mount Royal Hotel. Across the Atlantic and on the all-night train from New York I could see, taste and smell Ben's thick corned-beef-on-rye. I had to have one.

Five of us shared the fare and the fear of the wild bronco-busting ride in a Montreal taxicab. The driver reigned his snorting yellow beast to a screeching stop at Ben's front door.

The corned-beef-on-rye was just as thick, the meat just as red and the cafe just as cozy but it didn't quite match the mouth- watering image I had nursed across an ocean. Like the big house we used to live in, the hills we used to climb, and the long distances we used to walk to school, everything seemed smaller, lower and shorter thirty years later. But Ben's is still there. If I ever get to Montreal, I'll have another corned-beef-on-rye.

It took me five days to reach Vancouver. I stopped at Sudbury and spent two days with Jim and Gladys Davidson. I was living with them when I joined up and considered their place home away from home. I said hello to the Brownes, and the Austins, and visited the assay lab in Copper Cliff. I talked to Red Stewart at the Inco employment office and he offered to put me to work the next day. I didn't need a job. I was going home.

I couldn't sleep as the "Canadian" rumbled through the Rockies and twisted through the Fraser Canyon into a rain-freshened, sunny

Irene and Gladys Davidson, May, 1945.

Vancouver morning. Ivy, in a daffodil-yellow suit, looking as fresh and lovely as spring and more beautiful than I remembered, met me on the platform. We kissed, hugged, and held each other close. Her hair glistened — so clean, so healthy and so inviting. I ran my hand over its gentle waves, felt it tickle my nose, and inhaled the titillating womanly scent of freshly washed hair. We had a room at the Devonshire hotel, the same room we had when I left for overseas. For three days we honeymooned again. Stanley Park, beautiful in her robes of spring, shared our love. We dined, shopped and took in shows and enjoyed being one again.

I lay in bed and listened to the streets of Vancouver awaken. I watched the light of a new day undo the darkness of our room and uncovered Ivy's head and her pillow. *You've made it, Gordon. It's five years since Dr. Hogg gave you your first Air Force medical. You're home at last! The naturopaths, the amoeba, the jaundice, the carbuncles, the bedbugs, the Fenter Douglases, the Sergeant Boxhams, the Melanies and all the other tempting women are behind you. You've made it. That's your wife's hair you're touching. She's here. Right beside you. Remember how you used to fantasize in those rope beds in Chaklala? How in the Rawalpindi hospital you dreamed she was in your arms and woke to find yourself hugging a pillow? You're a married man now, Wagner. With three kids. Ivy's done more than her share to preserve the way of life you were supposed to be fighting for. She mothered our three children, built our home and loved you. Now it's your turn, Gordon. Nurture her love. Make it fulfil your dreams, your hopes, your fantasies. You've learned to live with all types of people in your five years of war. Temper your love for Ivy with tolerance. I wonder if she's awake?*

My diary says it all. About those three days I wrote, "Wonderful beyond words."

We took the CPR's Princess Elaine to Nanaimo, and the up-island bus to Courtenay. I was home at last with our rose-covered cottage only a few blocks away.

We walked up the Lake Trail Road into the glare of the setting sun. The lengthening shadows, the lazy hum of the quiet street, the well-tended lawns and flower beds all seemed to listen as a distant church bell tolled an unexpected welcome. We crossed the E & N Railway tracks and put down our luggage for another rest.

"There it is!" said Ivy with a mixture of pride and embarrassment in her voice.

Ivy's rose-covered cottage, vintage 1988.

The months of dreams vanished. I knew how Cinderella felt when the clock struck twelve. The roses turned to tar paper, the well- kept lawn and flower beds to bracken three feet high, and the flagstone walk to gravel. The children had ripped the tar paper off as high as they could reach. The steps were a couple of wooden blocks.

Two tiny faces waited at the window. Ivy opened the door. Keith and Linda rushed to greet her.

"Say hello to Daddy," she prompted. Linda hid behind her mother's skirt and Keith retreated to the sofa. Five-month old Shirley, propped up in her buggy, smiled.

"I'm surprised the children are so shy, Gordon. They were so happy when we heard you were coming home. Keith, did Mrs. Telosky bake a cake?"

"Yes, she did, Mummy. It's in de frig," chirped Linda before Keith had a chance to answer.

"Why don't we have the party we had planned for Daddy?" suggested Ivy.

"Can Keith and I have real tea, Mummy?"

Ivy put the kettle on and cut the cake. Linda pushed her high chair up to the table ready to eat. "Come Keith, get your chair to the table. Remember when we lived with Auntie Mae how you used to watch the buses every day to see if Daddy had come home. Gordon, I don't think he missed a day. When he'd hear the bus stop in front of the store he looked at me with those big blues and say, 'Daddy come'? I had to choke back the tears. He always looked so disappointed and sometimes he just sat and let the tears roll down his cheeks."

"Mummy when are we going to have our party?" Linda asked.

"Come Keith, and tell Daddy how we loved to read his letters. We used to put your picture on the coffee table and we'd sit together on the couch and pretend you listened with us. We loved Daddy's letters, didn't we Keith? Remember when we got the letter telling us Daddy was coming home and he wouldn't be in the war anymore? Linda was having her afternoon nap. We were so happy that we just hugged each other and cried."

I watched Keith as he listened to Ivy. Then I sat beside him on the couch. "You've grown to be a big boy while I was away. Thanks for taking such good care of Mummy while I was gone. Daddy loves you and I missed you so much. I'm never going away again and I'll help you take care of Mummy."

He looked up to me with those big blue eyes and long eyelashes and smiled. "I'm so glad you're home, Daddy. Will you still be flying in those big airplanes?"

"No Keith, I'm finished flying. I saved my flying cap for you."

Keith couldn't keep his eyes off my Air Force hat. I put it on his head and he wore it at the table while we drank real tea and demolished Mrs. Telosky's cake.

Keith pushed my Air

Force hat to the back of his head and turned his big blue eyes on me and said, "Did you win the war, Papa?"

"Yes, Keith, I did."

"Did you kill any Germans?"

"No Keith, I didn't kill anybody. Some day I'll tell you all about it."

"Ivy, it's so good to be home again. To have a home of our own to come to. I'm proud of you and the home and family you have given me. I do love you. I always have and always will."

At the children's bedtimes I watched as Ivy sat in her rocking chair with Keith and Linda on her lap. She helped them sing their nursery rhymes and finished by singing their favourite, "Bye, Bye, Blackbird."

We carried them to bed, tucked them in and I watched as Ivy read until they slipped into the land of their dreams. Oh, it was so good to be home!

I had three weeks leave, and by the time I had to report to the RCAF's No 3 Repair Depot the children had accepted me as the Daddy they had heard so much about.

No 3 RD was on Vancouver's Jericho Beach and the officers' mess had once been the residence of the department-store Spencer family. I spent nearly a month there having my liver probed, punched and tested. In the end they decided I was healthy but thought I should have a stay in a convalescent home.

The RCAF had converted the clubhouse of Victoria's Colwood Golf Club into a hospital. I enjoyed a month of fine weather, some golf, swimming in Lanford Lake and being entertained in the homes of some of the members. It was five months since I had been discharged from Bombay's BMH so I was probably the healthiest patient Colwood ever had.

I needed a job. I had lost five years and gained a wife and three children. I searched Vancouver, Victoria and Courtenay in vain. I made a late application to the College of Dentistry at the University of Alberta and was accepted. It was mid-September, and I had just been discharged without the expected pension for my damaged liver. We would have to give up our home in Courtenay, and I had to admit to myself that I didn't relish the thought of having to look into people's mouths for the rest of my life. Dentistry was out.

The colours of October gave way to the rains of November. Our savings were dwindling. I got three days work digging in two feet of mud to drain a railway siding. "Union Bay Joe" Walker and the CPR paid sixty-five cents an hour. I almost got a job as a "powder monkey" with Comox Logging but early snow got in the way.

A hundred and twenty returned soldiers were looking for work in the Comox Valley.

But there were the mines in Sudbury. I had three months from the date of my discharge to get my old job back with my five Air Force years added to my seniority. I had to be in Sudbury by the 19th of December.

"Ivy, I dread the thought of moving to Sudbury. Remember the winter we spent at Brentwood Bay? Christmas day was warm and sunny, the grass was green and we fed robins on our window sill. I want to stay on Vancouver Island."

"That was Keith's first Christmas and we haven't been together since. The kids will really miss you. You've always been so good with young children. I wish you didn't have to go."

"I'm all packed. I'll get the train Thursday morning and get to Sudbury with a day to spare."

"Don't forget to have your shoes half-soled. You should get a new pair but you'd better wait until you're working."

I took those black oxfords to the shoemaker in the back of Searle's Shoe Store in Courtenay, right where Searle's is today. The cobbler with a mouthful of tacks pounded them into the shoe he had on his last. "I'd like to have these oxfords half-soled. I need to have them tomorrow."

He waited until he'd emptied his mouth and driven the last tack. "We're not open on Wednesday. They'll be ready Thursday afternoon."

"But I have to have them. I'm catching the train to Nanaimo Thursday."

"I'll be here tomorrow. Come around to the back door, I'll be here.

The shoes will be ready."

Those shoes and Jimmy Ashton kept me in Courtenay. The diminutive cobbler, with one ear sort of corkscrewed to his head, loved to talk. He wanted to know where, how and why I was going. He listened with his good ear cocked towards me.

Then, with a fatherly tone in his Cockney accent he said, "If you can make a living in Sudbury, you can make a living here. I came to Courtenay forty years ago. This town has been good me." It was all I needed to hear. I unpacked my trunk and I have been in Courtenay ever since.

Gordon and Ivy Wagner, 1989

The Author

Gordon Wagner was born and raised in Markinch Saskatchewan. A graduate of the University of Saskatchewan, he worked two years underground in Sudbury's nickel mines and then he spent five years in the Royal Canadian Airforce, logging time in twenty-one countries. He settled in Courtenay after World War II, obtained a commission as British Columbia Land Surveyor and later qualified as a Notary Public.

Upon his retirement in 1980, his love for the land and the advice of his accountant prompted him to buy and clear twenty acres of swamp for his ranch, the Flying W.

In 1985 he took his first course in creative writing and decided to abandon his tax shelter and try to write. By 1987 he had accumulated enough assignments for a book. Six publishers said they couldn't look at his manuscripts for a year or two. At seventy-four, time is precious so he published it himself, calling it *From My Window*. In his enthusiasm he had five thousand copies printed and realized he would have to do his own promotion. His success amazed the staid publishing and bookstore people.

In *How Papa Won the War*, Gordon tells about the people he met and the friends he made in his five-year tour of those twenty-one countries.